Matt Whyman is a bestselling author of fiction and non-fiction, notably the critically acclaimed *Boy Kills Man*. He is married with four children and lives in West Sussex.

Matt Whyman

# Walking With Sausage Dogs

HODDER

First published in Great Britain in 2012 by Hodder & Stoughton
An Hachette UK company

First published in paperback in 2013

6

A CIP catalogue record for this title is available
from the British Library

ISBN 978 1 444 73427 0
eBook ISBN 978 1 444 73428 7

Typeset by Palimpsest Book Production Ltd. Falkirk, Stirlingshire

Printed and bound by Clays Ltd, St Ives plc

Hodder & Stoughton policy is to use papers that are natural,
renewable and recyclable products and made from wood grown
in sustainable forests. The logging and manufacturing processes
are expected to conform to the environmental regulations
of the country of origin.

Hodder & Stoughton Ltd
338 Euston Road
London NW1 3BH

www.hodder.co.uk

This book is dedicated to the medical team who treated Emma with such kindness, care and respect.

# Contents

'Nothing will turn a man's home into a castle more quickly and effectively than a Dachshund.'

*Queen Victoria*

# Prologue

Falling headlong down the stairs is never great. As soon as your balance slips, you just know it isn't going to end well. Still, my life didn't flash before my eyes when I took a tumble recently. To be honest, I had no time to reflect on the milestones of my existence. I didn't think of my dear wife, Emma, or our four children. I knew that I would miss them dearly if the final impact proved to be fatal, but my loved ones just weren't uppermost in my mind.

Instead, I thought of only one thing I would leave behind. He was watching me from the landing, where he had crossed my path without warning and left me with no room to manoeuvre. Mid-somersault, I had caught a glimpse of him. With his head tipped to one side, he didn't look at all horrified about the accident he'd just caused. He just appeared a bit baffled. Had he not been so long in the torso, I might've avoided tripping over him. As it was, in the final moment before I saw stars, just one thought travelled with me, and that was a simple fact.

Family life was about to change dramatically on account of a sausage dog, and not for the first time since his arrival.

One man and his proper dog.

'We're going to need a bigger pet carrier.'

# part one

Another back yard
break out.

Before the new dog
arrives, a test activates
Sesi's laser eyes.

# 1

# Full House

'Absolutely not. Out of the question. We just don't have the space.'

This was my response when Emma dropped the first hint as to what she'd like most for her birthday. We were standing in what was left of the garden at the time. A picket fence penned off much of it, which also contained the shed. At our feet, my four ex-battery chickens were scratching at the few remaining threads of grass that had previously missed their attention. On the other side of the fence, which was splattered with mud, Emma's two minipigs rooted enthusiastically in the soil.

By rights, we should've stopped referring to Butch and Roxi as minipigs some time ago. It's just that's how they'd been sold to Emma, arriving together in a little pet carrier, and the name just stuck. Nearly three years on, neither of them came close to fitting that description any more. While Butch was knee-high, and certainly small compared to a normal pig, Roxi had basically maxed out in every way possible. Weighing in at close to twenty stone, what we had here was a vaguely housetrained Hogzilla. The pair had started out under the same roof as us, but the arrangement didn't last long. Eventually, having become overrun by the new arrivals inside my own home, I saw sense and insisted that they relocate to the bottom of the garden. Even Emma accepted that they were happier in their natural environment. Privately, I figured a farm would have been more suitable, but by the time Butch and Roxi were fully grown they had become a part of the family. At that moment, however, it wasn't the size of our female minipig that concerned me but the determined look on Emma's face.

'*You* have a dog.' She gestured at the white Canadian Shepherd stationed at the gate to the pigpen. People often mistook Sesi for some kind of snow wolf, which was no bad thing, seeing that we lived on a quiet country lane, with fields and woodland behind us. If any household was going to be tied up by burglars and robbed of all their valuables, it wasn't ours. Still, it seemed my wife believed one burglar deterrent wasn't enough. 'Why can't I have a dog, too?'

'Sesi is not my dog as such,' I said. 'She belongs to everyone.'

'She's your dog.' Emma folded her arms. 'I would never have gone for something as huge as her.'

I looked over her shoulder at Roxi, the so-called minipig, but decided not to inflame the situation. Instead, I reminded Emma of Sesi's attitude towards other dogs.

'She hates her own kind. She always has done. As she's reached the canine equivalent of late middle age, I very much doubt you'll be able to change her outlook. She might be fine with children, chickens, minipigs and rabbits, but other dogs worry her. As you know, she expresses that fear by attacking them.'

'It's all show,' said Emma dismissively. 'Sesi's never drawn blood. She just likes to get in first in case the other dog decides to have a go.'

'Last month in the woods,' I told her, 'she picked a fight with a poodle. I hardly think a dog like that should present a major threat, but somehow that's the way Sesi sees it.'

4

'Another dog might help her settle down,' insisted Emma, whose ability to remain optimistic knew no bounds. Even when friends and family stopped dead in their tracks on seeing Roxi for the first time, my wife would always focus on her minipig's good nature instead of her spectacular size. 'Sesi would love a friend,' she added. 'I'm sure of it.'

'I just don't see what's brought this on. Why do you want a dog all of a sudden?'

'Because of the cats,' she said frankly.

We certainly had a problem here, but it wasn't with other people's moggies. The issue took the form of the lane. We didn't get much traffic at all, but what passed by tended to do so as a blur. We had lost three cats under speeding cars, and that was more than enough for us all. After the last one was run over, Emma agreed that we could have no more. It was just too upsetting. I also figured we had enough on our hands. Along with the minipigs, a bunch of ex-battery hens and a dog with issues, we also owned four rabbits, which always seemed excessive in my view. As a younger man, I'd have said the same thing about four children. That kind of number seemed feckless and irresponsible. Then Emma came into my life, and one pregnancy led to another.

Like the minipigs, our youngest children, Honey and Frank, were no longer so small. Even though they were six and eight respectively, we still referred to them as the little ones. Together, they had reached an age where their world revolved exclusively around the Nintendo DS handheld games console. We tried our hardest to introduce them to other interests, but short of furnishing the house with power ups and gold coins to collect it was almost impossible to peel them away from their bleeping screens. As for their elder sisters, thirteen-year-old May was a sensitive soul, prone to stewing on her worries.

Willowy and whisper-quiet, even when surrounded by chaos, she looked like the sort of girl who really ought to possess terrifying psychokinetic powers. As for Lou, her inner soul was generally available to view in the form of her regular Facebook status updates. At fifteen, our eldest daughter couldn't be trusted to keep anything in the family. If I happened to slip into Emma's pink Crocs just to step outside and collect the eggs from the hen house, I'd return to learn that several of her friends had already 'liked' my disregard for gender stereotyping. In short, all four kids were hugely rewarding and totally maddening in equal measure.

Parenting-wise, it was a lot of work, and at times the pet count pushed things into pandemonium. Even so, I wouldn't have changed a thing. Apart from the rabbits, of course. If the children needed an animal to love and cherish, I argued, when Emma began to replace my potted herbs in the yard with hutches, straw and sawdust, couldn't they have shared one bunny between them? Sure enough, the kids loved their fluffy charges. It's just that love didn't always extend to feeding and cleaning them. As I worked from home, while Emma had a proper career that involved dressing professionally, such tasks defaulted to me. I was well aware that my wife had a greater tolerance for the challenges a big family brings. Still, I figured enough was enough. Even without a cat, we were running at full capacity.

'Another dog would be madness,' I stressed. 'What's wrong with spending more time with the minipigs?'

I crossed to the picket fence. Both Butch and Roxi broke off from their excavations to greet me. After all this time in our care, we had done our utmost to make sure they had everything they needed. It meant as well as sacrificing much of my garden, I'd also given up the back of the shed, which was now sectioned off to cater for their sleeping arrangements. Every time Roxi lumbered out from the side entrance built for them, however, I did wonder whether I needed to look at strengthening the floor. The fact was these were much-loved, disarmingly-friendly and appallingly-researched pets. Despite their hefty size, Emma hadn't fallen out of love with pigs. In fact, she'd become one of those people who'd gone on to collect any kind of trinket that reflected her passion. As a result, our window ledges were cluttered with everything from stuffed cloth pigs to china pigs, wooden pigs, glass pigs and toy plastic pigs. Short of a sticker in the window that read **I ❤ PIGS**, she couldn't have made her porcine passion any clearer.

Given how big Butch and Roxi had become, Emma's continued commitment to them was admirable. I had to respect how she had stuck with a project long after it had exceeded her expectations. The breeder had assured her that such pigs would remain pint-sized when she first took them on, only to cease trading when it became abundantly clear that the whole concept was a myth. It was for this reason that I figured Emma had set her sights on the kind of pet that didn't have the potential to push through the garden fence.

'Butch and Roxi are great,' said Emma next, 'but they're not, you know . . .'

'Mini?'

Emma seemed relieved that I had just put the words in her mouth.

'I realise they can't come inside much any more.'

'Not if you want to run the risk of Roxi tipping over the TV,' I said, and reached over the fence to pat her flank. 'If there's so much as a crumb of food on the carpet or indeed underneath it, she'll sniff it out and let nothing stand in her way.'

'A little dog wouldn't do that,' she said after a moment.

Emma sounded hesitant, and for good reason. I just didn't click with little dogs, as she knew full well. They yapped uncontrollably, troubled your ankles, and provided no sense of security. When anyone knocked on our door, Sesi would make it very clear from the other side that we were not the sort of household who would easily hand over our valuables. What Emma had in mind would not be capable of giving off that kind of vibe. With a little dog patrolling the grounds, we might as well leave the front door wide open and invite the burglars to an open house day. We already had a dog. A big one. Under no circumstances did we need another.

# 2

# How Low Can You Go?

As far as I was concerned, Emma's desire for a second pooch was dead in the water. This wasn't because I loathed small dogs. She just didn't have a breed in mind.

'I'm not sure what I want,' she said when I pressed her. 'But I know what I like.'

Given how vague Emma seemed on the subject, I decided to let it lie. From experience, I hoped she would privately recognise all the drawbacks and come round to my way of thinking. If I ever pushed my wife to change her mind, she would always stick to her guns as a point of principle. By making no further comment, I would be giving her a chance to reconsider without losing face. Allowing Emma to see sense on her own terms had proven effective in the past. It's why we didn't have a death trap in the garden in the shape of a massive trampoline. I could hardly forget the last time I raised objections to something she had set her sights upon. We ended up with a pair of minipigs.

Going quiet about the issue was not without consequences. Over the following weeks, every time we came across a small dog it transformed into an elephant in the room. Stuck in traffic one day, neither of us could ignore the creature inside the car in front. It yapped and snarled at us from the parcel shelf with pure venom. I mustered a tut of disapproval, because it would've been wrong not to do so, before turning up the radio by a notch. Then there were those households along our lane that contained little terriers. I use 'contained' in the literal sense, for whenever someone passed by they would hurl themselves at the gates and fences, barking and snapping with sheer aggression. If I walked Sesi into the village, we would zigzag across the lane in a bid to keep our distance. She hated them, and I couldn't blame her. In my view, small dogs were basically demented. I saw no reason why my wife could possibly disagree.

I knew Emma had no desire for another big dog. Sesi was lovely, but we couldn't let her roam freely at home. She was just too big and unruly. As a result, with the help of two child gates, she happily inhabited her own space in the boot room between my office and the kitchen. It was constantly covered in a layer of mud, and served as a reminder of what the entire house would be like had we not used what was effectively police kettling tactics. With Butch, Roxi and the chickens laying claim to the garden, four rabbits occupying the yard and four kids everywhere I turned, it was my belief that another dog, big or small, would only upset the delicate balance of our family life.

Just as I was beginning to think that Emma had put the whole idea behind her, we were invited into London for supper with old friends. They didn't own a big dog or a little dog. Instead, what they had would convince my wife of the shape of things to come.

Emma had gone to University with Adam and Claire. Generally, I saw them at weddings and christenings, but we'd reached an age where those events were few and far between. Rather than gather dust at home, as I liked to do, they were easy and exuberant hosts who could happily invite a dozen or so people at one time. Emma and I could count on one hand the number of dinner parties we'd thrown in all our years of marriage. Even then, we'd never dare stage such a large-scale social event. Having got through a working day, and made sure both kids and animals were fed, clean, exercised and happy, the prospect of entertaining other people always felt like the last thing we wanted to do. Still, when the invitation came through, Emma declared that it was only right we made the effort. With a babysitter in position, we took a taxi to the station and a train to the capital. It felt like a huge hassle to begin with, until Emma reminded me that as well as being renowned for their big parties Adam and Claire also boasted an impressive fine wine collection. As a result, I arrived feeling relaxed and responsibility-free.

'Welcome, Whymans!' announced Adam at the door. 'I was half expecting you to be wearing wellington boots.'

Every time I saw Adam, he made a crack about country living. It was an easy source of humour for him, but I always held my tongue. They were Emma's friends, after all, and I didn't want to come between them by suggesting that the silk neckscarf Adam was sporting pushed the boundaries of metrosexuality.

'It's great to be here,' I said instead, and handed over the bottle we had brought as a gift – one I hoped we wouldn't have to drink that evening.

Inside, we didn't know anyone else except for the hosts, but Emma was unfazed. She was good at talking to strangers, while I was great at standing quietly beside her. I knew I had about ten minutes before my wife would leave me to fend for myself. Until then, and very probably afterwards as well, I was content to enjoy the wine that Adam had poured me.

'What are you doing?' asked Emma, scoping the other guests as I lifted the glass to the light.

'No idea,' I confessed under my breath. 'It's just that Adam is watching us.'

Emma looked across the room, smiled at the host and then tutted at me.

'You worry too much about what people think,' she said. 'Perhaps you should try to get out more.'

'With our pets, I'm never alone,' I reminded her, and decided to taste the wine one more time for good measure.

While Claire worked as a school teacher, Adam spent much of his time shuttling between offices in Mayfair and New York. Generally, I tended to travel no further from my desk than the foot of the garden. Our host, meanwhile, had enough air miles for a free trip to the moon. As well as being a successful fine art dealer, it was no surprise to learn that Adam was also an accomplished distance runner. With his lantern jaw and easy charm, I defaulted to feeling inadequate. I didn't have any stories to tell about spearheading an art fraud investigation, or hitting the wall during the *Marathon des Sables*. Still, I was happy to listen and just enjoy a calibre of vintage red which evidently hadn't been sitting on the 'Offers' shelf at the supermarket earlier that day.

'So,' Adam said a little later, having found me nursing a glass on my own, 'Claire tells me you have two unusual pets. Is that right?'

As soon as he asked the question, I was aware that a couple of people around me had turned to hear my response.

Adam really didn't look like the kind of man who would take pleasure in seeing me squirm. I figured he was genuinely interested. Nevertheless, I looked to my feet when I said: 'Pigs. We keep some pigs in our garden.'

'Claire told me they were little ones or something. *Minipigs?* Is that right?'

As ever, I felt myself going a bit red when he said this. I was never comfortable admitting that we had bought into the whole concept of pigs small enough to live indoors. As things had turned out, it was like admitting to a belief in unicorns.

'Butch and Roxi are a bit more midi nowadays,' I told him, by way of explanation. 'There's certainly a lot to love, if you see what I mean.'

Adam looked intrigued. He glanced around at those guests who had now joined our conversation, as if to gauge their feeling about the subject.

'A pig as a pet,' he said, returning his attention to me. 'Now there's a thing.'

I pretended to inspect the wine, wondering how I could change the subject. Ever since Butch and Roxi arrived, I'd found myself justifying their existence in our household to anyone who asked. And most people asked. I looked around for Emma, hoping she could rescue me, when something else caught my eye. My wife was deep in conversation with Claire, and appeared not to notice the dog that trundled in from the kitchen just then. At first, on seeing its floppy felt ears, I thought I was looking at some kind of stunted spaniel. The dog continued to advance into the room, but only when its rear quarters failed to emerge from behind the door frame did I realise it was something altogether more peculiar. To my eye, his body just went on and on. Finally, as if operating independently from its forelegs, the dog's back end waddled into full view.

'What the hell is that doing here?' I muttered under my breath, a little too loud for my liking, but mercifully Adam's attention was locked on this four-legged freak.

'*Dandelion!* There you are! Where have you been?' Dutifully, the dog honed in on him, though frankly she looked more like some hideous cross between a canine and an otter. 'My little Dandy-Doo! My girl, my doll . . . oh, come to Daddy!'

By now, Adam had entirely abandoned his wine-pouring duties, much like his dignity, and was preparing to greet her. He dropped down on one knee, which caused everyone around him to back off a bit, and then spread his arms wide. I glanced up at Emma, who had effortlessly read my mind because she mouthed something that warned me not to pass comment. As our host scooped up the dog in his hands, I felt embarrassed for him and turned my attention to the floor. There, I sensed that I wasn't alone in studying the tiles. From the corner of my eye, I noted two other guests had adopted my position.

'Unbelievable,' said one man quietly.

'Tragic,' the guy beside him added, and glanced across at me.

By now Adam was on his hands and knees so the dog could lick his face. I grimaced, and agreed under my breath that it was no way for a grown man to behave.

'It's wrong on every level,' I muttered. 'How low can you go?'

It wasn't until the last leg of our journey home that I chose to discuss the issue with Emma. This was because I'd had to wait for her to cool off a bit, following our discovery on the train that we were out of cash for a taxi. As our nearest station was in the middle of nowhere, and with the two cabs available taken by passengers who could pay, we had no option but to trudge back to the village. It wasn't far, but then we only had

Emma's keyfob light to guide us, which made things testing. I wasn't quite sure why I was being made to feel that it was entirely my fault. I just knew that it was best for me to wait for my wife to start talking about something other than forward thinking.

'Still,' she said as we reached the final stretch, 'it was good to see Claire and Adam.'

'It was great,' I agreed, 'apart from the moment when he *totally* embarrassed himself. What on earth does he see in a sausage dog?'

'It's a Dachshund,' replied Emma. 'I think Dandelion is a sweetie.'

Following the lane out of the village, we passed the small-holding that belonged to our friend, Tom. There he raised pigs properly, kept his wife's horses in a stable he had built himself and also tended to his chickens. Emma often looked at it with a sense of envy. On this occasion, she focused her attention on shining the keyfob light in my face, and I knew just why.

'I'm not going to say a word about that dog's name,' I assured her. 'Each to their own.'

Emma swung the tiny beam ahead of us, not that it did much good. The lane began to rise here, and we lived on the crest. Between us and home lay a peppering of cottages set back among woodland. As we walked, porch lights could be seen twinkling between the tree trunks and the branches.

'You're being horribly reasonable,' she said next. 'Normally you'd tear a name like that to shreds.'

'Dandelion,' I said out loud, and paused in my tracks for a moment. 'Dan-de-lion.'

Emma turned to face me.

'It's unusual, but she's sweet.'

'It's *ridiculous!*' I replied, unable to hold back any longer. 'A ridiculous name for a ridiculous creature. Why on earth that breed hasn't gone the way of the dodo is a mystery. Apart from transforming a strapping male like Adam into a simpering little girl, what purpose does it serve?'

'I knew you'd be like this about it,' said Emma after a moment. 'You're so judgmental.'

'As soon as she appeared, Dandelion was asking to be criticised. You could see it in her eyes.'

'You didn't get close enough,' said Emma. 'She steered clear of you all evening.'

'Even if I'd wanted to make friends,' I replied, as we trudged on up the lane, 'I'd never have got past Adam. Dandelion spent the entire time at his feet or on his lap. When he was telling me the story about art prodigies, I just couldn't take him seriously. He looked like a bad Bond villain.'

We walked on for a moment. Just ahead of us, two gate lamps cast a dim glow across the lane.

'Well, I liked that dog,' said Emma. 'I liked her a lot.'

All of a sudden, I realised where this was going. I stopped in front of the gates and waited for her to turn.

'Oh, *please*,' I said, reasoning with her. 'Anything but that!'

In the light from the gate lamps, Emma looked like she was ready with a response. It was as if she had been preparing for this moment ever since she laid eyes on Dandelion. Before she could speak, however, the sound of something scuttling urgently in our direction caused us both to start. We turned together, just as a terrier shot out of the darkness of the driveway and threw itself at the gates. Snarling and yapping, jumping and turning circles, this canine midget reacted as if the sole purpose of its existence was to irritate and annoy me.

By contrast, Emma regarded the terrier as some kind of living justification for what she had to say next.

'See that,' she said. 'That's a *little* dog. What I have in mind is something . . . longer.'

# 3

# Tough Love

So my wife dreamed of owning a Dachshund. As I saw things, she could dream as much as she liked. All she had to do was wake up and take a look through the bedroom window to realise we were running at full tilt in terms of pets.

When the minipigs joined our household, the pair were so small that we lost them at times. Butch and Roxi enjoyed snuffling under blankets and jostling for position with us on the sofa. With every week that passed, however, my spot in particular came under threat. Roxi was always the beefier of the two, but coupled with her stubborn will there reached a stage where I was forced to give up my seat to her completely. That was the tipping point for me. These minipigs belonged outside with the hens, where they were free to thrive.

Now that Butch and Roxi had reached their adult size, it seemed clear to me that we had sacrificed enough for the care and upkeep of family members in possession of a snout, twitching nose, muzzle or beak. Frankly, our days were dominated by demands from both children and animals. The minipigs would kick off first by joining in the dawn chorus. This was basically a ploy to be fed. Roxi was the main offender. She knew that sauntering out from the shed, filling her lungs and then squealing at a volume that made the windows rattle would prompt me to come running – usually in wellies and

18

a dressing gown I had failed to tie properly on account of being half asleep. We only had one immediate neighbour, but Roddie was an old boy who relished order, peace and quiet. The minipigs failed on all three counts. What's more, their dawn uprising would always wake the chickens, who would begin squawking to be let out from their roost. There was once a time when both minipigs and poultry lived in harmony. It was Roxi's appetite that put paid to the arrangement. Not only did she eat the eggs, in return for protection from foxes; there came a point last year when she threatened to eat the chickens. Consequently, my flock now roamed freely in the garden, making sure that any blade of grass that dared to flourish was quickly plucked from the soil.

By the time I had dealt with the outdoor brigade, which included feeding all the rabbits in the yard, I would head back to the house to find Sesi looking at me longingly. Then, just in case I was contemplating a quick cup of tea, she'd switch her attention pointedly to the dog lead on the hook.

As for Emma, she would rise at the same time as me. She also had a long list of duties. As she needed to power dress for work, however, her contribution revolved around tasks that didn't involve getting muddy or being forced to intervene in a dog fight. We both had careers, but only one of us counted people and not pets as colleagues. If I'm honest, I've never been entirely sure what she did for a living. I knew where she worked, of course, but her position in the company has always been a bit of a mystery to me. Whenever she explained her role and responsibilities, it involved so much interaction with actual humans during working hours that it seemed totally alien to me. Still, it explained why she could get ready for work while effortlessly marshalling the kids into some sense of school readiness. As a seasoned multitasker, she could have them washed, fed and dressed while jabbing away at her work BlackBerry at the same time. Watching her, you'd be forgiven for thinking the device was some kind of remote control for children.

Once Emma dropped the kids at school on her way to the office, I would be free to head for my desk. In reality, this meant reaching my chair feeling like I needed a soak in the bath. Even so, it was vital that I made the most of the time available to me. For a living, I write books for children and teenagers. Mostly these are novels, but I have also penned advice guides for young people. In my twenties, in order to fund the writing of my first novel, I took on any freelance writing job I could find. At one point, I was invited to answer questions in a monthly agony column for a popular teenage girl's magazine. My friends just laughed when I was offered the job. Just because I'd written a feature for the magazine, they said, it didn't qualify me to deal with young people's problems. As far as I was concerned, however, it meant a regular paycheck. I also saw the funny side, of course. This wasn't a lifetime ambition, after all. Then the post bag arrived. The first letter I opened came from a fourteen-year-old boy who was desperately worried that he had pubic lice. I read the letter with interest, only to drop it pretty smartly when he signed off with the line: 'I have taped a sample on the other side.' It was an unpleasant find, but also quite a wake-up call. This kid had written in because he was desperate, as were all those who put pen to paper about an issue in their lives. Mercifully, it turned out to be a one-of-a-kind question. The majority were penned by girls with boy troubles, but I realised very quickly that my role came with a great deal of responsibility. As a result, I figured I would last six issues at most.

Over fifteen years later, I was still in the job. It had been a steep learning curve, but given my terror of saying the wrong thing I'd tackled it with a passion. In that time, I never once visited the magazine's office. Nor had they ever updated the picture of me that accompanied the column. I could only assume they believed I was the Peter Pan of the problem page. The only drawback was that both May and Lou had reached an age where the magazine was often read in school by their fellow pupils. I couldn't imagine how appalling it must be to leaf through the latest issue together with your mates, only to find your old man gurning out from the page. Still, it helped me earn a living. Unless I was eased into retirement, I couldn't afford to spare their blushes.

It required a great deal of discipline to make the most of the working hours available to me, which would come to an end shortly before the school bell rang once again. By that time, I would bitterly regret wasting so much time putting together music playlists instead of actually doing some writing. Still, once Emma was home to take over with the household tasks I would always return to the keyboard. Panic-stricken by my lack of productivity, I would finally knuckle down to an honest day's graft. It was exhausting, but ultimately everyone was happy and that's how we got by.

Both Emma and I pulled our weight in different ways. Even so, it was always my belief that any upset to the domestic routine would reveal that we were effectively living in a house of cards. We'd already come close to one collapse when the minipigs arrived. For all the fun and games that came with accommodating them, even Emma acknowledged that it had been a strain. A dog wouldn't dig up the garden with quite such devastating consequences, but it was my view that another pet was just asking for trouble. On the evening that we finished traipsing up the hill from the train station, leaving the frenzied *yap-yap-yap* of the horrid little mutt behind us, I knew how I could prove it. Heading around the house for the back door, I stopped in the yard and drew Emma's attention to the rabbit hutches.

'When was the last time you cleaned them out?' I asked.

'That's the children's responsibility,' she said. 'If they're not doing it every week then you're not being tough enough on them.'

'I don't have time to be tough on them. I'm too busy cleaning them out myself as well as dealing with *your* minipigs.'

'And *your* hens and *your* dog,' added Emma.

Any pet was hard work, of course. Even the starter ones. A goldfish tank doesn't clean itself and you never see a gerbil or a hamster sweeping their droppings away. We'd done them all over time, but not once had I considered that their existence in our household should be a cause for division.

'I just think we should make the most of the animals we have,' I said, as we waited for the babysitter to unlock the back door from the inside. 'They won't be here forever, after all.'

It's often tempting to look back and wish you'd chosen a better way of saying things. I wasn't to know that several weeks later the rabbits would become a cause for concern. When one stopped eating, and took to sitting morosely in the corner of its hutch, I did wonder whether I would be held responsible.

On paper, Hansel belonged to Frank, our youngest child. Emma had come across the rabbit at a county fair, along with his sister, Gretel. As ex-show-bunnies, the pedigree pair sported velveteen black coats and looked utterly miserable inside their small, wire cage. Immediately, my wife's instinct to save and nurture them had kicked in. To be fair to Frank, he had only just turned four at the time. Nobody really expected him to embrace full responsibility for Hansel's welfare. Frank's sister, Honey, was keen to take on the task along with caring for Gretel. Realistically, at her age we couldn't entirely trust her to see it through, which is where I came in. Hansel and Gretel were easy rabbits to manage. They were used to being handled, and never scratched or scrabbled. So, on the day that I reached in to collect Hansel for his shuttle to the run in the garden, only for him to retreat from my reach, I knew that all was not well. By lunchtime, when I realised he was also off his food, I decided it was time to make an appointment with the vet.

'Why didn't you tell me?' asked Emma, when she returned from work to find a little paper bag of pet medication on the kitchen worktop.

'You're busy,' I said. 'And I didn't think it could wait.'

'Is he OK?'

'Not great, but hopefully we can turn him around. He's got some mystery bug, apparently. According to the vet it's quite common in rabbits and often impossible to pinpoint what's caused it. The main thing is that we need to keep his fluids up.'

Opening the bag, Emma peered at the array of sachets and droppers.

'I can do this,' she said, and slipped off her coat. 'Where is he?'

'In the isolation ward,' I said, and gestured at my office behind the boot room. 'I didn't want to upset the kids.'

That evening, Emma devoted herself to caring for Hansel. At first, he refused all attempts to drink from the syringe. Eventually she got him to take a few drops. Every half an hour, she would head back to my office to try again.

Inevitably, the children grew wise to the fact that all was not well. Honey was the first to follow her mother and see for herself. Within the space of a minute, all four were crowding at the door.

'He'll be fine,' I assured them, watching Emma cradle the rabbit like a newborn baby. He didn't look good, however, and twitched his head away when she encouraged him to drink a little more. 'Hansel will be hopping around in no time at all.'

May turned to me, looking most concerned. 'What have you done to him?'

'Me? Nothing! Well, I've fed him, just like I feed all your rabbits.'

May had no reply to this. Like Lou, Honey and Frank, they just assumed the bunny fairy took care of things whenever they forgot. Frank kneeled beside his mother, watching curiously with his Nintendo DS in his lap, while the three girls glanced at one another.

'We're going to check our rabbits,' said Lou eventually, and was the first to file out towards the back door.

Much to everyone's relief, the three remaining rabbits looked in fine health. Honey's bunny, Gretel, appeared a little lost without her brother, while the two that belonged to Lou and May looked the same as ever. These were no pedigree pair. They had pretty much come off the shelf from the pet shop, with lop ears, button eyes and a permanent look of shame whenever anyone addressed them. Unfortunately, I had to take full responsibility for what they were called. When they first came home, I had made my suggestion with an ironic grin directed at Emma. I didn't think any of the children would be old enough to understand the reference, and I was right. Even though it meant nothing to them, however, my names for them seemed to stick.

'There's nothing wrong with Starsky,' said May, on her return from the yard.

'Or Hutch,' Lou added, poker-faced.

I cringed to myself, as ever, before suggesting their pets might each like a carrot before bed time.

I had assumed that Emma would make Hansel comfortable before turning in for the night. Instead, having made sure he had enough straw in the pet carrier we were using to contain him, she set her alarm in order to wake every two hours. Each time she would creep downstairs and try to get the rabbit to drink something. I only got out of bed for the minipigs, which occurred like clockwork at the first gleam of daybreak. In effect, they had become my alarm.

'So, how is the patient?' I asked on my return from the garden.

Still in her nightshirt, Emma sat cross-legged on my office floor. Hansel was resting in her lap, eating rabbit feed from the palm of her hand. Even before she replied, I could see he was looking perkier.

'It's been exhausting,' she added, 'but worth it.'

Behind me, Sesi began to whine. I turned to find her looking at me pleadingly. If I didn't get out and walk her, this disruption to the morning routine would have an impact on us all.

'You need to get ready for work,' I pointed out, on searching for Sesi's leash. 'Leave Hansel in the office. I'll keep an eye on him throughout the day, but it looks like you don't need to worry about him any more.'

Shortly before lunchtime, I was back on the phone to the vet. Hansel had appeared to be fine when I sat down at my desk. Every now and then I would turn around to see how he was doing. There he was, looking settled, just gazing through the mesh gate of the pet carrier. I must have got a bit involved with my work at one point, because when I next checked up on him, about an hour later, he appeared to have collapsed. When the vet said I should bring him in straight away, I opted not to waste time calling Emma to let her know. I just grabbed the car keys, assured Sesi that I would be back soon, and headed out with the pet carrier on the passenger seat.

I made the return journey alone, with an empty carrier stowed in the boot. At some point that afternoon, once they were home from school, I would have to tell the children that Hansel had been put to sleep. First, I had to inform my wife. It wasn't a telephone call I felt comfortable making. Even before I broke the news, I knew she wouldn't just mark it down as one of those things.

'But he was on the mend!' she said. 'I spent all night taking care of him, and now you're telling me he's dead? What happened?'

'The vet said there was nothing more we could have done.'

'But did you do *anything*?'

'Nothing bad. Of course not.'

A pause came down the line.

'How are the others?' asked Emma finally.

'Gretel, Starsky and Hutch are all in good shape,' I confirmed without checking. 'At least that's something.'

Hansel's sister was the next rabbit to experience a downswing in health. As soon as I'd finished speaking to Emma, I thought I should just pop out and make sure I hadn't spoken too soon, and that's when I found her in the corner of the hutch. With an hour to spare before I had to collect the kids, it seemed only right that I returned to the vet. Hansel had at least received some shots, and though it didn't save him I hoped it might work this time. Ultimately, I couldn't let another one die on my watch. As carefully as I could, I transferred Gretel into the pet carrier. Before setting off, I made sure Sesi was secure inside the boot room, and then searched around for my car keys. Finally, I headed back out, scooped up the pet carrier and left the yard for the drive.

'Mr Whyman! So glad I've caught you.'

On seeing our neighbour in the lane, I smiled and cursed under my breath. Roddie was never one for a quick word.

'Is it about the minipigs again?' I asked, and prepared to apologise in advance.

As ever, Roddie was dressed in a golf blazer and tie. Soon after moving in next door to him, I had made the mistake of expressing absolutely no interest in the sport whatsoever. What's more, being left-handed, I had assumed they just didn't make clubs for people like me. Roddie often reminded me of this whenever I tried to muster enthusiasm for the sake of conversation. I always got the sense that he believed a family like mine were at odds with his idea of a quiet rural life. As we were here to stay, all I could do was be as genial as I could in his company while avoiding him where possible.

'I'm just here with some old apples from my orchard,' he said, and gestured at the carrier bag he was holding. 'Your pigs can be a nuisance but I know you do your best.'

'Oh, the health and welfare of our pets is a priority,' I replied, quick to capitalise on this unexpected compliment.

It was just a shame, I thought, that Roddie didn't appear to be listening. Instead, his attention had dropped to the pet carrier in my hand. Then his expression tensed, and I knew that all was not well. I raised the carrier to see for myself, which is when I realised that poor Gretel was no longer with us.

# 4

# The Bunny Crisis

In the hours after losing our second rabbit, I was ready for my wife's return from work. Frank, Honey, May and Lou had been informed. When it came to the loss of small animals, they were experienced grievers. There had been tears and then a subdued air for the rest of the day. At tea time, on hearing Emma's car pull up in the drive, I left the kids at the table and headed outside to meet her. I wanted to bring her up to speed in my own way, rather than risk one of the children blabbing in the kitchen before she'd even kicked off her shoes.

'How are the rabbits?'

This was the first thing she asked. No kiss. Not even a smile.

'Great!' I said, in a bit of a panic, as I'd been hoping to lead the conversation. 'Well, two of them are great . . . what I mean is Gretel isn't doing so well.'

Emma considered what I'd said for a moment.

'She's dead, isn't she?'

I hung my head, before nodding.

'And buried,' I confirmed, 'in the back garden.'

Emma sighed and fiddled with the car keys in her hand.

'What is going on with the poor things?'

'I called the vet,' I told her. 'Apparently bunnies are vulnerable to infection if a bug is doing the rounds, so I've been out with a bucket of hot and soapy water and disinfected every-thing. All we can do is take precautions. I've been very thorough.'

Emma collected her bag from the car. As she did so, I noted how her attention turned to the pile of splintered wood lying just outside the backyard.

'Is that part of the precautions?' she asked, observing what had been Hansel and Gretel's quarters.

'No, that's just me being practical,' I said, without first thinking 'yes' might've been a better answer. Aware that I needed to explain myself a bit more, and possibly sell what I'd done here, I added: 'It's freed up a huge amount of space for us! Plus we can use all this for the wood burner. Trust me, Emma; Hansel and Gretel haven't died in vain. Think of it as, well . . . recycling.'

Emma looked at me like I'd spoken in a language utterly alien to her.

'I'm worried about Starsky and Hutch,' she said, and hurried towards the yard door. Watching her show such concern, talking gently to both bunnies as she crouched down and opened their door, I realised just how much they meant to her. 'Oh, no,' she sighed, as I leaned in beside her. 'Not Starsky too.'

The lops were brothers, but different colouring. One was white and the other grey. Despite looking after them for several years, I didn't like to admit that I'd never got round to telling which was which. In my view, rabbits were high-maintenance pets. You fed them, watered them, changed their bedding and relocated them out in the garden when it was sunny so they could get some air. Looking after the infirm offered more reward than this, but as Emma cradled the grey rabbit it was quite plain that she did not share my view.

'Is he sick?' I asked. 'It's Hutch, isn't it?'

'Starsky.'

'That's what I meant to say.'

Emma rose to her feet with the rabbit in her arms. Starsky certainly looked lethargic all of a sudden, unlike his brother who was hoping for some food.

'I refuse to let another rabbit die,' she said and turned to head inside.

This time, Emma chose not to set her alarm to rise every two hours through the night. She just didn't go to bed. In the morning, I found her dozing in my office chair with the rabbit on her lap. A number of empty rehydration sachets and plastic droppers were scattered on the table behind her. Even before she stirred, however, I could see that all her efforts had come to nothing. Starsky looked like he had given up the fight just moments earlier. My first thought was that Emma would freak out if she woke up to find a deceased rabbit in her hands. I crept in to remove the body, which is when she opened her eyes.

'You did your best,' I said, and stood back in case she reacted badly. 'At least you can console yourself with that.'

She glanced down, caught her breath, and then looked to the door behind me. From the kitchen, I could hear the sound of small children bundling downstairs for breakfast.

'Don't let the little ones see this,' said Emma, blinking back tears.

I may not have shared her connection with the rabbits, but I could see what this meant to her. So I nodded, closed the door and turned to find Frank and Honey looking up at me expectantly. They were standing side by side at the child gate used to stop Sesi from running wild.

'Right!' I said decisively, and clapped my hands together. 'Who wants to put down their DS's and feed Hutch?'

When both children nodded, I invited them to follow me. It was only as I stepped out onto the yard that I realised I ought to have checked the rabbit in question was still with us. Seeing Hutch eagerly awaiting us with his front paws pressed to the mesh came as quite a relief to me. Nevertheless, as I left the little ones to overfeed him in order to serve breakfast to the minipigs and the chickens, I figured it could only be a matter of time.

That morning, alone at home, I couldn't help thinking ahead. Demolishing one hutch might've seemed a bit harsh, but it had also made me realise that we once enjoyed a yard where we could sit outside on sunny days. Since the rabbits' arrival, it had felt like we lost ownership somehow. I didn't want to wish Hutch away, but if it was going to happen anyway then a little part of me looked forward to the extra outdoor space in the summer.

After lunch, I popped outside to see how our one surviving rabbit was doing. In a way, it was a small mercy to find that Hutch had retired to his sleeping quarters. I assumed he had sought for himself a dark and quiet place in which to die. It wouldn't be long before I was digging another grave in the garden. Until then, I figured I should leave him in peace and just get on with my work.

Minutes later, despite feeling very bad about giving in to the first thought that came into my head, I was out in the yard once more. This time, I had a tape measure in hand. Having idly checked out the dimensions of a bistro table and two chairs I'd found online, I wanted to see if it would all fit once the last rabbit hutch had gone. Sesi had followed me outside. She was watching me intently. I tried to ignore her. If I caught her gaze, as true and devoted as ever, she'd only encourage me to take a long, hard look at myself. With my back turned to my dog, I measured the length and then the depth of the last bunny's quarters, only to realise I had forgotten some of the dimensions for the table. So, I set the tape on top of the hutch and popped back inside to check the details on my computer screen.

When I returned to the yard once more, I found Emma in her work coat, her bag on the flagstones, looking down at the hutch with her back turned to me.

'You're early,' I said, trying hard not to sound startled. At the same time I noticed what I had left on the roof of the hutch, and grimaced inwardly. To my relief, Emma turned to face me.

'I took a half day so I could look after the rabbit. Shifting my meetings was a nightmare, but I couldn't just leave all this to you.' Emma returned her attention to the hutch, dropping down to peer through the little entrance into the sleeping quarters. It was too dark to see any sign of life. 'How's he been?' she asked.

I waited for her to face me once more before assuring her that I'd been watching him closely. Even so, I said, it didn't look good for him. Emma appeared resigned, while I must've just seemed shifty.

'What are you looking at?' she asked, turning to the rabbit hutch once more. When she met my eyes once more, I just knew from her expression she had seen the tape measure on the roof.

I spread my arms, hoping she would be reasonable.

'I'm just thinking that when summer comes around it would be nice to sit outside with the newspapers. A table and two chairs would fit perfectly there.'

Emma held my gaze for a moment after I'd finished speaking. Her eyes tightened, ever so slightly, before she turned her back on me once more. Just as she crouched in front of the mesh, a white nose emerged from the gloom of the sleeping quarters, followed by a set of whiskers and then the rabbit itself. Hutch had never looked so good, I thought, as he hopped forward to greet her.

'Who needs newspapers,' she asked, having opened up the wire door to lift Hutch out and cradle him in her arms, 'when we can sit outside with the rabbit?'

# 5

# Endgame

I was well aware that I had been hasty in my bid to reclaim the yard. I had just assumed that Hutch was holed up in his sleeping quarters, quietly expiring.

As it turned out, he was in there for nothing more terminal than a lunchtime nap.

I still held out that Hutch would inevitably follow the fate of the three preceding rabbits. Whenever that happened, I figured I ought to wait a while before returning to the idea of turning the yard into a space for the family. When I did so, I would point out that spending time in the garden was no longer that relaxing. Sure, on a fine day you could sit out there, close your eyes and sun yourself. It's just the combination of clucking hens and grunting minipigs left you feeling more like you were occupying a particularly challenging level of Angry Birds.

In the end, my plans for the yard were put on permanent hold. In short, Hutch failed to show any sign of sickness whatsoever. Emma cared for him closely in the wake of his brother's passing, but the only change I could see was in his size on account of all the extra treats. Hutch belonged to Lou by rights. At her age, however, any leisure time spent away from Facebook often left her irritable and twitchy. As May and the little ones were so upset at the loss of their rabbits, our eldest seized the opportunity to appear generous while absolving herself of further responsibility for her pet. As a result, Honey, Frank and May took on joint ownership of Hutch. After a couple of weeks, that meant regular reminders from me to feed him before school, while I continued to clean his quarters myself because I couldn't be bothered to keep nagging them about it. This came as no surprise to me, unlike the lengths that Emma had gone to nurse the rabbits. In looking after them she had forgone both sleep and work. I was quietly impressed by her commitment in the face of an emergency. It reminded me that if it wasn't for her career then the daytime care for Butch and Roxi would be something she'd embrace with enthusiasm.

As for the ever-growing elephant in the room, our drama with the rabbits proved to be just a temporary distraction. Once it was clear that Hutch had cheated death, so the awkward pause on coming across little dogs returned to haunt me. Whenever an undersized ball of fury made its presence known, neither Emma nor I would pass comment. I said nothing for fear of starting something I would regret, while her silence told me what was uppermost on her mind. She might've claimed there was a big difference between a little dog and a long one. Being the owner of a proper dog, I simply kept my views to myself.

Eventually, the issue was forced into the open. It happened as we were heading for the seaside on a day trip. We had only recently taken to treating ourselves in this way on account of the people carrier that we had picked up second-hand. As a family, we couldn't fit into anything less, which was something we had only realised when Frank came into the world. For years after his birth, if we wanted to go anywhere we would have to travel in convoy using Emma's company car and our battered old Volvo. When the Volvo gave up the ghost, we went for the only vehicle that could squeeze us all in. Given the purpose of a people carrier, it was no surprise that it came with years of crisps and biscuit crumbs engrained into the fabric of the seats and a *Teletubbies* soundtrack jammed into the CD player. In a way, it felt like a home from home on wheels, and we made full use of the opportunity to travel en masse. On the downside, the boot was too deep for Sesi. She couldn't see out. In a bid to stop her complaining, we had taken to strapping her into a seat at the back.

It was our dog who was responsible for starting up the conversation I had been striving to avoid. We had arrived at the coast, where traffic along the seafront moved at a crawl. As a result, Sesi had plenty of time to scope out those people enjoying a walk on the promenade and then ruin it by barking at them as we passed. There wasn't much we could do to stop her. I just hoped the traffic would pick up the pace a bit as we headed for the car park. This became even more pressing for me when I caught sight of one man up ahead with a hound that just screamed *wrong*. As soon as I saw them, I wondered whether I could perform a u-turn before the rest of the family noticed. As the man drew closer I even tried to distract them by asking if Sesi was safely belted in, but by then it was too late.

'Look, kids!' said Emma, and sat up in her seat. 'A sausage dog.'

By now, the man was close to passing our car. With the traffic at a standstill once again, there was nothing I could do but watch along with the family as the Dachshund led the way. Straining on the leash, propelled by paddle feet, it looked about twice as long as Dandelion, and she was a mutant through my eyes. The dog also drew attention, not just from the kids in the back but other passers by. Smiling and nodding as he walked, the man didn't seem to mind one bit. Emma even swivelled in her seat to get a better look as he passed. Then she turned to face me. I tightened my grip on the wheel, fighting the urge to say something, only to catch sight of the pair in the wing mirror. The sausage dog was such a length that the man kept having to perform what looked like little ballet steps to avoid kicking it in the rear. The urge to pass comment suddenly proved irresistible.

'Well, my day just got a bit brighter,' I declared, and promptly burst out laughing. 'How can any man hold his head high with a pointless pooch like that? I mean, *really*? I'm sure the dog is great, but basically it shouldn't belong to anyone other than a Parisian housewife.'

'He looked like he loved that dog!' said Emma, who had clearly been waiting for a moment like this. 'Just as we would love one, too.'

I drew breath to suggest that she count me out, but the kids were in the back and chimed in with their enthusiasm.

'Sausage dogs sound on trend,' said Lou, and then addressed May. 'Do any celebrities have one? We could be the first!'

'But you're not famous,' I pointed out. 'And I don't want to be known around the village as a man who owns one. It's a girl's dog.'

'Don't be ridiculous,' scoffed Emma, just as the traffic ahead began to move.

'I'm serious! Look at Adam. You just know that Claire must've been the one who thought it would be a good idea. Mark my words, behind every sausage dog is a woman who got her own way. If I walked out with one, everyone would assume I'm henpecked.'

'You're not henpecked,' said Emma. 'It's just you're wrong about a lot of things and I'm right.'

'You weren't right about the minipigs,' I was quick to point out. 'I should've been firm when you first suggested we needed a pair to share our sofa.'

'This is different. This is about a dog that won't take up any of your time because he'll be mine. I'll do *everything*.'

I focused on the road ahead for a moment. Having seen the dedication Emma showed to the rabbits, I didn't doubt that she meant it. As far as I was concerned, she could take on any pet she liked if it never crossed my path. From experience, however, I just knew her job would get in the way.

'Who's going to look after it when you're at work?' I asked, with no need to remind her that in office hours I was Butch and Roxi's primary carer. 'This is why we can't have another dog, Emma. Whether it's a Dachshund or a Doberman, I'd be the one who has to deal with it during the day.'

'I'll take it with me,' she countered quickly.

I looked across at her. She seemed deadly serious.

'Really? Is that entirely professional?'

'It'll be fine,' Emma insisted. Then, with less conviction and in a quieter voice, she added: 'Lots of people take their pets to work.'

I glanced in the rear-view mirror. Lou and May met my gaze, evidently holding out for my response. Even the little ones had looked up from their Nintendos to see what I would say. I was beginning to feel like the victim of a grand family plot to force me into surrender. I could continue to stand my ground. I knew I had that option. I also sensed that Emma had no intention of quietly giving up. Every now and then, when I least expected it, she would return to the issue. And each time, I'd discover that somehow she'd moved one step closer to cranking up the size of our household. So, yes, I could protest, but there was a very good chance that I'd simply be delaying the inevitable. Once again, the cars in front slowed to a standstill. I brought the people carrier to a halt and sighed to myself.

'So, I'd have nothing to do with this new dog, right?'

'Nothing,' Emma said, echoed by several voices from the back seat. 'Nothing at all.'

Judging by the way she held my gaze so firmly, I realised I had revealed a crack in my convictions. It wasn't much, but I couldn't expect her to let it go now. Just one question from me, engaging her on the subject rather than resisting, had taken us all the way to the endgame in a matter of moments. From here on out, there could only be one outcome. In frustration, at myself more than the vehicles in front, I jabbed at the car horn. Then I raised my hands in surrender before anyone could tell me to relax. In the rear-view mirror, the only pair of eyes not locked onto mine belonged to the dog. Sesi was still looking out of the window, her tongue lolling, with not a clue about the course of our conversation. She adored being out with the family, especially the children. On the beach, I could expect her to sit protectively by the little ones as they made sandcastles, or accompany Lou and May for ice creams. She served a purpose. If another dog were to enter our lives, it needed to offer us something as well. Even if it was physically capable, I couldn't think of anything a Dachshund could bring to the table. Then I considered what was in it for me, which was an end to the unspoken pressure to cave in.

'Very well,' I said, with a long sigh. 'If you're so desperate for one of those stupid things then don't let me stand in your way. But I want to be completely clear here. Everything from feeding to exercising and clearing up after it is down to you. I can't guarantee that Sesi will be so agreeable, but that's my position. As far as I'm concerned, this dog doesn't exist.'

# 6

# A Dog Too Good To Be True

So, the Dachshund craved by Emma and the kids was to come under terms and conditions.

In some ways, I felt quite satisfied with the way it had all turned out. Even though I'd basically crumbled, somehow it seemed like I was the one who called all the shots. It gave me licence to pay no interest at all in the internet trawl for breeders; a search that commenced as soon as we returned from our day trip to the beach. Nobody rounded on me for failing to share in their coos of admiration at the puppy pictures they found. I wasn't accused of a lack of enthusiasm because basically I had ruled myself out of any role in this dog's life.

Despite my air of indifference, I found I had a few things to say when Emma checked her emails over breakfast one morning and announced their search was over.

'You're going to love this,' she said, switching from her BlackBerry to her laptop on the kitchen table. Quickly, the children abandoned their bowls and gathered around her. I remained at the sink with a half-washed-up cup in my hand. Even though my back was turned, I stopped scrubbing and listened intently. I could even see their reflection in the window in front of me. 'In a few weeks from now this little sausage dog mummy will give birth to babies,' she continued, pecking at the laptop keys, 'and one of them will be ours!'

'Awww!' Lou peered over the heads of the little ones, studying the screen intently. 'She has lovely eyes.'

'And a sweet face,' added May.

'And long hair,' I pointed out, standing behind them now. 'Long-haired dogs are a nightmare when they shed. It clogs the vacuum cleaner, sticks to furniture and clothes, and gets in your teeth at times.'

Emma seemed unsurprised to find me breathing down her neck. She clicked the mouse to bring up another shot of the dog. It was sandy in colour, shaggy and very, very long.

'That isn't something you need to worry about,' she reminded me. 'We'll make sure any Dachshund dog hair clings to our clothes and not yours.'

'Just look at Sesi,' I said, aware that I was already undermining my hands-off policy. Dutifully, everyone turned to regard the dog in the boot room. She was lying behind the child gate, watching us all. On finding everyone peering at her, she tipped her head and whined. 'Every spring and winter she sheds so badly I could stuff a duvet with it. Another long-haired dog would just make things worse.'

'So, you sweep up the Sesi hair. We'll take care of the sausage dog.'

This was Lou, who put her suggestion to me like I should've thought of it myself.

'It really wouldn't be as easy as that,' I explained. 'I'm just suggesting that a short-haired model would be lower maintenance for you all.'

Emma turned back to the screen. She clicked on the mouse once more. The next shot showed a picture of the dog stretched out under a radiator. It pretty much spanned the length of the thing.

'I still can't get over how long these dogs are,' I said. 'Long and useless. If it was long and had a function, I'd understand. Y'know, like a baguette.'

'Or a vibrator.'

The suggestion came out of nowhere, and left me lost for words. That it had been made by our thirteen-year-old caused Emma and I to stare at one another in disbelief, and then turn to May. She looked at us both, seemingly surprised by the attention.

'Sweetheart,' I said, and cleared my throat. 'How come you know what that is?'

May switched her attention to Lou, who smirked and dropped her gaze.

'I don't know,' she said with a shrug. 'Most probably I read about it in one of your advice books.'

'I see.' All of a sudden, it felt like it was *my* fault that May had spoken inappropriately. 'I didn't realise you were interested in my books.'

'Oh, I'm not,' she said brightly. 'Mum left a copy of one on my bed.'

I exchanged an awkward glance with Emma.

'Perhaps a talk might be better?' I suggested. 'You know? A *special* girls' chat about . . . stuff.'

I felt myself blushing as I spoke. Regardless of all those years spent writing advice for teenagers about sex and relationships, my record for communicating face to face with my offspring was dismal. My attitude was an uneasy mix of utter denial, which was the traditional paternal posture, combined with an evangelical willingness to address any question that they had. Of course, despite my experience as an agony uncle, I was the last person on earth that my children wanted to approach, which is why I relied on Emma to make sure they were informed.

'Can we discuss that later and get back to the Dachshund now?' Emma gestured at the image on the screen once more. I couldn't look at it in the same light, though I was relieved to be moving back on topic. 'I think a long dog is lovely.'

'I still think you'll regret choosing one with so much hair.'

'But if we backed out now,' she told me, sounding totally untroubled by the moulting issue, 'we'd lose the deposit.'

'You've paid money already?' I stopped myself there, and tried not to look shocked for the second time in a matter of moments. It was all very well keeping out of the search for a sausage dog pup, but now they had found one I suddenly questioned the wisdom behind it all over again. It didn't help having a visual right in front of me. I looked at the image once more. 'Don't you think it'll get under our feet?' I asked.

'Not yours,' said Emma, who checked the clock on her BlackBerry and promptly scrambled to get her bag ready. 'At this time during weekdays, the puppy will be heading off to work with me.'

By now, the little ones had decided some drawings of the new dog were needed. Despite the fact that we had wasted several minutes of our busy early morning schedule, I couldn't get them to return to their bowls to finish breakfast. As for Lou and May, they were never great at speeding up when short for time. Even though they only popped back to their bedrooms to pick up their school bags, sometimes it felt more like they'd gone on to climb through a wardrobe and lose themselves in an enchanted kingdom or something. Even if I was to stand at the foot of the stairs and bellow at them to hurry up because we had a house fire on our hands, they'd still finish doing their hair.

It was only later, after having just made the school run, that I found myself looking at the drawings Honey and Frank had made. My son's took a while to interpret. Rendered in red and black felt tip, it featured six figures with circular torsos, oversized arms and a gigantic worm underneath them. I was well aware that the worm was in fact his interpretation of a sausage dog. What struck me most was the happy face he'd drawn inside the sun.

Honey's offering was a little more studied. She used a wider range of colours, and included not just her immediate family but the minipigs, the chickens, Sesi and four rabbits in fine health. She had appointed herself to be the one holding the Dachshund's lead. I couldn't help noticing that she had set me apart from the rest of the family. I was also alone in having an unhappy face.

'Already the dog is a problem,' I muttered to myself, and folded away both pictures.

I should've put the subject out of my mind when I settled down to work. With Sesi snoozing beside me, Hutch out in his run, the chickens patrolling the lawn and the minipigs sleeping off their breakfast in the shed, I was free to close the office door and knuckle down. Five minutes in, however, and I was scrolling through the search return for *Dachshund*.

To my surprise, the breed hadn't come to prominence five hundred years ago merely for the comic entertainment of the German nobility. What they were drawn to was a bold, confident working dog whose long trunk, paddle paws and powerful shoulders made it ideal for tracking down rabbits and badgers in their burrows and setts. Never mind that their heads looked too big for their bodies, a Dachshund had a reputation for being lively and courageous. In fact, the more I learned, the clearer it became that we were talking about a ballsy, idiotic-looking dog who had never once looked in the mirror. I came away from my research with a grudging respect for the fact that the breed hadn't become overwhelmed by shame and retreated into the wilderness away from public view. If anything, their popularity had been on the upswing for some time.

As for work, when I finally got around to it I began by wading through my emails. Mostly these suggested my penis could benefit from enlargement and my bank account from an overseas lottery win – if I'd just like to hand over my card details. Beyond the junk, I didn't really get much proper correspondence. Apart from Emma, the only other people I tended to hear from regularly was my children's books editor, ever anxious that I deliver on time, and a pet-sitting service that Emma had once signed up to on my behalf. The time had long gone since we could afford to pay the costs involved in hiring people to take care of all the animals in our household so that we could go on holiday. Even so, it was a professional outfit that maintained a high profile with a regular e-newsletter. I always made a point of reading it, not because I lived in hope that we would one day enjoy a break without squealing or barking to bother us. To be honest, I skipped the stuff about rates and discounts in favour of the list at the end. It was one that detailed those customers who sought to rehome their animals. Often there was too much information, but it always satisfied my nosy streak. From these despatches, I learned that Vincent the Siamese cat needed a new home, 'preferably with hard flooring' on account of his incontinence issues, while an Afghan Hound called Dolly was looking for a family prepared to put her on webcam each week so her former owners could stop pining from their new home in Australia. I didn't need to know any of this. I just liked to be reminded that I wasn't alone in sharing my life with challenging pets.

Opening up the newsletter, I looked forward to reading about other people's predicaments. A cursory glance told me there was nothing this time around that would raise a wry smile. Instead, what I found sharpened my attention and brought me closer to the screen.

By the time Emma came home from work, I had already sold my discovery to the little ones. Before she'd even had time to shed her coat, Frank and Honey were closing in to show her a new set of drawings especially commissioned by me. I had decided not to involve Lou and May until I had brought their mother onside. For what I had to propose here was an alternative dog to the Dachshund. Had I breathed a word to them in advance, there was a good chance they'd have phoned Emma in the office and I'd have been greeted by her with an unequivocal *no*.

'These are lovely,' she said instead, on admiring Frank and Honey's artwork. 'Is it supposed to be Sesi?'

'Sesi has pointy ears,' I reminded her, and prepared to begin my pitch. 'This is a Labrador.'

Emma looked back at the pictures.

'How nice,' she said, forcing a smile. 'What a handsome-looking Lab.' With their efforts duly praised, the little ones took off to tack the pictures on their bedroom wall. Emma waited for them to leave the kitchen before adding quietly: 'The world's most boring dog.'

I affected a look of surprise. Even though I totally agreed with her, I couldn't lose my momentum.

'Labradors are far from dull,' I said. 'I know of one that is too good to be true.'

As I spoke, Emma kicked off her heels and hung up her coat.

'I don't have anything personal against Labs,' she said. 'It's just they lack a little spark. They're loving, gentle family dogs, for sure, but in my experience they always grow fat and spend their time snoring in the sun.'

'Some can do more than that,' I said, and seized my moment. 'Check this out.'

I invited her to sit at her laptop, which I had preloaded with the email in question.

'It's the newsletter from the pet-sitting people,' she said, brightening up as she took a seat. 'Are you about to propose a holiday?'

'Something much better than that,' I said, and pointed out the paragraph for her attention.

As Emma settled in front of the screen, I stood back awaiting the moment she realised that this could be the dog of our dreams.

'I don't believe a word of it,' she said eventually. 'It must be a hoax.'

'That's what I thought,' I pressed on, 'but I called the owner and he said it's for real.'

I took myself to the chair opposite Emma, who finally looked over the laptop at me.

'No dog can do the things it lists here,' she said, sounding a little uncertain now. 'Can they?'

I beamed broadly.

'Ossie can help you dress in the morning and put you to bed at night. He's been trained to load and unload the washing machine, as well as pick up everything from the phone to the post. He knows how to fetch the TV remote when you need it and carry a shopping basket in his jaws.'

'That's not a dog,' she cut in. 'It's a housekeeper.'

I shot her a look that told her this was not a joke.

'There are people whose lives depend on an assistance dog. If you have trouble standing upright, for example, Ossie here is the pet for you.'

'But you don't have trouble standing upright,' Emma pointed out. 'Not always.'

When she returned her attention to the details on the screen, I sensed that I was beginning to get through to her. We didn't need some overpriced and overlong pooch. What we wanted was a dog like Ossie! When I woke up in the night and shuffled off to pee, he would be right there to switch on the light for me, ease the lid up with his nose and even operate the flush with a bit of practice. In short, he could cover for all the things I so often failed to do. It was a Lab who would have my back. Patiently I waited for Emma to read through the details all over again.

'If this dog is so highly skilled,' she said eventually, 'why isn't it working with the disabled?'

'According to the trainer,' I told her, ready with my answer, 'Ossie passed every test but one with flying colours. He's clearly really talented, but standards are so high that he didn't quite make the grade to look after someone in need. It just means they have no option but to find him a family home. A home like ours, in fact. The trainer has even been good enough to hold him for us until I talked to you.'

'But it's too late,' she said. 'I've even been to the pet store at lunchtime. I've bought a sausage-dog-sized crate and everything the new puppy needs. It's all in the back of the car.'

I knew what Emma was talking about. We'd used a crate for Sesi when she was younger. It was basically a wire mesh cage that served as a sort of safe den for the dog. Sesi used to take herself there to nap during the day, and we'd shut her in at night for her own safety as much as ours. I could only think that a crate custom-built for a Dachshund pup would look more like the sort of trap you'd find on riverbanks. As for Ossie, if he found time between tasks to take a break he could probably pop out and pick one up for himself.

'A dog is for life,' I reminded her. 'It's important we make the right decision here.'

Emma scrolled back to the accompanying picture. He did just look like a young, industry-standard Labrador. Then again, Clark Kent didn't seem up to much until he'd found a phone booth.

'I suppose he is kind of endearing,' said Emma, tipping her head to one side.

'Just think,' I added, placing my hands gently on her shoulders now. 'Some help with the chores at last.'

It may not have seemed like a big incentive, but I knew my wife well enough. Being at home, the cooking and the cleaning fell to me. Nevertheless, when Emma finished work there would always be things she would do again because it hadn't met her standards. They weren't unrealistically high. It's just mine were a little bit lower than hers. I fell short when it came to folding clothes, for example, or putting away the plates once they've dried in the rack. A dog who could take over where I left off would mean a great deal to us both.

A moment later, watching Emma direct the cursor on the screen towards the print button, I smiled to myself victoriously.

# 7

# Outdoor Kind of People

Just one obstacle stood in the way of Ossie joining the family, and that was the Dachshund. Emma had placed a deposit with the breeder, after all. We couldn't afford to lose the kind of money she had put down, which meant everything rested on the phone call she went on to make. I left the room so she could focus on appealing to the breeder's good nature, and then listened closely at the door. Much to my surprise and delight, the lady proved no obstacle whatsoever.

Ossie sounded like a one-in-a-million dog, she told Emma, and I couldn't disagree.

When it came to winning over the children, we presented a united front. I pitched it to May and Lou by explaining that Ossie was a pet who could also keep their rooms nice and tidy. The little ones proved to be tricky about it. This was mostly down to the fact that they'd been playing a canine simulation game on their DS's. Having each adopted a sausage dog, it was quite a challenge to persuade them to delete them and select Labradors instead. With the promise that Ossie's first task would be to accompany them to the village shop for sweets, we got there in the end.

With the family onside, I called the assistance dog trainer

back and arranged for us to visit. If we could demonstrate the right qualities, Ossie would be ours to take home.

Two days later, we pulled up outside a terraced house in a market town to the south of the county and prepared to make a positive impression.

'The game consoles stay in the car, OK?' I had turned in the driving seat to address the little ones. 'I want no squabbling or fiddling with things that don't belong to you, and when Mum and Dad are talking to the nice man do *not* interrupt.'

'Can't Frank and Honey stay in the car?' asked Lou.

'No, but your mobile phone can keep your seat warm,' I told her. 'We can't have you uploading pictures of the poor dog to your profile before we've even become his rightful owners.'

Immediately, Lou lodged an appeal with her mother.

'Your father's right,' said Emma, and unbuckled her seat belt. 'At least let's aim to give the impression that we're a *normal* family.'

I caught May's eye as she said this.

'Just try to stay calm,' I asked her, before swinging open the car door. 'If Ossie doesn't come to you first, that's not a sign he hates you.'

We had left Sesi at home. I had even explained my reasoning over the phone to the trainer, who sounded impressed by my sense of responsibility. When I went on to tell him about our chickens and the rabbit, he assured me that a dog like Ossie would take them all in his stride. I decided not to mention that we also owned a pair of minipigs.

Nervous with anticipation, we assembled outside the trainer's house. Emma pressed the buzzer. In response came a bark from somewhere inside, followed by the sound of padding feet.

'I imagine that's Ossie,' I said quietly, and wondered if the dog himself would open the door, welcome us in and offer us tea and biscuits. When a human form took shape through the frosted glass, I decided perhaps that was too much to ask.

'Hi, there!' I said cheerily to the man who greeted us. He was a trim fiftysomething with a pressed shirt tucked into his jeans and the air of early retirement. I introduced the family as we shook hands, and though I missed what he was called there was only one name on my lips. 'And this must be Ossie!'

Sitting dutifully beside him was the dog himself. Ossie looked up at me, and then raised one front paw.

'He wants to say hello,' said the trainer, and stood aside for us. 'Shake hands, Ossie!'

From the moment I felt the pads of his paw in my palm, I was totally sold. So too were the rest of the family as they took turns to meet and greet a dog who had our name all over him.

'I'm impressed already,' I said, before the trainer invited us to follow him through into the kitchen. The dog waited for us to file in before bringing up the rear. There the trainer turned and gestured at the front door. Obediently, the dog switched back to push it shut. I glanced at Emma, nodding my appreciation.

'Do you have your car keys?' the trainer asked next. 'Ossie can take care of them for you.'

As I reached into my pocket, the Labrador moved across to sit in front of me, as if awaiting a treat. When I produced my keys, he took the fob lightly between his teeth, carried the set across the kitchen tiles then hopped up on his hind legs to deposit them on the counter. I was busting to ask if we could teach him valet parking, but reminded myself not to overstep the mark.

'Incredible,' said Emma instead. 'What a useful companion he must be for some people.'

'Oh, dogs like this are a lifeline,' said the trainer. 'Most owners genuinely couldn't manage without their help.'

As he went on to explain how assistance dogs were trained, I eyed the Labrador and wondered if he could do essential stuff for me like open a wine bottle or even feed the minipigs their breakfast in the morning. I could just see Ossie setting his own alarm clock so he was ready with the feed bucket before Roxi and Butch began to bellow. I couldn't expect him to brew a pot of tea on his way back in, of course. It wasn't in any dog's best interest to deal with boiling water. He could take responsibility for the toast instead.

'Is there anything that Ossie can't do?' I asked at one point as the kids gave in to temptation and set about petting him.

Observing his canine student, the trainer folded his arms tight across his chest. 'Assistance dogs carry so much responsibility it's vital that they finish their training with top marks in every discipline. Ossie here was perfect in terms of his skills and ability. It's his personality that let him down.'

'But he's adorable,' said Lou, clearly itching to grab her phone from the car. 'How could anyone fail him?'

'In the right household, he'd be perfect,' the trainer observed, and then addressed me directly. 'On the phone you said you live in the countryside, right? I assume that means you're outdoor kind of people?'

'We *love* it!' I assured him, because I felt sure that's what he wanted to hear. So too did the kids, who swiftly backed me up. 'There's nothing we like better than spending time in the fresh air.'

'Then there won't be a problem,' said the trainer, sounding mightily relieved. 'I do believe that Ossie here has found himself a good home.'

'Hold on,' said Emma, who had been unusually quiet. 'I think we should at least know why he didn't make the grade.'

I found myself cringing inwardly. It was a perfectly acceptable question to ask. I just would've taken a different approach from my wife, because she had made it sound like the man had something to hide.

'I'm sure it's nothing,' I said before he could speak. 'A dog this useful is more than welcome to live with us.'

'It's only a problem for some people.' The trainer summoned Ossie to his side. 'But you don't look like couch potatoes to me.'

I wasn't quite sure what he meant by this. Still, I watched along with everyone else as he commanded the dog's full attention by snapping his fingers. Then he pointed at a small flat-screen television on a cabinet in the corner.

In response, a deep growl built in the back of the dog's throat.

It was a noise that turned to a snarl when the trainer crossed the room. He collected the remote control himself, which seemed a bit of a wasted opportunity from where I was standing. Then he used it to switch on the television, and that's when Ossie went nuts.

'What's got into him?' I asked, as the kids kept their distance from the Lab now baying and barking at the screen.

'It's just his background,' the trainer said with a shrug. 'The household where he was raised didn't own a television. They brought him up beautifully but it's a formative stage for any dog. Now, Ossie just sees it as a threat. Since he came to us, my wife and I haven't watched a programme in peace. That's why I'm keen that he goes to a family like yours.' He switched off the set. At once the dog calmed down and returned to the trainer's side. 'So,' he said, and clapped his hands together, 'any questions?'

I looked to Emma and then the children. All of them were waiting for me to respond.

'How about video games?' I asked feebly, mindful of my late-night weekend habit once everyone else had gone to bed.

'Same response. Worse, in fact. My son spends more time at his friend's house nowadays because Ossie refuses to let him play.'

'Will he grow out of it?'

The trainer shrugged.

'He'll fetch your newspaper,' he offered instead. 'And books!'

I tried to picture what life would be like without the television. Yes, we lived beside swathes of fields and woodland. The air was fresh and the walks could be nice, especially when the bluebells emerged in the late spring, but ultimately we were a family who depended on the tube for so many different reasons. It served as a sort of liquid-crystal child-minder for the little ones when I was preparing the tea, while the end of each day would always find most of us flopped on the sofa half-watching anything that happened to be on. In terms of viewing habits, our quality threshold was shamefully low. In particular we liked the kind of programme where people signed up in search of celebrity and yet inevitably exposed themselves to ridicule. Anything highbrow that caught our eye we recorded. And there it would remain until we ran out of space and had to delete it. In short, our days were busy and this was how we unwound. When I thought of the sacrifice we would have to make for this dog, the prospect of dressing myself in the morning didn't seem like such a chore.

'What do you think?' asked Emma, and shot me a look that made it clear Ossie was no longer an option. Whatever happened, I was painfully aware that there would be in-house repercussions once we'd extracted ourselves from this predicament.

'He's a brilliant companion in every other respect,' said the trainer, who showed no sign of suspecting that our desire to embrace the great outdoors tended to be fulfilled by *Total Wipeout.*

As I struggled to find a way to eat my words, May sneezed several times in succession. I glanced at my daughter, who sniffed and rubbed her nose. She'd been brewing a cold for a little while, but all of a sudden I saw it as the only exit strategy that would preserve the dignity of my family.

'Is that an allergic reaction,' I asked, and raised my eyebrows at her, 'to Ossie?'

The wrong answer would spell an end to her evening soap opera habit. May looked at the dog; the one that could make life easier for us all in so many ways, and who came at a price that none of us were prepared to pay.

'I think it is,' she said, nodding sadly, much to our collective relief.

# 8

# The Road Home

I was in the dog house. From the moment we beat a hasty retreat from the trainer's front door, my family held me entirely responsible for dropping the Dachshund in favour of a Labrador with a profound dislike for downtime.

Every now and then, when we sat around the television, someone would mutter about what a mistake I had made. To make things worse, when Emma called the Dachshund breeder to see if she could reinstate her deposit, she learned that her chosen puppy had been snapped up by another family. As for the crate she had bought in advance, that remained flat-packed in the boot room. I could only think she hadn't returned it for a reason, which left me with no choice.

In order to regain respect in my household, I knew what I had to do. It was a journey that started with me secretly scouring the classified ads in pet magazines, and ended some weeks later, one storm-lashed night, when I came home in more ways than one.

*   *   *

The long drive out to my destination was fine, even though dark clouds were massing. It was the ride back that proved to be diabolical, and not just because of the downpour.

'You can do it,' I muttered, addressing more than just myself. 'Hang in there.'

We'd been on the road for about an hour, with another one to go. Night had only just fallen. Thanks to the storm, however, the darkness was absolute. As for the rain, it was coming down so hard it felt like I was driving through a car wash. I glanced at the speedometer. We weren't exactly stationary, but the needle looked like it was nodding off. As for my stress levels, those had hit the red just as soon as I set out on the return trip. The forecast had warned that conditions would take a turn for the worse. Even so, nothing could prepare me for this. I could only think the deluge didn't bother the driver of the truck that filled my rear-view mirror.

'We'll get there,' I said, through gritted teeth. 'No need for alarm.'

The truck wasn't the only thing to be giving me grief. The passenger on the back seat had started complaining from the moment I started the engine. It was understandable. I had effectively showed up at his home, popped him in the pet carrier and permanently extracted him from his family. That he had been the last of his litter to leave left me thinking I was breaking a very big bond indeed. As money had changed hands, his anguished howls made me feel like some kind of heartless trafficker. With a straight stretch of road ahead, and no oncoming traffic, I dared to glance over my shoulder. The carrier was safely strapped in behind the seat belt. I didn't get a chance to see the occupant through the mesh. He probably saw me when lightning knifed out of the sky, but that was enough to remind me that I really needed both eyes facing forward. It also served to crank up his squeaks of terror by several decibels.

'Oh, come on! *Relax*. Get some sleep or something.'

With my plea ignored, and the truck in my mirror looking all the more menacing, I did my level best to tune out from the noise. This was basically done by focusing on not meeting my maker in the form of the ditch or a tree. I considered switching on the radio, but the rain was hammering down so hard it would've just been more noise to distress my passenger. Eventually I grew deaf to the din. What bothered me was the nagging voice in my head that questioned whether I was doing the right thing. My thoughts were only interrupted when my mobile started to ring. With no verge for me to safely pull in to, I put the call on loudspeaker and rested the phone on the dash.

'Dad? Where are you?'

This was Lou. She sounded tired, almost bored, which wasn't unusual for a fifteen-year-old at any time of day. Even though my eldest had called me, it was as if she was trying to forewarn me to keep it brief so I didn't clog the line and risk her missing a call from friends.

'I'm on the road,' I told her simply. 'Home shortly.'

'I mean what are you up to? Mum says you were acting suspiciously when you left.' Before setting out, I had told Emma I would be helping Tom for the afternoon. Unlike me, he was a hugely practical man. Tom had done all the hard work when it came to customising the shed for the minipigs and also fencing them in properly. As he always only charged me for materials, it seemed quite plausible that Tom would call upon me for a job that required an extra pair of hands. Mine might have been unskilled in his line as a landscape gardener and soft as a little princess's on account of my work at the typeface, but I was always happy to help out. With Lou on the phone, it was the whining from the back seat that I knew I'd find much harder to explain away.

'What was that?' she asked. 'Is there something in the car with you?'

'Got to go,' I said, and reached for the red button. 'Bye!'

After the debacle with the assistance dog, I wanted this to be a happy surprise for my family. I decided that I would spin it as a late birthday present for my wife. Emma was born on Halloween. I have never dared to read anything into this, though I did question what kind of offspring we were raising when Lou arrived on a Friday 13th. As it turned out, with three girls and a boy who all naturally hovered between good and evil, our brood was much like any other. It was just big, prone to bedlam and little scope for keeping secrets from one another. So when my phone rang once again, moments after I had ended the call, I just knew that Lou was onto me.

'Dad, that was a *puppy*!'

'I don't know what you're talking about,' I replied, in a weak bid to mask the sound of whimpering. 'OK,' I confessed after a moment. 'But *promise* you won't breathe a word to Mum?' From the other end of the phone, my confession was marked by a shriek of delight. 'Lou!' I hissed. 'Keep it to yourself!'

'Hold on. I've just got to tell May.'

I sighed to myself as Lou informed her sister. May was only eighteen months younger. They were as different from each other as they were close. While Lou would simply be thinking ahead to the photo opportunities, May's first thoughts were for the animal's welfare.

'That puppy sounds sad,' she said, having taken Lou's phone to speak to me. 'You have a puppy in the car who's *crying*!'

'Everything is fine,' I assured her, 'but it won't be if I come home to find your mother knows all about it. You have to keep this to yourselves. So, don't breathe a word to the little ones. Is that understood?'

I waited for May to respond. As I pushed on through the lashing rain, the silence was broken by further sorrowful whining from the back seat.

'So, what did you do to upset it?' she asked me.

* * *

I had plenty of time to think on the road home. Mostly, it concerned Emma's desire to keep stocking her family. She wasn't driven by any sense of unhappiness with her lot in life. Far from it. She was just one of those people who thrived on keeping busy at the heart of a chaotic family. Solitude, peace and quiet just didn't register with her, which often made me wonder what she saw in me, a writer. We were polar opposites in many respects, but like so many couples I doubted that one could function without the other. All I knew was that if we lived apart, one of us would have a whole lot more pets for company and trinkets to match.

With just a mile or so left of my journey, disaster struck. I didn't slide off the road or crash into one of the few other vehicles braving the atrocious conditions. At that moment in time, it seemed even worse. First the pitiful yelps from the back seat stopped. Seconds later, they were replaced by the sound of heaving.

'Don't be sick!' I pleaded. 'We're almost there!'

In response, the abrupt splashing sound on the floor of the pet carrier told me I should save my breath. What reached my nostrils a moment later made me wonder whether I could just stop breathing altogether. For judging by the awful smell, I realised my passenger had just lost control at both ends.

After several hours battling the elements, it was a huge relief to reach our house. Pulling into the drive, I killed the wipers, switched off the engine and removed the key. The interior lights came on automatically.

'We made it,' I said, resting my head on the back of the seat for a moment. 'You can relax now.'

Home at last; I knew the family would be waiting for me. As I hurried through the rain with the pet carrier in hand, it was no surprise to see Lou at the back door. May was standing behind her. The little ones were also poised to see what I had brought with me, even if their attention at that moment was nailed to their Nintendo screens.

'You've earned a welcoming party,' I said to my travelling companion. 'They're going to love you.'

I raised the carrier to glance inside, but it was just too dark to see much. At the same time, Sesi pushed past the kids to greet me. Unwilling to let her create a scene, I twisted around so that she couldn't see what I had in my hands.

'Where have you been?' This was Emma, dishcloth slung over one shoulder, who joined the others from the kitchen now. 'And what have you got there?' she asked as I stepped inside.

'If you'll just let me through,' I said, still holding the carrier from the reach of grasping hands. 'I have a late birthday present for you.'

'I didn't blab to Mum that you had a puppy,' Lou said, a little too loudly for my liking. 'It was May who told Frank and Honey.'

'That's not true!' May reacted with such raw indignation I feared the ceiling lights might flicker and pop. 'They just overheard you!'

'Guys,' I said, easing my way towards the kitchen. 'Let's all calm down. We don't want to frighten my little friend here.'

I caught Emma's eye. She looked somewhat taken aback,

but not in a bad way, so I invited her and the kids to follow me from the boot room. Sesi seemed put out when Frank closed the child gate so she couldn't join us. It was for the best, despite her disappointment. My dog needed introducing carefully. I wanted this moment to be marked by joy, not bloodshed. Keen to really milk things here, I placed the pet carrier on the table facing away from the family.

'Let me show you the last word in loveable,' I announced, aware that I now had everyone's full attention. 'Prepare for your hearts to melt.'

Then, with great reverence, I swivelled the carrier around. As I unclasped the mesh door, Emma gasped, so too did May and Lou. The little ones made noises, too. That it sounded like 'yuck' led me to glance over my shoulder at them. To my surprise, I found every member of my family grimacing in horror.

'What's wrong?' I asked, before turning to find the answer to my question.

'*Gross!*' gasped Lou, and placed her sleeve across her nose. 'What is it?'

At first, it did indeed feel like I was looking at some kind of swamp monster. All I could really see were two big, sorrowful eyes. The rest of the creature was so caked in a porridge of sick and diarrhoea that it barely looked like a dog at all.

# 9

## Way Better Than Bublé

'That's a puppy?'

Even though she sounded uncertain, Lou was the first to identify the wretched, stinking animal that blinked back at them through the mesh of the pet carrier.

'I think you'll find it's just what you've always wanted,' I said, and moved to release the fastenings. Immediately, my wife and children took a step back. As I reached into the carrier, the occupant looked up at me fearfully. I didn't want to distress the poor thing any further, which meant holding back my disgust at the state of the interior. Quite frankly, it looked and smelled like a prison cell protest. I figured the pup could only be relieved when I liberated him. 'Easy does it,' I said, and lifted him gingerly into the open. 'He's the runt of the litter. All his brothers and sisters went to homes before him, which is why he's been with the owner a while. On the upside, he had all his jabs yesterday, so that saves on one more visit to the vet.'

When the new arrival continued to emerge I heard several gasps behind me.

'A sausage dog!' gasped Emma, the first to recognise what I had here, and clapped her hands together.

'One that won't get in the way of our viewing habits,' I added.

Finally, as the pup's rear quarters exited the pet carrier, I swung around carefully so that Emma could take him from me. Instead of embracing my gift to the family, however, she just looked alarmed.

'Don't you think it needs a wash?' she suggested. 'Take it to the sink in the back room.'

'*It* is a little boy,' I said, feeling somewhat put out by the reception so far. At the very least, I had expected Lou to fire up the camera on her mobile phone. 'Doesn't anyone want to hold him?'

As I waited for someone to accept, the poor pup was just hanging from my hands, looking lost. The breeder had told me that when carrying a dog with such an elongated spine the hind quarters needed support at all times. It didn't seem like a problem to me. Then again, the puppy hadn't soiled himself at that point. All I could do was remind myself of my responsibilities, and clutch him to my chest. Lou and May looked appalled. The little ones simply stepped apart so I could make my way to the back room.

'He'll scrub up,' I assured them. 'He really is adorable!'

I noted that nobody followed me. In silence, I negotiated a path around Sesi. Normally if anyone entered her domain in the boot room, she would be up on all fours and circling them in a bid for some attention. To my surprise, as I opened the gate with one hand, Sesi retreated to her bed. I figured the repellant stench had to be masking the puppy's normal canine smell, otherwise she'd have been all over me.

It was May who read the situation completely differently.

'Sesi *loathes* him,' she declared. 'You can see it in her eyes, Dad. What are you thinking bringing a puppy into the house? You know she doesn't get on with other dogs.'

Facing her, I struggled to get a handle on how I had done the wrong thing yet again. I wanted to remind her how bad I had been made to feel in recent weeks about having only one dog in the household. *A dog that didn't count*, so everyone told me in their own way, because Sesi wasn't the cuddly kind who could frolic happily with other dogs in the village. Just then, the puppy in my arms began to struggle. I could only think he was alarmed to be in the presence of such a wolf-like breed, which persuaded me to push on for the sink.

'You need to strip off once you've finished,' said Emma, in such a way that I couldn't get excited. 'And put your clothes in a bin-bag.'

The back room was located just behind Sesi's lair. Along with the sink and a washing machine, it contained all the things in our house that were too useful to be stored in the loft, even though we never touched them. Carefully I picked my way around the portable radiator, cleared a space beside the cappuccino maker and then turned the taps so the water ran warm. By now my shirt was filthy. I smelled as bad as the puppy, but it would be a little while yet before I could clean up. As I watched the sink fill, Lou appeared beside me and squirted a dash of baby bath into the water.

'Mum has gone to fetch a towel,' she said, as May and the little ones joined her. 'She says you'll have to replace it.'

'How welcoming you all are,' I said, and stopped the taps. 'No doubt Randy is delighted to be here.'

With great care, I lowered the trembling pup into the suds. As I began to wash him, I heard Lou and then May repeat his name. Then Emma chimed in, with a tone that didn't sound as if she was just trying it out to see how it sounded.

'Randy is the worst name in the world for a sausage dog,' she added just to clarify.

'What's the problem with it?' asked Lou. 'Randy is a cool name.'

'Do you know what it can mean?' Emma asked her.

Lou looked blank.

'Randy is what you call someone who likes a lot of sex.'

This was May, whose interjection left her parents lost for words once more. Emma looked at me pointedly.

'We can discuss that later,' I said, and returned to washing down the puppy. 'The breeder is a Randy Newman fan. It's a musical reference. Randy in the other sense didn't even cross my mind.'

'A dog called Randy is wrong,' said Emma. 'We can do so much better than that.'

I looked back down at the puppy in the sink, as if seeking inspiration. In response he peered back up at me and whimpered.

'Are you ready?' I asked Emma, who had the towel with her. 'The pup with no name is about to come out.'

As he emerged from the water, we could've been looking at a different animal altogether. A seal was what sprung to mind, given his proportions and air of utter helplessness. With all the clag removed, his coat was visible to all. I had chosen a long-haired variety because despite my misgivings that's what the family had favoured. This one was predominately black with a cream muzzle that matched the colour of his paws and the underside of a tail that looked like it belonged by rights to a squirrel. Emma collected the puppy in the towel and folded him into it. I moved to take him in order to dry him off, only to find her hold had tightened. I looked up and found her gazing at his long face and almond eyes.

'Matt,' she said, in a way that left me uncertain what I had done now. 'He's *soooo* cute!'

I matched her smile, feeling only relief. This was no minipig. There was zero danger that the little Dachshund in her arms was going to surprise us in terms of sheer size. In fact, I had something else to share about the dog that I knew would delight them all.

'He isn't just an ordinary Dachshund,' I told them, as Emma placed a kiss on the crown of his head.

'No Dachshund is ordinary,' she said, still cradling the puppy as the kids gathered round to pet him. 'They're all gorgeous.'

'Well, this one,' I announced, 'is a *miniature* Dachshund.'

Sure enough, this earned me the full attention of my family.

'Really?' Lou whipped out her phone and fired up the camera app.

'Well, he won't fit inside a Facebook profile picture without a little cropping,' I told her, 'but we're talking no more than fifteen pounds in weight when fully grown.'

I had come across this sub-group of the standard breed quite by chance. As soon as I did so, I figured it would more than make up for what had happened with the minipigs.

'Fifteen pounds?' Emma looked astonished, and then appeared to question it in her mind. 'Roxi weighed less than that when she arrived,' she added. 'Are you sure this dog isn't going to go the same way?'

May counted quickly through her fingers, and seemed suddenly alarmed.

'We don't want a gigantic Dachshund in the house, Dad! There's no more space!'

'Your mother isn't talking literally,' I assured her. 'She's just a bit wary after the minipig experience, but this is different. A miniature Dachshund is a pedigree. This little chap's bloodline goes way back. Unlike Butch and Roxi, I even have the paperwork to prove it. Trust me, he isn't packing any surprises.'

By now, the pup had been thoroughly dried. He looked a little less freaked out and a lot more frizzy. Above all, with so many hands stroking him, he just seemed stunned.

'So, what shall we call him?' asked Lou, returning to the crucial question. 'How about Bieber?'

'Behave,' I said. 'Billy is good.'

'I like Bublé,' decreed Emma, without acknowledging my suggestion, 'as in Michael.'

'Bublé?' I wasn't alone in sounding aghast at the suggestion. Lou and May looked like they would rather return the dog than be forced to name it after a crooner they only ever heard on their mother's favoured radio station. 'Emma, be sensible. You can't call the dog Bublé.'

'But I thought you wanted nothing to do with him?' she said, and turned to take the towel-swaddled pup back into the kitchen. 'What does it matter if we call him Bublé?'

'I'm not thinking of me,' I said, as we followed behind. 'It's the dog's self-esteem I'm concerned about. He needs a name that makes him feel big and strong, because with a body that shape he's going to face a lifetime of being laughed at.'

Emma hugged the pup closer, and shot me a look like I had just hurt his feelings.

'So what do you have in mind?' asked May, as we crossed the boot room once more. 'Something macho like Tyson, Vinnie, He Man or Hercules?' I trailed to a halt. The little ones flowed around me from behind, while Emma, Lou and May faced me from the kitchen. Sesi must've got a whiff of washed dog just then. She lifted her muzzle, sniffing sharply, and then growled. Everyone else told her to calm down, while I just stared at a point midway between my family and me.

'Hercules,' I said, and nodded to myself.

'No!' declared Emma straight away. 'Not that.'

'It's way better than Bublé,' I said. 'And let's face it, he's going to need an epic name to survive life with a big old Canadian Shepherd. Hercules speaks volumes!'

'For a Rottweiler, maybe, or a Great Dane, but we're talking about a sausage dog here. A mini one.'

I joined them in the kitchen, closing the child gate behind me in case Sesi launched a pre-emptive puppy strike. Bringing a Dachshund into the household was one thing. Allowing my family to rename it was quite another, which was why I played my winning card.

'On paper,' I told them, and reached for a plastic wallet the breeder had given me, 'he's *my* dog. I signed the forms, see?'

I handed Emma the wallet. Without looking at the documentation inside, she returned it to the worktop.

'I'm thrilled that you've done this for us,' she said, 'but are you disowning him, like you promised you would when we first decided on a Dachshund, or does this mean you've had a change of heart?'

I looked at the puppy, swaddled in his towel. Emma looked as if she was holding some kind of canine Baby Jesus. He seemed soothed by the way she handled him. It didn't bode well.

'In every respect, he's your dog,' I said. 'But if you call him anything other than Hercules, you'll avoid years of tutting from me every time you say his name.'

Emma swapped glances with Lou and May.

'I don't think he's joking,' said Lou. 'Maybe Bieber can be his middle name.'

'You can call him as many middle names as you like,' I said, now totally sold on May's initial suggestion, even if she probably wished she'd kept it to herself, 'so long as it begins with Hercules.'

'What do you think, little ones?' asked Emma.

'You can't ask them,' I pointed out, before either Honey or Frank could draw breath to speak. 'The only names they know come from Nintendo games. I'm not having a dog in this house called Mario or Luigi.'

Straight away, the little ones protested to their mother at the sheer unfairness of it all. Emma responded by shushing them, which made me think she shared my opinion. We had a new pet here, after all. Not a plumber.

'Let's take a look at him,' she suggested next, and lowered the puppy to the floor. 'It's really important to choose a name that feels right.'

We crouched in a circle, waiting expectantly as Emma began to unfold the towel. As she did so, the pup seemed so much smaller than he had appeared in her arms. It was as if she was stripping him of a protective coat. From behind the bars of the child gates, Sesi growled at her first clear sighting of the new arrival. I wasn't surprised, though even she fell into a kind of stunned silence when Emma removed the last fold of the towel. The miniature Dachshund appeared totally exposed. With his head bowed, looking lost and forlorn once more, his proportions were quite breathtaking. Even though he was so little I could've scooped him up in my hands, his stumpy legs supported a square chest and a body that seemed almost telescopic in length. A moment later he shook himself down, and then peered around at the new family staring intently at him.

'That's no Bublé,' I said quietly, which caused him to sniff the floor and wander towards me.

'Sizzles?' May suggested hopefully, only for Emma to point out how inappropriate that might be for a sausage dog.

'It's a Hercules for sure,' I said, as the pup attempted to pop his little front paws onto my knee. It was a struggle for him to reach, taking several attempts before he made it, which I felt was more than enough to justify my suggestion. 'Just look at him,' I added. 'This is a pup with *passion!*'

It took a moment for me to realise what was going on as the new dog began to move back and forth on his hind legs. It was then I stopped tickling the top of his head.

'Oh, gross!' said Lou, and clapped a hand to her mouth. 'He's . . . doing it with you!'

'He's too young!' I protested, and attempted to push him away. 'It's just a reflex action.' The puppy responded by just climbing back on board again, while my wife and children looked on and laughed. 'Cool it, buddy! Get off!'

'Well, he's randy by nature,' chuckled Emma as she lifted him away. 'But not by name.'

I rose to my feet, trying hard to bring my dignity with me, and brushed myself down.

'If that puppy attempts to score on me again,' I said, 'he's going back to the breeder.'

Emma responded by lifting the sausage dog close to her face and breathing in the smell of his freshly washed coat. 'Not after that,' she said, and posed for Lou so she could take a snap. '*Hercules* is here to stay.'

Straight into the sink.

One dog's dream, another's nightmare.

# part two

'Herculeses Toy Box' as created by the little ones.

Chickens? Where?

# 10

## Early Riser

The first night is always the toughest. You bring a puppy into the house, often a youngster freshly weaned from its mother. Understandably it's frightened, but with care and affection it quickly settles in. The kids can't get enough of the new arrival. They help to make its bed, set up bowls for food and water, and then forfeit valuable screen-time to play with their young four-legged friend. Such a scene reminds you why it was a good idea to get a dog. In many ways, it brings everyone together. A family companion for years to come.

Then you turn in after such a momentous day, and the true nature of your commitment becomes apparent.

\* \* \*

'This is ridiculous, Emma! How can something so little make such a big noise?'

'He'll learn. It's all about sleep-training.'

We were having this discussion in bed. Downstairs, crated in the boot room, Hercules was howling. His abrupt squeaks reminded me of the kind of sound that came out of a squash court. In this case, there could be no winner. It had been going on for hours. The last time I'd looked at my bedside clock, it was four in the morning. I couldn't say how much time had

passed since then as I'd placed a pillow over my head in a bid
to block out the noise.

'I really think you should go down,' I said, as I had many
times over. 'Just so he knows that he hasn't been abandoned.'

'That would be giving in,' Emma insisted. 'Hercules will be
totally safe inside his crate.'

From the moment the pup had kicked off, we'd had a
steady stream of visits and complaints from the kids. The
little ones were the first to shuffle in and ask if they could
play their DS's until the little Dachshund decided to call it
a night. The request was refused, of course, though I did
come close to changing my mind after their fifth appearance
at our bedroom door. As for May and Lou, their level of teen
hysteria hit new heights after the first hour. Lou was
concerned about what a loss of sleep would do for her skin,
while May chose to believe that Hercules was in fact crying
out in pain.

'He could be *dying* down there!' she insisted, after Emma
had instructed her not to give in and check on him.

'The only thing that's dying,' I told her, 'is my patience.'

As the canine protest continued, Emma sent May back to
her bedroom and then sighed to herself.

'When you collected him,' she asked me, 'was his mother
noisy by any chance?'

'She was asleep in her basket actually.' For a moment, I
considered what I'd just said. 'Maybe she'd been up all night
on account of her offspring.'

As well as the squeaking, the little Dachshund could be
heard frantically scrabbling in a bid to burrow through wire
mesh. It was pitiful, futile and totally annoying. I felt tired
and also increasingly frustrated with Emma for being so hardline with her training. Hercules was only a couple of months

old, I reminded myself. The puppy deserved a break. We all did, in fact.

'That's it,' I said finally, and snapped open the duvet. 'One of us has to do something.'

'Mark my words. You won't be helping him.'

'Yeah, but I'll be helping us all to get some *sleep!*'

I reached for the dressing gown hanging on the door. It turned out to be a short silk one belonging to Emma, but that didn't matter at such an antisocial hour. The little ones shared a bedroom. They were peering from their door as I headed for the stairs. Then, when I reached the top, I sensed a presence close behind.

'May!' I said with a start, on turning to find my pale, ethereal daughter in the gloom. 'You gave me quite a fright!'

'Hercules is definitely hurt, Dad,' she said. 'I can't believe you've ignored him for so long.'

'Will you just relax?' I hissed, feeling even more tense now I had to deal with this. 'Come with me and see for yourself, if it makes you feel any better. He's not in any pain. He's just being one.'

As May followed me down the stairs, Hercules must have picked up on our footsteps because his howling and whining cranked up by another decibel. Before bed, Emma and the kids had settled him in his crate in the boot room. It made sense to keep him in the same place as Sesi. Even though he would be accompanying Emma to work, they had to get used to each other at night. With careful management, I figured she would recognise that this was just a youngster, and not tear him to shreds at the first opportunity. Crossing the kitchen, with May close behind, I suddenly realised that the din coming from the other side of the door must be ten times worse for our poor Canadian Shepherd.

She was getting on a bit in age and, like us all, enjoyed her sleep.

I opened the door to the boot room by a notch. At the same time the scrabbling and howling subsided, and then switched to a whimper.

'Quick,' said May, panicking now. 'Before he dies!'

I frowned at her, swung the door back and faced the scene before me. Sure enough, the miniature sausage dog was alive and well in his crate, which was stationed in the middle of the room. Having left him there at bedtime with Sesi circling, the whole set-up reminded me of a diver's cage on the bed of a shark-infested ocean.

And yet I saw no sign of our resident predator.

'Sesi?' I called out quietly. 'Where are you?'

Assured that Hercules wasn't mortally wounded, May immediately refocused her anxieties.

'Has she escaped?'

I stepped into the boot room. Inside the crate, Hercules was sitting on his cushion, wagging his tail with excitement, but Sesi's bed was unoccupied. Much to the disappointment of the sausage dog, I stepped over the crate and peered into the utility room. She wasn't in there either. Puzzled, and a little panicked, I turned and looked around. The back door was locked. Unless Sesi had been secretly attending assistance dog training, there was no way she could've let herself out. Then I heard some movement from the room behind me. I glanced over my shoulder at my office door, and realised what had happened here.

'Hey there,' I said, on flicking on the light and spotting my dog. She was under my desk, her head on her front paws, looking totally fed up. Clearly the noise had been too much for her. Firstly Sesi had jumped the child gate that normally prevented her from causing chaos in my office. What's more, once inside she had gone on to push the door shut behind her. It was impressive, but still didn't mean she could be trusted to help anyone walk in a straight line. In my experience, when on a leash Sesi was quite capable of dragging me in any direction she chose. I watched her dark eyes flick from me to the crate in the boot room. She looked a little wary, I thought, which was a first. Even so, given the late hour and the fact that she had behaved herself, I couldn't order her back to her bed. Instead, I bid my dog goodnight and closed the office door.

'OK, young fella,' I said, turning my attention to Hercules once again. 'There are some house rules you need to know about.'

As I crouched before his crate, the pup looked overcome by excitement. His bushy tail wasn't the only indication of this. There was also the puddle of wee that pooled underneath him.

'Shall I tell Mum?' asked May.

Technically, this was Emma's responsibility. Then again, I knew that dragging her down to deal with it wouldn't bring out her best side.

'It's fine,' I said with a sigh. 'Go tell your sister she's good to get her beauty sleep, and be sure to turn in yourself. It's crazy that he's kept us all awake so long.'

Sending May on her way, I returned my attention to the puppy and the sodden cushion underneath him. It took another five minutes for me to sort him out. With Hercules scooped up in the crook of my arm, I replaced the cushion with a towel I found in the laundry basket and then returned him to the crate. He didn't make a fuss. Like everyone else in the family, I could only think his nocturnal activity had left him exhausted.

'You should've left him,' murmured Emma, when I finally slipped back into bed. 'Nobody will get any sleep with all this coming and going.'

I lay propped upon my elbows, looking across at her incredulously.

'I don't hear him whining any more,' I pointed out. 'Perhaps if you'd have gone downstairs when he first started up we'd both be getting the full eight hours.'

Emma was facing me on the pillow. She opened her eyes and smiled dozily.

'I appreciate the effort you've made, but surely after sleep-training four babies you'd know the drill by now?'

'Well, perhaps I should use the silence to think about it,' I said, and settled in to get some shut eye.

For a while I stared at the ceiling and listened out for the slightest whine. I heard nothing, much to my satisfaction, though it was a shame that Emma missed out. She seemed to find no difficulty in dropping off once more. In a way, that made it harder for me to relax. I wriggled in a bid to get comfortable. Clearing up puppy wee wasn't the same as sipping from a cup of chamomile tea in terms of winding down. Even so, I was determined to make the most of what little remained of the night. Aware that the shard-like space between the curtains was beginning to turn from black to grey, I closed my eyes and focused on taking myself to a special place. A hammock between two palm trees seemed like a good choice, accompanied by the lapping of waves on a shore. The odd bar of birdsong wasn't something I consciously slipped into the mix, but it seemed in keeping with the picture in my mind. Unlike the subsequent sound of two waking minipigs as they jostled from their quarters and drew breath to serenade the new day.

# 11

## Pets for Life

On the subject of dogs, Emma and I came from very different backgrounds.

We grew up in the same town in the Home Counties, and knew each other as teenagers. Her sister, younger by two years, was closer to my age. Rachel and I shared the same circle of friends. I was always wary whenever I dropped round, however. Not because I secretly hoped that Emma would answer the door, but on account of the huge Doberman that pretty much served as their personal bodyguard.

Bill was built like a bouncer on four legs. He was all meat and menace, though Emma and her sister didn't see him as a threat. Whenever I rang the bell and a booming bark filled the house, I would stand there feeling tense and unsettled. It was bad enough trying to look cool and relaxed. Doing so with a dog's nose buried in my groin was next to impossible.

The intimidation didn't stop at the doorstep. Inside, Bill would continue to sniff at me as if I had a marrowbone stashed inside my underpants. Rachel and Emma never appeared to register my unease, or if they did then they secretly relished it. Either way, my time at their kitchen table, with one hand on a cup of coffee and another fending off what was frankly an interspecies sexual assault, didn't leave me with a massive desire for dogs. If anything, it simply reinforced a view that my father had done his level best to instil in me.

Dad really wasn't a canine kind of man. Dogs were just a hassle to him, as indeed was any kind of pet. When pressed, usually by my animal-loving younger brother and sister, he would come up with a list of reasons as to why it would be a bad idea. He'd cite everything from vet bills to the difficulties associated with going away, plus the grieving that would follow when they died. Through his eyes, taking on a pet was nothing but a trap and a shortcut to misery and sadness.

In a way, his opinion was proven right over the years. It began when my mum's elderly father was forced to give up his beloved budgerigars. Ever since I could remember, he had kept a thriving flock in an aviary attached to his house. As a child, I was struck by their colour and song. He and my grandmother also owned two Labradors. Liza was lovely, and I always thought Nelson was good fun too. Until one day, alone in a sunny garden aged five or so, I wandered up to see if he wanted to play, only for the dog to raise his head from the grass and growl at me.

I vividly remember the jolt of shock, disbelief and fear. At that age, a Labrador like Nelson seemed huge. In that moment, the back door to my grandparents' house might as well have been a million miles away. All I could do was turn from the dog and make my retreat with my little heart racing.

The experience left me wary. As a result, I didn't consider growing up without a dog to be the very definition of a deprived childhood. Despite my dad's view that pets were a pain, he made an exception when my grandfather became too old to take care of his budgerigars. As I had shown an interest at such a young age, he offered the flock to me. It was a great honour, and a thrill when my mum persuaded my dad to agree.

To his credit, he helped transport the half dozen budgerigars and the aviary, which he retooled to fit against the side wall of our house.

At last, we had pets! The budgies didn't come inside the house, fetch sticks, catch mice or bask in front of the fire, but those birds meant the world to me. That autumn, I did everything by the book. I undertook all the feeding and the cleaning, hung cuttlefish from the roof joists and spent time inside the wire frame with the beautiful sea green, cobalt blue, and buttery yellow birds. I felt sure my dad would look upon this experiment and consider it to be a success. If I could take care of budgerigars, surely he would be happy for me to take on all manner of different creatures.

Then came a change in the season, and the onset of frost and bitter winds. We had chosen the wall outside our back door for the aviary because it was sheltered. Even so, the conditions were severe. When I found the first bird in the grit, my dad took steps to insulate their sleeping area against draughts. I felt really bad that we had let one die. That would never have happened under my grandfather's watchful eye. When another one expired, I began to worry that I would get into trouble. Between us, my dad and I did everything we could to protect the flock. As the winter deepened, however, the budgerigar number continued to dwindle. When the last one gave up the fight, I knew that my grandfather would have to be informed. We couldn't lie to him, after all, though I worried about just what I'd say. When the moment came, the next time we saw him, my dad broke the news before he could ask after them. I remember holding my breath I was so nervous. My grandfather, with his sparkling eyes and neat, grey moustache, simply blinked and sat back in his chair. Then he offered me a gentle smile.

'Never mind, my boy. Never mind.'

His sense of forgiveness stayed with me. It was something I would go on to share with our wider family as a teenager when asked to give the eulogy at his funeral. As well as leaving me with great respect for my grandfather, it put me off pets for some time. As far as I was concerned, I should've listened to my dad. He had been a huge source of support in the battle to see the budgerigars through the winter, but ultimately our efforts came to nothing. My brother and sister continued to lobby, of course; only now he could call upon that disaster to justify his view. There was no need for him to rattle off every single possible problem associated with pets. When asked, he simply said, 'The budgies,' and left it at that.

Next door's cat was responsible for softening my dad's position. He didn't actually like the creature. It considered our garden to be a toilet and also a hunting ground. One spring, the cat dislodged a bird's nest from the gutter behind our shed. I was about ten years old at the time, and had just come home from playing football at school. I wasn't very good at the game, but determined to get better, and so I'd taken myself into the garden to annoy my mum by repeatedly kicking the ball against the back wall. On hearing the commotion, and catching sight of the cat as it high-tailed over the fence, I went to investigate. The nest was upended in the grass. When I lifted it away, I found two helpless, grasping newborn blackbirds. One more had died in the fall. My instinct was to save the pair. Running back to the house, I found an empty ice-cream container. Without stopping to tell Mum about my rescue bid, I took it out to the compost heap and lined it with leaves and grass clippings. When I returned to the baby birds, one of the two had fallen still. The cat had come back by this time, watching from the fence, and so I placed the nest inside the container and then scooped up the surviving bird.

My mum had mixed feelings when I finally told her what I had done. Her first thought was that the mother bird might come back if we replaced the nest in the guttering. It was the presence of the cat that persuaded us to keep watch from a distance. Eventually, with every indication that the baby bird had been abandoned, she gave me the key to the shed and told me I could keep it in there. My brother and sister shared my excitement. Having placed the container on my dad's workbench, we headed out to look for worms. They weren't hard to find in the compost. We kept them in a jam jar filled with soil. As soon as I dangled a worm over the nest, the blackbird reached up and opened its beak hungrily. My little brother was next. I stepped back so he could give it a go. This time, the bird paid him no attention. It just sat there, breathing so hard that it rocked back and forth. Then my sister gave it a shot, only for the same flat refusal. Out of curiosity, I offered up another worm.

The bird reacted like it hadn't been fed for a week.

Regardless of their disappointment, my brother and sister lost no interest in our adopted pet. For the rest of the afternoon, every half an hour or so, they would join me as I popped out to feed the blackbird another worm. Each time, the little thing seized it hungrily. When anyone but me had a go, however, the bird continued to ignore them. When my dad came home from work, despite being in our pyjamas, we led him out to the shed in a state of pride and excitement. He was impressed by my rescue story and the care and attention we'd paid to the sole survivor from the nest. He watched as I plucked a worm from the jam jar. When the bird turned its beak away from my offering, he carefully suggested I shouldn't hold out hope that it would survive the night.

I was up at first light. Dew coated the grass. In bare feet, I hurried across to the shed. Mindful of my dad's warning, I was delighted to find the little blackbird waiting for me. Even so, just as I had the evening before, I returned to the house disappointed.

'It's stopped eating,' I told my mum, who was loading the washing machine at the time. 'It's like it doesn't recognise me any more.'

My dad hadn't left for work at that point. He rode a scooter to the train station, for the commute into London, wearing a helmet that mortified my mum. On the back, as a deterrent, so he said, he'd painted the scooter's registration number and **'stolen from:'** above it. Clutching the helmet and his briefcase, he'd just come through to say goodbye to us. Having overheard our exchange, he suggested that perhaps I should wear something a bit more blackbird-friendly than my bright red dressing gown.

'How about your school uniform?' he offered, as a subtle way of hurrying me up to be ready for the day. 'A grey, black or brown might work.'

It seemed like a sensible idea to me, but then my mum took an alternative take on the predicament.

'What about the clothes you were wearing when you first fed the bird?'

The items in question had just gone into the drum. They were far from subdued in colour. My school football strip was yellow with black stripes. If anything, heading back out to the shed in the unwashed top, I worried the bird would mistake me for a huge wasp with limbs. Instead, to my surprise and delight, it fed from me without hesitation.

Over the next week, as word spread through my primary school, I took on the reputation for being a kind of middle-class *Kes*.

The bird thrived, so long as I was wearing the same football top. In that time, it took to hopping up onto the edge of the ice-cream container, and even making little ventures across the workbench. One day, when I found the fledgling blackbird watching me from the shelf at the back of the shed, my dad advised me that I should leave the door open. I was aware that the bird wouldn't be reliant on me forever. Even so, I held out hope that some magical bond had been formed. The next day, on discovering the bird had flown the nest I'd made, I decided to leave some worms out just in case. For a minute or so I stood outside the shed, and was thrilled when my adopted pet appeared on the gutter. I held out my arm. A moment later, the bird was using me as a perch. It stayed there for a short while and then flitted off over the garden. Grinning to myself, I hurried inside to tell the rest of my family. Dutifully, everyone traipsed out to see for themselves. With my parents, my brother and my sister gathered at a suitable distance, I held out my arm once more, whistled and then waited.

We never saw the blackbird again.

I didn't take it personally. Even my brother and sister understood that a bird like this belonged in its natural environment. At the same time, I suppose we had demonstrated to my parents that we could look after something without it keeling over, and even when a sad thing happened we took it in our stride. Certainly something persuaded my dad to recognise that we were old enough for pets. A dog was unthinkable, of course, and none of us had any desire for more budgerigars.

Sensibly, so he thought, we started with rabbits. We were allowed to choose a pair from the pet store and loved them to bits. Only the rabbits seemed to love each other a little bit more. Finding homes for the litter they produced proved to be a challenge, but we cared for them nonetheless. As I grew out of the appeal, so my sister took over, followed by my brother, and that's how we saw them through their natural lives. Having proven ourselves, my dad finally caved in properly and agreed to a cat. Smokey arrived as I turned fifteen. He was around for many events in our family life, from three grown-up children leaving home in turn, to the early deaths from cancer of my sister and then my mother within months of one another. With nobody else left in the house, Smokey went on to serve as a consoling presence to my dad. He wouldn't go away unless a neighbour was on hand to take over feeding duties. In his view, a cattery was simply out of the question. Whenever I called to see how he was doing, he'd often update me on the cat's welfare first.

Smokey passed away some years ago, having lived to a grand old age, and yet a framed photograph of him as a kitten still hangs in the kitchen. Mounted a couple of inches above the skirting board, where his feeding bowls used to be, it's pretty much the first thing you see on stepping through the front door. My dad put it up shortly after Smokey's arrival, so the cat knew where his place was in the household.

# 12

## More Pets for Life

In a way, cats were responsible for bringing Emma and I together.

I was living in the West Country at the time. I'd finished university, but having bailed from a disastrous year teaching English in Italy, I returned with designs on becoming a writer. In effect, this meant living in a bedsit in a run-down quarter of Bristol, working part-time to pay the rent and wondering if I'd just buried myself in the graveyard of ambition. To keep me company, a friend persuaded me to take on two kittens. It turned out that their alleycat mother belonged to a drug dealer who'd been talking darkly of taking them into the city and losing them unless a home was found within the week. The visit was intimidating and didn't last long. Under more comfortable circumstances, I would've asked after the pair's background and health. As it was, he just handed them to me in a cardboard box, growled something about fleas, and sent me on my way.

Mungo and Nancy were a pedigree crossbreed, if cats could be recognised in this way. In short, they had *everything* in them and it all just sort of fitted. You could tell they were brother and sister, because their mixed-up markings were pretty much the same. Anxious to do something with my life, I spent every spare moment writing while two little cats barrelled around my bedsit. Eventually, my first break came in the shape of a short story. I'd had it accepted for publication in an anthology, and duly made my way to literary London for the launch party. I knew nobody, but for one blonde, beaming young woman with pool-blue eyes who I hadn't seen since leaving home.

Unlike me, Emma was forging a career that earned her a living. She loved her job in publishing and had a passion for books. To my disappointment, she also seemed to feel the same way about the man with his arm wrapped around her waist. When I asked after her family, she told me Bill the Doberman had passed away some time ago. It prompted me to mention that I had just taken on two kittens. Emma asked me to post her some pictures, which I duly did on my return. We struck up correspondence over the following months, during which time she was unceremoniously dumped by the man I had met at the launch party. Despite the years that had passed since I last sat at her kitchen table, I found it easy to open up to her, as she did with me. Despite the heartbreak she was going through, Emma always asked after Mungo and Nancy, who were now a regular feature in the backyards under my window. Eventually, I plucked up courage to ask her if she'd like to visit the kittens for real. Short of throwing in some sweeties, I felt a bit sleazy in making such an invitation. It meant I was mightily relieved when she didn't just go silent on me.

Emma and I were married two years later. With the cats in tow, we then set about laying the foundations for our family.

We first set up home in the East End of London. Having saved hard for a deposit, and with Emma heavily pregnant with Lou, we took out a mortgage on a terraced house in need of some love and repair. On receiving the keys, I opened up to find the place stripped down to its ice-cream pink flock wallpaper. The only items left by the previous owners were two tins of cat food, along with a note to say they hadn't been able to find their timid little tabby, Bella, before setting out for a new life in the West Country. I was astounded. How could anyone just abandon a cat like that? What's more, I was due to collect Mungo and Nancy, along with Emma, from the flat we were renting on the other side of the city.

The previous owners had left a number at the bottom of the note, which I phoned straight away. As politely as possible, I told them that adopting Bella would be impossible. We had cats of our own, after all. Whether or not they truly appreciated our position, it was agreed that I should drop off Bella at a friend of theirs who lived in our new neighbourhood, and they would travel back to pick her up. The exchange left me feeling grumpy and in no mood to mess around with an evasive moggy. I had arrived in advance of Emma to spend a couple of days decorating. Having opened up the kitchen door, I went back out to my car to bring in the gear I'd hired to strip the walls. When I returned to the kitchen, despite the colour pink screaming for my attention, the sight of a tabby cat high-tailing it into the yard took priority.

'Bella!' I called out, and hurried after it. 'Come back!'

I found the cat preparing to leap the fence. She looked very nervous, which was no surprise seeing that her family had walked out on her. I crouched down so as not to disturb her, and held out my hand. At once the cat disappeared from sight. It was a disappointment, but as I headed inside to start work I figured it wouldn't be long before she came home.

Bella kept me company through the rest of that day. Every time I turned around she would be there, only to melt away as soon as I laid eyes on her. That evening, as I set up my camp bed, she pawed at the back door to be let in. When I opened up, she panicked, and so I decided to leave her some food outside. It was a question of building up trust. Once the cat let her guard drop, I would pounce.

The moment arrived towards the end of the next day. I was stripping a wall upstairs when Bella appeared on the landing. What I wanted to do was get behind her, and then head downstairs to close the kitchen door. It worked on the first attempt, but only because Bella darted into one of the bedrooms to avoid me. As calmly as possible, I made my way to the kitchen and clicked the door shut. Then with a cardboard box I had already reserved for the task, I crept back to the landing.

'Here, puss! Time to pack your bags!'

Clearly Bella detected a hint of menace in my tone, because she shot from one room to another before I had drawn breath. The game of cat and Matt that ensued quickly became desperate. Having kept cool and calm to build up a bond, I left nothing unturned in my bid to capture her. Eventually, I cornered my prey. Desperate scrabbling ensued, and not just from Bella. Despite the scratches to my wrists, as soon as I had sealed down the last flap on the box I was on my way to the halfway house to offload a cat that hardly qualified as a fixture or fitting.

The next day, on the drive to our new place, with Mungo and Nancy yowling inside the pet carrier, I told Emma all about what had happened. She seemed pleased to know that I had sorted it out, but also slightly apprehensive – and I knew why. At the time, London's East End had yet to become a popular choice for first-time buyers from outside the area. It had a reputation for being rough around the edges and even closed off to outsiders in places. Having worked in the area as an assistant to a journalist for a little while, I thought this was unfair. It took me some time to convince Emma that the reality was very different from the mythical East End full of wide boys and shifty geezers. I felt sure that as soon as she settled in, she would recognise that was just a monstrous cartoon cliché, and all would be well.

Had I known what was happening that day I might've waited an hour or so before making the journey to the house. As it was, I picked the same moment to turn into our high street as the tail end of the funeral procession passed by for the infamous crime overlord, Ronnie Kray.

'Oh my God,' breathed Emma, as we found ourselves at a standstill amid what was clearly a street thronging with sharp-suited gangsters. Many were about eight feet wide at the shoulder, wearing dark glasses and tans picked up in the Costa del Sol. 'Lock the doors,' she whispered. 'Just don't make it obvious.'

Up ahead, a black carriage, festooned with floral dedications and drawn by horses complete with peacock plumes, made its way towards the church. Bystanders lined the procession, many of whom looked like they'd last left the house in the sixties.

'There's nothing to worry about,' I said, and tightened my grip on the wheel. 'The road will be clear in a minute.'

'We can turn around now,' replied Emma, as a bullet-headed man sporting a huge gold necklace and fur-lined black jacket crossed in front of the car. 'Just don't hit anyone.'

'Relax!' I said, avoiding eye contact with the man as he prowled by. 'It's just a funeral.'

'Just a funeral?' she repeated, keeping her voice in check. 'It's like a criminal Mardi Gras! What the hell are we doing here?'

'It's home,' I stressed, as a side road appeared up ahead. 'Everything will be fine.'

When we finally pulled into our street, we found dozens of residents had stepped out from their houses to witness the procession. As I helped Emma from the car, families spanning generations mingled in the sunshine. I even overheard some talk about the good old days, which did little to reinforce my assurances that the East End was a progressive part of London. Then, before I'd even closed the passenger door behind her, some bare-chested little kid on a bike wheeled out and pointed directly at me.

'This is the geezer,' he cried, with his eyes locked upon me, and then turned to address a whip-thin couple who I assumed were his parents. '*Look*! The cat snatcher's come back!'

'What?' Before I could say any more, the couple relayed the boy's news to a small group of people further down the road. I turned to Emma, feeling a hint of panic. 'There's some mistake,' I insisted, and then addressed the boy once more. 'We've only just moved here.'

By now, we were really beginning to draw attention. As well as the boy's parents, several other people had begun moving closer towards us. It felt like some kind of cockney zombie strike at the time, though fleeing was hardly an option. Not with Emma in her condition. Besides, the kid was still standing before me, hands on his waist, grinning provocatively.

'You pinched our cat,' he said, relishing my discomfort. 'I hope you haven't skinned it or anything!'

Helplessly, I turned to his parents for some explanation. My head was spinning, but I did note how the woman was smiling in a way that assured me I wasn't about to be shaken down for protection money.

'It's just a mix-up,' the woman said sweetly. 'Don't tease the poor bloke.'

'What's happened?' Emma sounded a little alarmed.

'The cat your husband caught,' said the mother, 'it was the wrong one.'

I glanced at my wife, who closed her eyes for a moment.

'But the owner left me with clear instructions,' I said. 'I delivered it to their friends, just as they asked.'

'Yes, you did,' the boy's mum confirmed. 'Only it wasn't Bella.'

'You took our Floss,' the father chimed in, looking far from amused. 'Floss doesn't like being far from home. She's on medication. For her nerves.'

'I wasn't to know,' I reasoned weakly. 'I just assumed the cat that came in was wondering what had happened to its family.'

'They were next door.' The man jabbed his thumb across at the house beside ours. 'Watching *Countdown.*'

I drew breathe to apologise, only to be stopped by the sound of a muffled meow from the car.

'That's one of our cats,' I said, and forced a smile. 'Really. We've had them for years.'

The couple looked at Emma, as if perhaps my word couldn't be trusted.

'I'm just so sorry,' she offered, seemingly on my behalf. 'Matt did say the cat had put up a fight when he boxed it.'

'Also when I handed it over to their friends,' I added, before realising this probably wasn't going to help matters.

By now, the woman had stopped smiling. She looked across at her partner, who clearly had something to add.

'Poor old Floss was so traumatised that she made a break for it as soon as they opened the box,' he said. 'It took them three hours to remove the kitchen worktop so they could extract her from behind the units.'

'The same time it took for our old neighbours to travel back from their new place,' the woman finished with a sigh. 'Which was a wasted journey.'

'Is Floss alright?' asked Emma, clearly concerned.

'She'll live.' The man shrugged and pulled a pouch of rolling tobacco from the back pocket of his jeans. 'So,' he said a moment later, 'you're new here?'

That night, we sat in the kitchen at the back of the house. Neither of us felt comfortable in the front room. It wasn't so much because we had yet to fit any curtains. We just didn't like the number of people who paused outside our house to peer in.

'I can't believe you got the wrong cat,' grumbled Emma. 'Now everyone will think their animals aren't safe with you around. Next they'll be asking to put you on some kind of cat protection register.'

'They were both tabbies,' I said, as I had repeated many times over. 'Anyone would've made the same mistake. I'll make it up to the neighbours. They'll soon realise I can be trusted.'

We were sitting at the table, toasting our arrival with a cheap bottle of fizz. It had gone flat within minutes of popping the cork. Emma wasn't too upset, being teetotal on account of her pregnancy, while I struggled not to dwell on other matters. Upstairs, our two cats were curled up at the foot of our bed. I was determined not to let this episode cloud what should've been a momentous event in our lives: our first home. Instead, I sat there grimacing my way through a couple of glasses, wondering what I would have to do to restore my standing in the street.

A little later, over fish and chips that I had scurried out to pick up, somebody knocked at the front door. As I set down my supper to answer it, I had visions of some intimidating pet racketeer, dead set on shaking me down for stealing the wrong cat. Instead, I opened up to find the lad from next door. Even before he spoke, I became dimly aware of the fact that the road was teeming with over-excited kids.

'We found Bella,' he said, and jabbed a thumb over his shoulder. 'All we have to do now is catch her.'

It was then I took in the scene. Under the street lights, the children were swarming from one side of the road to the other. The object of their pursuit, I realised, looked utterly terrified. Some of the kids were clutching boxes of cat food, which they shook furiously as if that might pacify the poor thing. More people began to appear at their doors, drawn out by the commotion. By the time I fetched Emma, it looked like the real Bella was likely to die of fright unless we intervened.

'I have an idea,' I said, and stepped out to share it with the street.

It only took a couple of minutes to drive the cat into our house. It was where she once belonged, after all, and had rapidly become a less frightening environment to be in than the street. Bella looked hungry, totally freaked out and unwilling to let us go near her. Still, with the front door shut and away from the crowd, we finally managed to corner her. Our cats simply looked on with disdain as we manhandled Bella into their pet carrier. It wasn't pretty, but at last she was in a safe place.

'Do you realise what this means?' asked Emma, who looked genuinely relieved. 'We can stay here!'

I wasn't sure whether she was being entirely serious.

Nevertheless, it was with some sense of ceremony that she opened up the front door for me. Before my eyes could adjust to the glare from the streetlamp outside, I stepped forward, lifted the pet carrier high and basked in the cheers and applause from the assembled crowd.

We had arrived. Thanks to the rescue of an abandoned cat, we were free to focus on the imminent arrival of our firstborn and the creation of the family Emma had always dreamed about. I never anticipated that it would feature more than two children, let alone four. Nor did I have any idea that pets would continue to shape our lives in ways that went beyond my imagination and into the realms of the ridiculous.

# 13

## Gone to the Dogs

The sausage dog formerly known as Randy had been with us for one night only. In that time, I felt as if I had aged by several years.

I was too old to go without a proper night's rest. It was OK as a new father in my twenties, but with every child the experience required just a little more effort. Now Frank slept through without waking, the last of our brood to do so. In response, we had brought a new kind of infant into the house. Hercules and his constant crying left me exhausted. I knew that Emma felt the same, and yet there was no way that she was going to admit it.

'Isn't he gorgeous!' she remarked the next morning, while stifling a yawn. Hercules had been fed, and was busy investigating the kitchen. Lou, May, Honey and Frank served as moving obstacles to the Dachshund, such was their fascination with him.

'You probably shouldn't get down to his level,' I warned them. 'He'll mistake you for puppies and then there could be trouble in store.'

'Oh, I don't think we have to worry about that.' Emma was nursing a coffee. She peered at me from over the rim of her mug. 'Hercules is a very different dog to Sesi.'

From behind the child gate in the boot room, my Canadian

Shepherd was doing her level best to look put out. Sesi was only allowed into the kitchen and the front room when we said so. She had permission most evenings, when things were calm, because at any other time she would serve as a catalyst for chaos. We had set such limits when Sesi was a young dog, following the advice of a trainer, after she had developed an interest in rounding up Lou and May. It was instinctive canine behaviour, but as both kids were very small at the time we had to put their safety first. The arrangement had worked wonders. Sesi occupied a place she called her own, while Lou and May could grow up without fear of being pinned to the ground by an overexcited pet. Looking at Hercules, I could appreciate that he didn't present the same kind of threat. Even so, I felt it was important that both dogs were treated in the same way.

'We really should put him in the boot room,' I suggested. 'The sooner he bonds with Sesi, the better.'

'You can't do that, Dad!' May was the first to raise an objection. 'Sesi will savage him!'

'She'll do no such thing,' I said, as the little sausage dog waddled into Sesi's line of sight. In response, a long, threatening growl rose up over the child gates. 'They'll get used to each other. Just you watch.'

All I did was bend down to collect the puppy in my hands. In response, every member of my family beseeched me not to do it.

'You *can't!*' cried Lou, who had been taking pictures of the new dog on her camera phone. 'What will I tell my friends if something bad happens?'

I looked to Emma for support, only to find her regarding me like I'd just revealed an aspect of my personality she had never encountered before.

'Hercules is my responsibility,' she reminded me. 'Right now, there's no way that I'd dream of letting *your* dog anywhere near him.'

It was still a surprise to me that I owned a dog at all. Having grown up in a canine-free household, and faced intimidation from a domineering Doberman in my bid to see the girl I'd quietly admired throughout my teenage years, you'd think a four-legged friend would be the last thing I needed. I certainly didn't consider it when we lived in London. In my view, they existed just to foul pavements. Ten years later, when we moved to the countryside, all of a sudden a dog made perfect sense. It had nothing to do with finding an incentive to make the most of the fields and woodland. My reason for deciding that we needed a big one that would guard us was entirely down to being terrified at night.

It never truly got dark in the capital. Nor were you ever alone in the true sense. Out here, when the sun went down, the sense of isolation quickly got the better of both Emma and I. After a week of snapping awake in bed at every creak in the rafters or rustling leaves outside, I knew just what we needed in order to sleep through, which is how Sesi came into our lives.

Despite being banned from much of the house during daylight hours, our Canadian Shepherd was very much at the heart of the family. I was well aware that introducing another dog might cause some upset to begin with. I also knew that Hercules would be with Emma throughout the working week, and not my concern. I still wanted both dogs to bond, of course. I just figured that wasn't going to happen until the novelty of a new pup had died down.

\*   \*   \*

Seeing that my attempt to place Hercules in the boot room had been overruled, I decided both Sesi and I needed a break from it all, and so we had headed out for the woods. I was happy to see Emma and the kids go soppy over a miniature sausage dog, but it really wasn't my thing. Out in the open air, striding just ahead of me, Sesi really did look quite lupine and intimidating. I could walk her with my head held high, unless of course we came across another dog. In which case I would have to frantically lock her back onto the leash before the red mist descended over her eyes. Whenever that happened, she didn't feel so big and clever to me, but we could work on that now.

Despite the fact that Hercules looked all wrong through my eyes, privately I had come round to the idea that he could be good for Sesi. Under controlled conditions, here was a chance for her to get to know another dog. Once Emma stopped being so precious about her new pooch, we could begin the training. Until then, I was happy for my Canadian Shepherd and I to enjoy some time out while my wife and children worked through their clucking and cooing phase. What's more, it was shaping up to be a bright, beautiful day. Just the right conditions for a leisurely walk.

Later that morning, I returned to the house with a hatchet face and an inability to even look at my dog.

'What's the matter?' asked Emma, as I closed the child gate behind me.

'Have a guess,' I said, ignoring the puppy as it padded across the kitchen floor to greet me.

Emma considered Sesi, who had settled on her bed but was panting hard.

'Any bloodshed?' she asked. 'What was it this time?'

'A little one. Like Toto from *The Wizard of Oz.*'

'So, hardly a menace.'

'It never is,' I told her, sounding as stressed as I felt. 'Every time, she steams in snarling and just sort of smothers them. She's all bark and no bite, but it's frightening. I have to wade in and haul her off, and then apologise profusely to the owner. I can't keep saying she's never done it before because she's pretty much had a go at every dog in the village. It's like I'm exercising a mugger!'

As I spoke, Emma trained her gaze on the puppy. Hercules was investigating a curl of fluff in the corner of the kitchen. Somehow he had got it attached to his nose, and it was making him sneeze repeatedly.

'It's really important that you keep Sesi away from him,' she said, crouching now to free him from his torment.

It was then I noticed the band that had been fastened around Hercules's neck. I couldn't really miss it, in fact.

'Never mind Sesi,' I said. 'What's that?'

Emma stroked the puppy from one end to the other, which took a moment.

'His collar,' she said. 'Every dog needs one.'

'But it's pink,' I pointed out, as if she hadn't noticed.

'*Hot* pink,' she said to correct me. 'Sweet, isn't it?'

'It's also sparkling.' I moved around for a better look. The collar twinkled madly in the sunlight. 'Please tell me those aren't diamonds.'

'They're plastic, silly!' Emma chuckled, still petting the puppy. 'What do you think I'm like?'

I opted not to answer her question.

'It's certainly striking,' I remarked.

Emma rose to her feet, leaving Hercules to poke around the floor.

'I know he's a boy dog, and no doubt you think it's inappropriate.'

'I didn't say that.' I mustered a look of indignation. 'Did I say that?'

'You didn't need to. The fact is, I chose this collar when I picked up the crate for the puppy you made me cancel. Which was a bitch.'

'We've been through this,' I said, and scratched at the nape of my neck. 'Hercules is my way of apologising for the whole assistance dog disaster.'

Emma only had to lift her brow for me to realise she hadn't meant it like that.

'I'm not going to let a perfectly good puppy collar go to waste,' she said after a moment. 'These things are expensive. It might be for a girl dog, but it looks just fine on Hercules.'

I considered the young Dachshund and reminded myself that he was not my concern.

'I suppose it doesn't matter,' I said, sensing the weekend stretch ahead of me. 'He can wear any collar you choose during office hours.'

Emma looked up. She seemed surprised.

'Hercules can't come with me yet,' she said. 'If he's only just had his inoculations then he isn't allowed out for a fortnight. I remember the process with Sesi.'

She was right. This was something I had completely overlooked. The breeder had even spelled it out to me, but at the time I just nodded at everything. My only concern had been in hoping to beat the storm home. At our feet, Hercules switched his attention to his tail. I watched him turning very large circles as he tried to chase it down.

'So, he's here for the next two weeks,' I said to double-check. 'Can you work from home?'

'Sure,' she said reassuringly. 'I'll take the day off on Monday.'

'Is that all? What about your promise to take care of him?'

'That still stands,' she said. 'As soon as it's safe for him to come to the office with me.'

A few years earlier, when Emma brought two minipigs home in the same pet carrier I had used to transport Hercules, their presence in the house stopped me from working for weeks. In sole charge of what were supposed to be pint-sized porkers, Butch and Roxi had set about driving me to distraction. Even when I'd had enough of the wire chewing and the squealing every time my phone rang, their relocation to the garden hadn't done much for my focus and concentration. By then, I was broken. It had taken ages before things returned to what passed as normality. As I was the one who had brought back a puppy that wasn't quite old enough to leave the house, I figured I would have to take time out yet again. Even so, compared to the minipigs, I really didn't see how Hercules could be that much trouble. So long as he learned to sleep at night, the next two weeks would be a minor inconvenience at most. If anything, I could use the opportunity to introduce him to Sesi without anyone around to get hysterical.

I certainly didn't have to get involved for the rest of that day. Between Emma and the kids, Hercules could count on the constant presence of junior playmates and an attentive cleaner. He left plenty of puddles, but each time my wife was there with the kitchen roll and the antibacterial spray. Together with the children, she couldn't do enough for the young Dachshund, while I watched from a distance and did nothing at all to help them. I wasn't being lazy. I just wanted to make it clear that, bar the next fortnight, this dog was off my radar. By the time night fell, everyone but me was exhausted. The little ones took themselves to bed, which was a family first, while Lou logged into Facebook and set about befriending everyone in a group dedicated to Dachshunds. May remained downstairs with us for a short time, but only after I apologised for saying that Hercules was beginning to 'sizzle nicely' as he slumbered in front of the wood burner.

'He's quite happy where he is,' I went on to assure her. 'Why don't you run a bath? It'll help you to unwind.'

May nodded solemnly. 'OK,' she said, having cast her eye over the puppy one more time. 'But first I'm going to check on Sesi. I don't want her to think we've forgotten about her.'

As May left the room, I looked across at Emma. She was on the sofa beside me, feet up on the coffee table, tapping away at the laptop.

'Are you working?' I asked, idly, and began to flick through the channels with the remote.

'I'm just chatting to the breeder,' she said, and chuckled at something that scrolled up the little window on her screen. 'Her details were with the documents that came back with Hercules. I'm just telling her what a good boy I've been.'

I looked at her side on.

'Eh?' When Emma chose to respond to the breeder instead of me, I leaned across to take a closer look at the screen. '*I have had a lovely day,*' I read out loud. '*My new owners are such fun. I think I will be very happy here.*' I stopped there, and faced my wife once more. I really didn't think I needed to spell out what I made of all this.

'Wait,' she said, as the breeder wrote back to her. 'His mummy wants to say goodnight.'

'His mummy?'

'She's writing on the dog's behalf,' said Emma with a smile.

'Did you start this?'

'She did. It's just a bit of fun.'

'It's a Saturday night.' I reminded her. 'A time to watch a movie, not channel sausage dogs.'

'We're nearly through,' she said, tapping away. 'She just wants to know he's alright.'

'The dog is fine. It's you I'm worried about now.'

'Oh, let me have a laugh,' said Emma. 'Look, she's just signed off with a great big "woof"!'

'I had no idea she was like this when I met her,' I said, shaking my head. 'The same goes for you too.'

Emma set her laptop on the coffee table. On the other side, stretched out somewhat ridiculously across the hearth, her new puppy continued to slumber blissfully. After his first day with us, he didn't look like he had the energy to give us grief throughout another night.

'I'm really happy that he's here,' she said, and found my hand with hers. 'I do appreciate what you've done.'

I couldn't help thinking about Ossie once again. We may not have been able to watch the film we went on to play, but when Emma fell asleep within half an hour of the start, I could at least have counted on the assistance dog to put her to bed while I made it to the credits.

# 14

# Dog Tired

Asleep routine is vital for a new puppy. It helps them to settle and feel secure. Hercules certainly seemed to understand the importance of a regular pattern. The problem for us was that his downtime didn't coincide with the hours when we were trying to get some kip.

I managed to ignore the constant crying through his second night in the house. On the third, when Sesi lost the plot in the early hours of the morning and started barking at him, it was Emma who overturned her hands-off policy.

'I'll have a word with them,' she said, on hauling herself out of bed.

'I don't think asking Hercules politely to shut the hell up will work,' I warned. 'We need to sound-proof his crate. Entomb it in concrete or something.'

Emma wrapped herself into her dressing gown.

'I'll be speaking to them both,' she said. 'It sounds like Sesi is upsetting him.'

'This is Sesi's fault?' I pushed the pillow off my head so I could take Emma to task. 'She's just had enough of the racket. We all have.'

'I'm sure my dog would settle down without her,' she replied, on tying her dressing gown cord.

'*Your* dog?' All of a sudden, I began to feel as if I was being made indirectly responsible for the situation. I rubbed my eyes, adjusting to the landing light as Emma opened the door. 'Come back to bed,' I reasoned, aware that we were both frazzled. 'I'm sure things will calm down. He's just being a puppy. Until then, we mustn't let this come between us.'

For a moment, Hercules fell silent. Unlike Sesi, who continued to rage at him. When she tailed off, Emma sighed, closed the door once more and did as I had asked.

'I'm sorry,' she said, and climbed back under the duvet. 'I just struggle without sleep.'

'It's lucky you haven't got work tomorrow,' I pointed out, as she settled her head against my shoulder. 'You're on dog duty, remember?'

'I'm looking forward to it,' she said. 'With the kids at school, I'll be free to start some intensive puppy training.'

'Well, maybe you should start by teaching him the command to sleep.'

Reaching for the pillow once more, I positioned it over my head as Hercules tried in vain this time to divide and conquer us.

It was a rare thing for my wife to be at home on a working day. She didn't believe in being off sick, and when she took holiday leave it was to do just that. Nowadays that was limited to day trips on account of the minipigs. We couldn't bring them with us, and the pet-minding people charged too much to climb out of bed before daylight to feed them. Even so, Emma made full use of her allowance on beachside breaks that generally lasted as long as it took to eat an ice cream. She was away from the office for each maternity leave, of course, but then she had a baby to distract her. I had assumed that Hercules would keep her busy, and so did she. Instead, following the school run, the puppy took to his crate. Having been up all night, he then embarked on some much needed sleep. It left Emma with no choice but to open up her laptop and work from the kitchen table.

'Another cup of tea?' she asked, as I popped out to switch on the kettle. 'That's your second since you sat down at your desk.'

'Would you like one?' I asked.

'No, thanks. I'm too busy.'

As much as it was good to have some company for a change, I reminded myself that it was for one day only. Taking my cup back to my office, I decided it would be rude to close the door behind me. With Sesi settled beside my chair, I returned to the work on my screen. I had an agony column to deliver to the magazine by lunchtime. This involved editing three suitable questions and then answering them. The word count wasn't huge, but it took a lot of thinking time before I composed each response. Having Emma in earshot didn't help. While I sipped at my tea and considered what to write, I could hear her clattering away at her keyboard. Finally, after twenty minutes or so, the noise went quiet. I assumed she was taking a break. Instead, just as I drained my cup, I realised she was standing right behind me.

'Is that all you've done?'

I swivelled around in my chair to face her. With her lips bunched to one side, Emma peered at the screen.

'I work for myself,' I reminded her. 'I am my own boss.'

'If I was your boss, we'd need a review,' she said, and promptly broke into a grin. 'Sorry. I'm just a bit bored.'

Behind her, crated in the boot room, Hercules continued to sleep soundly. The Dachshund's curled-up position pretty much took him round by a loop and a half.

'So, this review,' I said, aware that we were alone in the house for once. 'I don't suppose now would be a good time, would it?'

Emma looked mystified for a second. Then a bit pained.

'I'm on call,' she said, and showed me her BlackBerry. 'In fact, I might as well be in the office.'

The puppy sighed in his sleep just then. It was as if he was channelling Emma's mood. As well as being disappointed that he hadn't stirred, I felt sure she must also be feeling as wiped out as me. We hadn't slept properly for two nights now, which was my excuse when Emma returned to the subject of my output so far.

'OK,' she said, reading the question on the screen, 'a teenage girl has written to you because her friends are laughing at her love bite.'

'That's right.'

'In which case you just need to let her know that's because it makes her look cheap. Then you can crack on with answering the next question.'

'It isn't as simple as that,' I reasoned. 'The subject might seem trivial, but if someone has been moved to write in then it's a big deal for them. Plus I don't offer a view. Whatever the question, I aim to provide all the information and options that person needs so they can make decisions that feel right for them.'

Emma folded her arms, considering what I had just said.

'If Lou or May came home with a love bite, I'd give them the option to cancel all social activities for a fortnight or provide me the name of the person responsible so I could speak to them.'

'How considerate,' I said. 'Then parents like you express surprise when their kids choose to write to people like me for advice instead.'

For once, I felt some ownership over the debate. When Emma chose not to pursue it, I believed that the message might well have got through.

'We need to talk about May,' she said eventually. 'Some of the things she's mentioned lately have left me lost for words.'

'She won't talk to me,' I told her. 'The same with Lou. I'm relying on *you*.'

Emma flicked her gaze at the screen once more. At the same time, her BlackBerry began to ring.

'The trouble is finding a good time,' she said, while reaching for her phone.

'If you don't then she'll just write to the likes of me.'

Emma took the call, but not before first masking the mouthpiece.

'Then she could be waiting a long time for a response,' she said.

I glanced around at the screen as she gestured at it. When I looked back she planted a kiss on the crown of my head before devoting herself to the call.

As puppies go, Hercules impressed me greatly throughout the rest of that morning. He didn't stir every time I left my office to reheat the kettle. He even resisted being poked by Emma who wanted to check he was still alive. It was quite clear to me that he was just sleeping. When that continued through lunch, I decided that what I had picked out here was the world's most perfect miniature dog. In daylight hours, at least. It was everything I wanted from something so little. In short, he didn't bother me.

Finally, some seven hours after he nodded off, Hercules arose for the first time since breakfast. It was the chaos created by the little ones that stirred him. I had just picked them up from school. As ever, they kicked their shoes off in the boot room and hung their coats on invisible hooks so they landed in a heap on the floor. With Sesi bouncing around them, Honey and Frank jostled with one another to be first into the kitchen. As my Shepherd settled on her bed once more, a sleepy-eyed and bewildered-looking puppy sat up inside his crate.

'Emma,' I called into the kitchen, as our youngest children told her about their day. 'Your dog will need a toilet break. Now would be good if you want to avoid an accident.'

I was determined not to be drawn into dealing with the latest pet to join the family. I might've been responsible for bringing Hercules into the house, but it was on the same terms that we had agreed on before Ossie foolishly turned my head. A long dog was not my thing. I didn't mind managing his time in the house for the next two weeks. As soon as Hercules was fit for the outside world, however, he would be free to join my wife at work. Just because Honey and Frank were enjoying the novelty of finding their mother in the kitchen after school, it didn't change the fact that Emma owned a puppy who looked like he really needed a wee.

To be fair, she answered my call straight away.

'You go back to work,' she told me. 'We can handle Hercules, can't we kids?'

As she crouched to open up the crate, Emma glanced over her shoulder. Honey and Frank were nowhere to be seen. From the hallway came the sound of little feet ascending the staircase.

'They've gone to find their DS's,' I told her. 'It's what they do after school if there's no homework. Don't take it personally.'

Emma looked crestfallen. Then the puppy emerged from the crate – front feet first, followed by his body, which then extended even further as he stopped to stretch himself from nose to tail.

'Never mind,' she said, and collected the puppy in her arms. 'Hercules and I can have some special time.'

'You never say that to me any more,' I complained, smiling all the same.

'That's because you're toilet-trained,' she replied, and slipped into her shoes to take the puppy out into the garden. As she did so, she paused and returned my gaze. 'You know, as birthday presents go, I really couldn't ask for more.' She cuddled the puppy nestled in the crook of her elbow. 'Hercules is just what I always wanted.'

'You said that about Butch and Roxi,' I reminded her. 'Until they became huge.'

'That's not true,' she said, though she failed to sound outraged. 'I wouldn't be without our minipigs.'

'Really? If you were given the chance to do it all over again, you'd still take them on?'

Emma confirmed that she would, but not without hesitating first.

'OK,' she admitted. 'Their size has been a complete surprise, but what do you suggest we do with them?'

'Nothing.' I shrugged. 'We'll just carry on doing the best we can. So long as Butch and Roxi have everything they need, we'll retain our reputation as being the family with two huge pigs as pets.'

Emma turned her attention to the puppy in her arms once more.

'And a sweet little sausage dog who goes to work with me.'

I watched her leave, and then glanced at Sesi on her bed. Her huge ears were turned inwards just a little, which told me she had been tuned into every word.

'Let's not forget the big dog in the boot room,' I remarked to myself. 'The one that keeps us safe at night.'

It was unusual for me to have the chance to work once the little ones were back from school. With Emma at home, I opened up the manuscript for a children's book I was writing and prepared to earn myself the evening off. Such quality time lasted all of five minutes before my office door crashed open. I didn't turn around at first because I assumed it would be Frank or Honey. Every now and then they fell out because one wasn't playing nicely. Then Emma's voice reached my ears, and prompted me to swivel round to face her.

'Your hens are a menace!' she announced, still holding Hercules against her chest. 'I can't put the poor thing on the grass without them stalking him.'

'They're just being curious,' I said, but Emma wasn't listening.

'Do you have to let them out into the garden all the time? Why can't they stay in their run?'

'Because I don't want to keep cooped-up ex-battery chickens,' I said. 'They've come from the worst existence imaginable. They should at least be free to roam.'

We were straying onto sensitive territory here. Before Butch and Roxi arrived, the enclosure at the back of the garden had been designed for use by hens. I kept their roost and run in there, but always left it open so that they could come and go. Having come from an industrial farming outfit, I considered it to be the very least I could do for them. Then the minipigs grew to become a threat to their safety, which forced me to evict them. As a result, we had ended up with displaced poultry in our back garden. Free to roam, they quickly trashed the lawn and turned the borders into dust baths, all of which I considered a price we just had to pay.

'Damaging the garden is one thing,' said Emma, 'but we can't risk them harming Hercules.'

By now it was clear that I wasn't going to be able to return to work without getting involved. With a sigh, I left my chair and told her I would find Sesi's lead.

'So long as you have control of the dog,' I said, 'you have control of the situation.'

I collected what I was looking for from the hook in the boot room, but when I turned around I found Emma looking at me aghast.

'You can't use that on Hercules,' she said, practically shielding him from me. 'It'll have germs on it!'

'What?' I regarded the lead, a long, knotted leather strap, and then my poor dog on her bed. 'Hercules can't catch anything from Sesi. For one thing, there's nothing on Sesi to catch.'

'It's OK.' Emma cut across the boot room and began to rummage in the bag of things she had amassed for her new puppy. 'I bought one along with the collar.'

'Is it pink?' I asked.

'No,' she said, and turned around with the object in hand. 'But it's clean.'

What Emma had was one of those retractable affairs with a plastic handle. I watched her attach the end to Hercules's pink collar while whispering soothing words of nonsense to him.

'I'll come with you,' I said. 'I don't want to be held responsible for any kind of stand-off between poultry and puppy.'

'If the hens were in their run,' she replied, 'Hercules could explore the garden.'

Emma stepped out into the yard. I followed behind, having instructed Sesi to stay put. My wife didn't wait for me to close the door. She strode purposefully towards the garden gate, and only stopped when I asked what she was doing.

'Hercules isn't going to explore anything unless you put him down,' I pointed out. 'If you carry him around everywhere he'll just get used to it. Let him use what legs he's got.'

Still clutching him protectively, Emma looked at the ground and then back at me.

'When did you last wash the yard down?' she asked.

'Oh, for goodness sake. It's perfectly clean!' I strode towards her with my hands outstretched. 'Give me the lead. Let me show you how it's done.'

With some reluctance, Emma passed me the plastic handle. I assumed she would set the dog down when I continued on towards the gate. In response, the cord began to unspool. I flipped on the lock with my thumb and faced her once more. Hercules remained in her arms. She hadn't moved at all.

'He's quite capable of walking there,' I said. 'The last thing you want is a pampered pet.'

'I'm only worried about infection,' said Emma. 'Just until his jabs have kicked in.'

'The risk of infection comes from other dogs that haven't been inoculated. Sesi's up to date on that score and the chickens won't pose a threat.'

'Physically they do,' she said. 'I dread to think what would've happened if I'd actually put Hercules on the grass.'

I thought about this for a moment.

'To toilet-train a puppy,' I said next, 'you really need to let him get on with it. You can't just hold him out and hope that he'll do the business. You'll give him a complex.'

'I am aware of that,' she muttered, and crouched down to

set Hercules on the ground. 'OK,' she said next, and let go of the puppy. 'Do your thing.'

'Observe.'

I called the Dachshund's name. Hercules didn't respond. He just sat with his hind legs slumped to one side. In a bid to encourage him, by giving him a little tug, I released the lock button. I didn't think it would have that much effect. Instead of drawing Hercules onto all fours, however, the retracting line yanked the little puppy clean off his feet.

'What are you doing?' Emma shrieked as the leash snapped backwards with the Dachshund still attached to the end. 'For crying out loud, Matt!'

Shocked by what had just happened, I found the presence of mind to cradle the poor puppy as it dangled in the air. Hercules looked both startled and relieved to be in safe hands. Aghast, Emma seized him from me.

'It was an accident,' I protested. 'This leash isn't suitable for a puppy. The spring is too strong for his size!'

Clutching Hercules to her breast, she unclipped the leash from his collar. It zipped back inside the handle, clipping my knuckles at the same time.

'Let's just get him into the garden,' she said. 'You watch out for the chickens, I'll worry about my baby boy.'

I watched her turn for the gate with the sausage dog in her arms, and then soundlessly repeated what she'd just said. Of all the pets that had joined our household in the twenty years we had been together, this was the first time Emma had referred to one in this way.

I just wasn't sure whether I should be encouraged by the nature of this bond, given that the dog would be her responsibility, or utterly appalled.

# 15

## Desperate Measures

The air of excitement that filled the family home came to an end the next day. Why? Because with the children in school and Emma back at work, the new arrival found himself under my care.

Given that Hercules had cried throughout the night, I was in no mood to indulge him. As far as I was concerned, the puppy would have to fit in around my schedule, just like all the other animals. As he slept throughout the morning once more, I had no cause to grumble. It didn't stop me, of course, when Emma called to check up on him.

'He's fine,' I whispered down the line, anxious not to wake him. 'Unlike me, thanks for asking. I'm exhausted.'

'But you slept through the worst of it.'

'Did I?'

'You were sound asleep. Even when the little ones came in because they'd had enough of all the yelping.'

'How are *you* feeling?' I remembered to ask after a moment.

'Tired,' she said. 'Tired but happy. Above all, I'm pleased I didn't give in last night. I just let him cry and cry.'

'So, it's working then?'

'Oh, it will,' she assured me. 'I can't wait to come home and see Hercles.'

'Hercles?' I furrowed my brow. 'Emma, you can't shorten a

name like Hercules. It doesn't work. Hercles sounds like a sexually transmitted disease.'

'Nonsense,' she said, before announcing that she had to go as people were waiting for her to start a meeting.

Having replaced the handset, I paused before returning to work and just listened out for a moment. I'd purposely shut the office door so as not to disturb the puppy. Sesi was in the office with me, lying on her back with legs akimbo, which told me she was out for the count. Satisfied that my conversation with Emma hadn't awoken Hercules, I settled in front of my keyboard once more. I needed a wee and a cup of tea. I just didn't want to risk stirring him. As soon as he surfaced, I could say goodbye to any chance of being productive, and so I worked in silence.

Towards lunchtime, my bladder was so full I'd been forced to unbuckle my belt so I could remain seated. Even that proved so uncomfortable that I'd taken to standing at my desk with my keyboard in one hand so I could continue typing. Several times I'd cracked open the door to check on Hercules. Part of me hoped I'd find him sitting up and waiting to be let out so I could rush to relieve myself. On both occasions, however, I saw no sign that he was set to wake. The second time I decided I should go for it. Creeping out as quietly as I could, I made my way towards the kitchen. Halfway across, the puppy's ears began to twitch. I froze, holding my breath at the same time. I had about an hour left to go before it was time to collect the kids from school. That was valuable working time. I really didn't want to spend it dealing with a hyperactive puppy, which ruled out opening the kitchen child gate with a rousing creak. So, as Hercules settled once again, I retraced my steps and closed the office door.

Minutes later, in desperation, I found myself scanning the

office in search of a means of emptying my bladder. My chosen receptacle took the form of a candle holder on my bookshelf. It wasn't very deep, but just then I didn't care. I figured it would serve as a kind of pressure release. Taking care to be sure I wasn't about to be spotted by a passing horse-rider, I unzipped my trousers and, with candle holder in hand, prepared to relieve myself. The trouble was I'd been holding on for so long that the opening salvo took me by surprise. The splash-back was intense, and also hard to stop.

'Bloody hell!' I hissed, having finally got a grip on the situation. I was still fit to burst, despite filling the candlestick to the brim and splashing my shirt and the floor. I glanced at Sesi, who had been watching me with interest. 'Don't say a word,' I told her. 'Desperate times call for desperate measures.'

I turned to set the candlestick on the shelf, with a view to dealing with it later, which is when Hercules chose his moment to announce that he was in fact awake.

From that moment on, until school finished, Emma's sausage dog took up every moment of my time.

This came as no surprise. After all, here was a young puppy still adjusting to life in a new home. He was curious, energetic, untrained and incontinent. Fortunately, we had hard flooring in the kitchen, which is where we took ourselves so I could keep an eye on him. Sesi observed with a mixture of jealousy and intrigue from behind the child gate. In return, Hercules showed a keen interest in my dog, as well as the cable from the corner lamp. Emma had also bought him some toys, which I used to distract him. Hercules ignored the chewy nylon bone in favour of the stuffed pheasant. I lost count of the number of times he mounted the poor thing, twice from the wrong end, but soon gave up trying to stop him. Instead, having got over the length of his torso, I began to note other aspects of his build. At first sight, his legs looked quite feeble. If anything, he reminded me of that primordial period when fish first hauled themselves from the water on what would eventually evolve into limbs. Then, as I observed him moving around, it became clear that in fact these bandy stubs were really quite strong. With his oversized paws, he could happily play tug-of-war with me over the pheasant. Whether or not he thought I was trying to confiscate the object of his affections, I was struck by the strength he displayed.

At the same time, when Hercules became too boisterous it was no effort to simply scoop him up in one hand. With my fingers cradling his chest, and his back legs splayed at my wrist, the puppy seemed quite content to be carried around. Not that I planned to encourage bad habits.

'Emma might treat you like a handbag,' I said, setting him on the floor at one point. 'But not me.'

Despite being so low to the ground, Hercules still made every effort to look me in the eye. With his head tipped right back, he peered up in a way that would make anyone want to collect him into their arms for a cuddle. Anyone except for me, of course. He had just two weeks in my company. I didn't want him to think of me as his master. I considered myself to be more like the owner of a bed and breakfast. I was here to keep him fed and sheltered. As soon as I was off duty, that was it.

Later, once the children were home, I decided it was time to introduce Sesi to the puppy. Since he arrived, she had studied Hercules from behind bars or through the mesh of the crate. Her track record with other dogs was despicable, but I felt this time she'd at least had a chance to grow used to him. Sesi didn't like little breeds, but this was different. Hercules was a puppy. He couldn't even bark properly yet. All he did was squeak like a toy. Surely even she wouldn't turn on something so young? Naturally, I had to minimise the risks, which is why I enrolled Lou and May to help me out.

'Life would just be a lot easier if they got along,' I told them. 'If we can send your mother a picture of the two dogs together, I think we'll all relax.'

Lou seemed to light up at the photograph opportunity. May looked more reserved.

'What if it goes wrong?' she asked. 'Mum won't be pleased if Hercules gets torn to bits.'

'Give Sesi a chance to prove herself,' I said. 'We're going to bring them together in a controlled manner, and if anything goes wrong I'm on hand to intervene, OK?'

May just stared at me, seemingly unsure if I was being serious.

'Where is Hercules now?'

'Humping Frank's ankle in the front room,' said Lou, who was busy fiddling with the settings on her camera phone. 'Only Frank's too caught up with his DS to notice.'

'You know, he isn't really humping,' I told them, and prepared to rescue my son. 'At his age, it's just an instinct because it feels nice.'

'Dad!' May cut in. 'If this is your way of starting up a chat about sex then you can stop right there!'

'It wasn't,' I protested quite genuinely, though on reflection it would've been a good move.

Lou glanced up from her camera phone, grinning.

'Face it,' she told me. '*That* talk's never going to happen.'

Before I could reply, Hercules waddled into the kitchen.

Seeing me, he rolled his head on his shoulders and bowled across the floor.

'Someone's pleased to see you,' May remarked. 'Perhaps you're the one he really wants to hump.'

'Girls,' I said sternly, ignoring the pup at my feet. 'That's enough. I'm just trying to do the right thing as a father. You know if there's anything on your minds, or if you need to know the facts about the birds and the bees, you can turn to me.'

'But we won't,' said Lou, who seemed to be relishing how helpless I was feeling. 'Precisely because you're our dad. You can save your chats for Frank. We're not going there.'

'When we want to know about stuff like contraception,' May added. 'We'll ask Mum.'

'But she's had four children!' I said, without really thinking. The pair just stood there, waiting for me to explain myself. I drew breath and started again. 'What I mean to say is that I've been writing about young people's issues for years. I'm comfortable talking about stuff like the choices you face, safer sex . . .'

'*No more!*' yelled May, and covered her ears. 'It's bad enough having to hear it from teachers at school.'

'How is that going?' I asked. 'What have you learned in class?'

'Just stuff like you can *die* during childbirth.'

'That's helpful,' I said. 'Anything more?'

'In our year we're doing a thing about being a responsible parent,' said Lou.

'Which tells you most new mothers survive,' I replied, looking at May.

'Our next assignment is about flour babies,' Lou went on. 'We each have to look after one for a fortnight. We're supposed to take it everywhere, and even get up in the night to feed it, but y'know . . .' The way her explanation trailed into a shrug told me she wasn't taking this seriously.

'You can't neglect a flour baby,' I told her. 'Just because it's a doll, it's still a vital life lesson.'

May was listening intently.

'Dad's right,' she said. 'Otherwise it might be miserable.'

Rolling her eyes, Lou returned her attention to her phone. 'Aren't we here to take a photograph?'

By now, drawn by our exchange, Sesi had left my office to join us. Seeing her, Hercules squeaked so excitedly that his front paws left the ground.

'OK, everyone outside. At least I know the dogs will listen to me.'

Our yard runs along the back of the house, which is where I planned to bring them together. What passed as a garden was to the side, bordering the lane. I was reluctant to allow Hercules and Sesi to get to know each other while the chickens were roaming freely. The risk of fur and feathers flying was just too great.

'I have a bad feeling about this,' said May, as I carried Hercules out into the daylight.

'You have a bad feeling about everything,' I pointed out. 'Now take Sesi to the other end of the yard. Let's give them the space they need.'

'To do what?' she asked. 'Dog jousting?'

I offered my daughter a look that persuaded her to do as I had asked. Sesi seemed keyed up by the fact that Hercules was within her reach. I still held out hope that she wouldn't harm him, however. She had been in my life for years now. If she could be trusted with grasping babies, I reasoned with myself, she'd handle an irritating little sausage dog.

'I'm ready,' said Lou, who was crouching at the door with her camera phone in hand. 'Unleash the beasts!'

Now it was her turn to receive a steely glare from me. This was no time to mess around. I had the welfare of Emma's puppy to consider.

'Here we go,' I said, and gently set Hercules on the flagstones. 'May, you can stop holding Sesi's collar now. I promise you she isn't going to pounce.'

'Oh Dad, you had better not be wrong.'

May took a second before she let go of her collar. Sesi watched Hercules intently, but I could tell she wasn't about to attack. Her ears would've flattened if she had a fight in mind. If anything, they were tipped forward, as if straining to anticipate the puppy's next move. Hercules, meanwhile, advanced across the yard with his nose close to the ground. Pretty much everything else about him followed suit, but I could see his attention hadn't quite reached the intimidating creature at the far end of the yard. Nevertheless, with every step he made I missed another opportunity to breathe.

'Take it easy, Sesi,' I muttered, and then with some urgency as the little sausage dog suddenly picked up on her presence.

# 16

## Mad Dogs and an Englishman

There was a reason why Sesi had such issues with her own kind. As a puppy, on her first walk into the woods, she was attacked by another dog.

The aggressor, a Boxer, belonged to a gentle old boy down the lane. He was left as shaken as both Sesi and me. We decided it had to be a territorial thing, and though it wasn't serious the experience left a deep impression on her. For weeks afterwards, she would run away from any dog that came near. Then she began to mature and muscle up. Finally, having grown larger than the dog responsible for rattling her in the first place, she exacted righteous justice with vengeful fury. Sesi didn't do enough damage to earn me a vet bill. That would come later. Instead, having left the Boxer on the ropes, she took on any canine contender that dared to invade her personal space. The problem for me, and other dogs, was that the space in question steadily increased. What started out as being a radius of no more than a matter of metres steadily expanded until it effectively embraced the village.

Things got so bad that I returned to our local dog behaviourist for help. The woman in question had worked wonders with Sesi when it came to socialising her in the house, and I hoped that she could do the same thing with her in the outside world. Tanya was renowned across the county for having a way with dogs that defied explanation. In particular, she specialised in dealing with dangerous breeds, and was often called upon to rehabilitate snarling hellhounds that would otherwise face a destruction order. Her training school was basically a boot camp for badly behaved canines. It even looked like a prison facility. You had to buzz to gain access through the main gates, and then park in a courtyard surrounded by mesh-walled kennels. Each one contained a dog that looked like it was in the psychosis stage of the rabies virus. Step out of your vehicle and the entire place erupted. It was an unnerving experience. All you could do was stand there and wait until Tanya made her presence known. You knew she was on her way when every inmate in the facility stopped raging and backed away from the mesh. A moment later, she would stride into view wearing high boots, a deerstalking jacket and her trademark broad-brimmed hat.

'Can you hear that?' she would say, over the dwindling whines and grumbles. 'That is the sound of respect. These dogs know who is in charge!'

Then Tanya would offer her hand in greeting and you too would bow to her authority.

The first time she shook my hand, I had to stop myself from taking a sharp intake of breath. The dog behaviourist didn't even blink. She just pinned me with such a penetrating gaze that I figured she had a measure of my soul before I'd even spoken a word. In direct contrast to her hands, which were covered in fading bite scars, her face was practically without a single line or crease. I put this down to her being the kind of person who had probably only cracked a smile about a dozen times in her life. Tanya was perfectly pleasant, but her core was formed from cold steel. She passed no comment when I inched open the boot of the car, only for my dog to bundle out and bark ferociously as if quite ready to take on every last mutt in the facility. Instead of offering to help, Tanya simply observed with her hands clasped behind her back.

'I think you can see my problem,' I said, while struggling to bring Sesi under control.

'The dog isn't the main problem,' said Tanya, and proceeded to walk so quickly that I lost sight of her as she left the courtyard.

I found her waiting for me outside the sand school. This was a large, windowless barn where she ran training classes for the general public. I had long since abandoned these because Sesi proved so disruptive. Instead of spending an hour learning to walk to heel in a line, my dog had devoted her entire time to lunging at her classmates. Eventually, for the sake of a quiet life, I had just given up.

This time, alone with Tanya, I hoped that Sesi would shape up her act considerably.

'So,' she said, having led us to the centre of the sand school, 'I want you to ignore your dog, take her off the leash and tell me how the problem began.'

She had positioned herself directly in front of me. We were close enough to look like lovers. All of a sudden, I knew how Sesi felt to have her personal space invaded.

'It's been a nightmare,' I said to begin, and promptly unloaded my story as if speaking to a shrink. While I did so, Sesi investigated the large ring in which we were standing. Eventually, aware that I was paying her no attention, she barked at me.

In response, Tanya curled a finger and thumb to her lips and then whistled so loudly that I took a step backwards. Sesi looked totally surprised. She cocked her head, and then spread her forelegs as if preparing to bounce about and play. In response, the dog behaviourist dropped to one knee and dipped her head.

'Come here, then, you *beautiful* girl. We haven't said hello yet!'

Sensing a game at hand, Sesi bounded across, circled Tanya once and then painted her neck with her tongue.

'Oh God! Sorry,' I said, on instinct, for I couldn't stand it when Sesi tried to do the same thing to me. Tanya didn't hear me, however. If anything, she seemed to be in a state of some bliss as my dog continued to lick her face until it glistened. 'Sesi, *please!*'

'She's just getting to know me,' said Tanya, who then rose to her feet and proceeded to skip away.

Immediately, Sesi gave chase. With her tongue lolling as she attempted to round up the trainer, I could see that my dog was having the time of her life. As for me, aware that this hour was costing me good money, I wondered what on earth was going on. Had Tanya lost the plot? This wasn't what I expected from a local legend in canine behavioural theory. As she practically danced her way around the perimeter of the sand school, with Sesi at her side, I felt slightly embarrassed to keep watching.

And then, without warning, she stopped dead in her tracks. Sesi took a moment to realise that her new special friend was no longer moving like a lunatic woman child. My dog turned to face Tanya, only to find she was no longer smiling happily but glaring fiercely. To underline this inexplicable mood swing, she curled her arms in front of her chest like a bodybuilder displaying her biceps.

Then a low grumble built in Tanya's throat. It took a moment for me to realise she was growling like a dog. Sesi looked shocked and also a bit fearful – as indeed did I.

'This is crazy,' I whispered to myself, quietly enough not to be overheard, so I had thought, only for the growling to halt.

'Oh, it's all part of the process,' Tanya replied breezily, and promptly broke out of the strange stance she had adopted. 'Heel!'

Without any hesitation, Sesi trotted across to the dog trainer, who held out the back of her hand as if she was some kind of royalty. This time my dog didn't attempt to drown Tanya in saliva. Instead, she nuzzled her hand before sitting dutifully beside her. Throughout, Sesi didn't once take her eyes off the trainer. She looked totally relaxed and completely obedient. 'Right,' said Tanya, and switched her attention to me. 'I have dominance over your dog. Now it's time to retrain *you*.'

'Me? I don't have a problem with other people's pets.'

'Yes, you do,' she said, and reached for a walkie-talkie that was clipped to the belt of her trousers. Pressing the button on the side, the device crackled briefly as she held it to her mouth. 'OK. Let's bring in the stunt dog.'

Before I could ask her what that involved, Tanya had attached Sesi back on her leash and handed control to me. She then retreated to the far end of the sand school. Making a circling motion with her fingers, she encouraged me to face the main entrance. The door was open. Sunlight flooded in, making it hard to see outside.

Just then, a knot of fear formed in my stomach. Memories of Bill the Doberman returned. Without further thought, I quietly covered my groin with my spare hand.

'Is this wise?' With my back still turned to Tanya, I felt vulnerable from both sides.

'We'll see,' she said cheerily.

The sound of footsteps crunching on the gravel outside

seized my attention next, along with the panting of a creature straining to be unleashed.

'Easy,' I instructed Sesi as she bristled visibly. 'Be good.'

I'm not sure what kind of stunt dog I was expecting. Certainly something with a bigger presence than the terrier that flung itself sideways into the sand school. Recovering from a terrific skid, the little dog then set about hurtling manically around the perimeter.

Predictably, at least in my experience, Sesi reacted with such force that she broke free from me effortlessly. The handle of the leash snapped from my hand, causing me to gasp at the stinging burn it left behind. Within a second or so, she was in the terrier's slipstream, preparing to leap. I stood there watching uselessly, unlike Tanya who issued her trademark whistle once more as both dogs raced by.

The noise acted like an invisible brake. Both dogs dug their forelegs into the sand, before turning to pad happily towards Tanya as if the pair were the best of friends.

'You did that quite wrong,' she said, addressing me. 'Sesi is about one percent to blame for her behaviour here.'

'One percent? How can that be right? I didn't *make* her do that.'

'No, but your body language is leaving her feeling vulnerable and frightened. What you're witnessing here is acute fear aggression. Sesi is terrified of other dogs, and you're showing no sign of protecting her. As a result, she strikes first in the hope that she can neutralise the problem. If anything, she's picking up on the surge in your adrenalin. Quite literally, she can smell your fear.'

I looked at my dog. All of a sudden, I felt a bit unwashed. 'Really?'

'As soon as you heard my stunt dog approaching, you tensed

up. No doubt your sweat output increased dramatically, and that's what Sesi would've picked up on.'

The way Tanya described this made me feel as if I had spontaneously soaked through my shirt.

'So what should I have done?' I asked. 'Attacked the dog first?'

Tanya almost cracked a smile, but her lips didn't quite part.

'Sesi just wants to feel secure. You need to be boss dog. At the moment, she's looking to you for leadership and protection, and you're not giving her what she needs.'

'Story of my life,' I muttered under my breath, and then addressed Tanya once more. 'So, I need to be more dominant? I have to be frank with you, that doesn't come naturally. I'm happy as I am.'

'But Sesi isn't,' she pointed out. 'If you took charge I guarantee she'd be a lot more relaxed. Start by standing upright. You're slouching!'

I felt as if she was addressing the ten-year-old boy in me. Once again, I wondered whether I was getting value for money.

'I understand what you're telling me,' I said. 'But I'm not so sure it'll do much good.'

Tanya rested her hands on her waist and continued to appraise me. Both the stunt dog and Sesi didn't once take their eyes from her.

'Let's put it to the test,' she said eventually. 'If you can take Sesi into the lower field, I'll join you in a moment with my attack dogs.'

If I had been concerned before the arrival of Tanya's stunt terrier, I was determined not to let Sesi detect a note of how I was feeling about the next test. This wasn't easy, waiting with her out in the field. It was a bright but breezy morning.

Birds trilled and chattered in the woods that bordered the training school. Despite this, I felt a rising sense of dread about what was set to happen.

'You don't need to worry,' I made myself tell my dog. 'I'm in charge here. Nothing can go wrong.'

I heard Tanya's voice before I saw her. When she appeared at the gate to the field, I was both surprised and unsettled by the shape and size of the dog pack surrounding her. That Sesi had yet to kick off wasn't down to my sense of calm and composure. It was plainly obvious that, like me, she had made like a statue in the hope that the pack of muscular-looking Ridgebacks wouldn't notice us.

At first I thought Tanya was set to let them loose in the field. Instead, she ushered every last dog through a gate in the side fencing, into an adjoining paddock.

In turn, as each dog filed through with great obedience, a transformation took place in their demeanour. It was as if a spell had been lifted, such was the change from servility to savagery. With a snarl, each one locked their attention on Sesi and me. They then set about menacing us from the other side of the fence.

'Shoulders straight, Mr Whyman,' the dog trainer reminded me, having raised her voice to be heard over the baying and the barking. 'Sesi wants to know that you're in control of the situation.'

I was relieved to see Tanya close the side gate and shoot the bolt across to secure it. Even so, it did little to ease my clammy palms. I glanced at Sesi. She showed absolutely no sign of squaring up to the pack behind the fence. She was headstrong and domineering, but not a kamikaze kind of canine.

'To be fair, I think *you're* in control,' I said. 'Are those dogs safe?'

'Not at the moment,' she told me casually. 'They're trained to patrol that side of the fence. It's where I keep them at night. We've never been burgled, you know.'

'Is that because nobody tried,' I asked, 'or because there's nothing left of them?'

Ignoring my comment, or perhaps to punish me for it, Tanya summoned one of the Ridgebacks and opened the gate to let it back in.

'Sesi is behaving beautifully at the moment,' she said, as her dog returned in an instant to its placid state. 'She has you to thank for that. Now let's see what happens at closer quarters. If you'll just release Sesi from her leash, Mr Whyman.'

In doing as she asked, I felt like I was setting up my poor dog to be torn to shreds. By now the Ridgeback had left her mistress to investigate the field. A moment after I unclipped Sesi, she did just the same thing. As far from the Ridgeback as possible. Sensing her retreat, the attack dog focused its attention onto me.

'He could destroy you,' said Tanya, striding over to join me, 'but you don't have to worry about that while you're with me.'

I tried not to tense when the Ridgeback reached me, which frankly was a challenge. Quite simply, every instinct in my body was urging me to run. Then the attack dog turned side on to me, and pressed his rear flank hard against my thigh.

'What's he doing?' I asked, struggling not to lose my balance.

'He's telling you that you're OK,' she said. 'For now.'

I looked over my shoulder. Sesi was stationed in the far corner of the field, doing her level best to be invisible. When I looked back, Tanya had left me to return to the side gate.

'Let's bring some more in,' she said. 'Shoulders squared, remember?'

The dog at my side was packed with muscle. It continued

to lean against me, panting rhythmically. Frankly it was a struggle for me not to start openly hyperventilating when Tanya invited the rest of the baying mob to surge back into the field. Once again they appeared to come through shorn of all aggression. Even so, as they joined the first dog and basically surrounded me, I was in no doubt just how easily they could tear me to bits.

'OK, this isn't something I'd choose to do,' I said, aware that my heart rate had risen. With about a dozen dogs pressing in on me, and Sesi nowhere to be seen, I realised I was entirely at the mercy of Tanya's pack. 'I hope this is going to be worthwhile.'

'Oh, Sesi is taking notes,' Tanya assured me. 'She's watching closely.'

I could sense a drop of sweat forming on my temple. It was the last thing I needed.

'What happens if they detect that I'm scared?' I asked.

'But you're not scared,' she said. 'Are you scared?'

I was more than scared. I had never felt such terror before. As carefully as I could, I reached up and wiped the prickle of perspiration. Unwilling to have my sweat-scented fingers chewed, I then clasped my hands in front of my chest.

'How much longer?' I asked, feeling dizzy and sick as I spoke. 'I think Sesi has learned her lesson.'

Tanya studied me for a moment, and then worked her magic with a forceful whistle.

'You can summon your dog now,' she said as the pack broke away. 'I think you'll be surprised.'

I turned to sight my cowardly, owner-abandoning Shepherd, stationed at least thirty metres from me, and glowered at her.

'Come on, then! You're safe now.'

When Sesi didn't move, I looked around to see what was

going on. Tanya was just ushering the last of the Ridgebacks into the side paddock. Once again, from the other side, they went completely wild. I'd had enough of feeling intimidated, however. If I got my kicks from this kind of thing I'd have squandered my money on an entirely different kind of service. Instead, I'd tasted pure fear for the sake of one unruly pet. As soon as the gate was closed, my dog came alive and bounded back to my side.

'Look at that,' said Tanya, who was too far away to see the look of sheer relief in Sesi's eyes. 'At last you have her at your beck and call!'

# 17

# A Handful of Hercules

I came away from the session feeling like I had wasted my time. It was only when I realised it had changed my dog for the better that I began to reconsider. Tanya hadn't set out to terrify me. It was simply an exercise in encouraging me to be the boss dog. So long as I maintained an authoritative manner on walks, I found that Sesi looked to me whenever we encountered another dog. She still succumbed to temptation fairly regularly, but that initial glance in my direction gave me hope. I just considered it to be my cue to become yet more masterful.

Privately, I held out hope that my dog's newfound respect for me would one day extend to the rest of my family. At the very least, as I set about introducing Hercules to Sesi, I figured the Dachshund would effortlessly submit to my command.

Like a boxing referee before the first round, I stood midway between the two dogs and switched my gaze from one to the other.

'Easy does it,' I said with my arms spread wide and my palms in their field of vision. I hardened my stare at Sesi, just to remind her that I called the shots. It was the sausage dog I should've been watching, however. Hercules was quite oblivious to me as he increased his pace across the yard towards the bigger dog.

'Dad, he's going to get hurt. *Do something!*'

For once, May's air of concern was shared by Lou. When Sesi rose and took a step towards Hercules, my eldest even broke off from filming to urge me to intervene.

'You can't let this happen!' she pleaded. 'YouTube will just take it down straight away.'

'Everybody stay calm,' I instructed them, for I knew what to do. Quickly I dropped to one knee in front of Hercules and pulled the bodybuilder's pose, just as Tanya had done in the sand school. I was boss dog here, after all, even if I did come across more like Brucie on steroids. Sesi certainly saw that I meant business. She stopped in her tracks, and even backed up into a sit. Hercules, meantime, paid me no attention whatsoever. He just scuttled wide in a bid to get around me. Abandoning my pose, I reached out to grab him. Hercules responded by just throwing himself at my Canadian Shepherd.

'You're too late!' yelled May, and covered her hands with her face.

Sesi was up on her feet before I could do likewise. She snarled and bared her teeth as the puppy bounced repeatedly into her chest. The little sausage dog pup showed not a hint of fear or trepidation. He just kept on jumping up at her as if to test her mettle.

'That's quite enough, mister!' I said, on snatching him into my arms. 'You need to learn what you're messing with here. Sesi could devour you.'

'But she didn't,' said Lou, who'd evidently been unable to resist the temptation to film the moment regardless.

'That's because I'm here,' I reminded her. 'In control of the situation.'

'Right,' she said with some uncertainty.

I was set to assure Lou that nothing bad could happen on my watch, only Hercules started wriggling and writhing in my arms. Eventually, fearing he would fall, I put him down again. Straight away, the overexcited puppy scampered for Sesi and executed a low-level head-butt that by rights should've earned him a full-scale fight back. Instead, Sesi growled and shrunk away. She didn't appear fearful. Just fed up with the hassle from a puppy who didn't know any better. When my dog looked to me as Hercules got in her face once more, I recognised that she was at the limits of her patience.

'OK, I think this introduction is over,' I said. 'Sesi, take yourself inside for some downtime.'

She didn't waste the opportunity. As soon as I opened the back door for her, my dog stepped right over the pup and hurried for the boot room. I closed the door behind her, stopping Hercules in his tracks.

'That was insane,' observed May. 'Hercules, you're going to get yourself killed!'

Lou was inspecting the screen on her phone.

'I've got the shot,' she said, smiling to herself. 'Mum is going to love this.'

'Hold on!' I stepped across with my hand outstretched. 'Let me see.'

As soon as I took the phone from my eldest daughter, it beeped to confirm that the picture had just been sent. With a frown, I studied the slightly blurred image of Sesi doing her utmost to escape from what was shaping up to be the world's most irritating puppy.

'That wasn't helpful,' I told Lou, and handed her phone back. A moment later, my office line began to ring. 'I think we all know who wants a word with me.'

\*   \*   \*

Emma wasn't upset, so she told me. Just disappointed. I immediately assumed that this was because I had disregarded her feelings about introducing Hercules to Sesi. *On the contrary*, she had said to correct me. Judging by the picture, both dogs looked like they were having a marvellous time. My wife was just sorry that she hadn't been there to witness it for herself.

'Hercules is clearly in safe hands with you,' she said. 'I'm pleased you're looking after him for now.'

I considered pointing out that the photograph didn't tell the whole story. Her puppy had shown absolutely no sense of self-preservation. Even if he was just out to make a friend, his behaviour had been hugely provocative for what was essentially a deeply grumpy dog. One prone to cystitis and the downturn in mood that went with it. I just didn't think Emma would ever accept that her sausage dog was anything less than perfect.

'Hercules is looking forward to seeing you,' I said instead, and glanced at the clock on my wall. 'We're counting down the hours, in fact.'

Taking care of the kids during the working week required a routine. After school, the children liked to know what to expect from their afternoons as much as I did. Everything from clubs to seeing friends was written down on the chalkboard in the boot room. Even Sesi was aware that she would get her walk just as soon as I had served tea. Not that she could read. She just knew that once the kids were eating we could head out to the woods.

Then Hercules arrived and put paid to the best laid plans. By the time Emma stepped through the back door and hung her work coat on the children's peg rack, I was still at the cooker.

'How come you're so late?' she asked, squeezing my arm in greeting before dipping a finger into a pan of pasta sauce.

'Ask him,' I said, stirring the sauce a little more vigorously than necessary. I was so angry with the new arrival that I couldn't even bring myself to call him by his name.

'Hercules?' Emma looked around, but saw no sign of him. Half an hour earlier I'd decided to contain him for his own safety. Any more misdemeanours and I worried that I might've lost it completely and added him to the pasta. Spotting him behind the bars of his crate, looking a little sorry for himself, Emma took herself back to the boot room. Sesi lay on her bed, watching warily. 'What's he done?' she asked.

'I can't leave him alone for a moment,' I said. 'Not only is he a walking trickle of wee, he's gnawed his way through the buckle on Honey's school bag, and created three holes in the rug in front of the wood burner. *Three!* That's pure provocation.'

'It's what puppies do,' she reasoned, opening up the crate. 'We have to accept this kind of thing will happen for a while, but he'll grow out of it.'

'Then there's the problem with upstairs,' I added. 'He can get up there easily enough. Coming down again is the issue. He's just too long for the steps. Twice he's finished the last flight like a slinky toy, which is just dangerous.'

'So we'll put a child gate at the bottom.' Emma kissed the puppy on the head and then set him on the floor. 'It's a simple solution.'

'I haven't told you the worst,' I went on as the sauce simmered away. 'You know those nice shoes you bought for special occasions?'

'The ones with the straps?' Emma stopped there. I could

144

tell she knew just what had happened to them. 'I can always save for another pair,' she said quietly.

Sesi chewed up other dogs, but had never done the same thing to footwear. Had she done so, I felt certain that Emma would not be so reasonable about it.

'He's unstoppable,' I went on. 'And the little ones don't help.'

'Where's he gone?' she asked, and looked around. 'He was here a moment ago.'

'Most probably running riot in the front room with Honey and Frank,' I said. 'I've given up trying to stop them from building a Super Mario level for him out of boxes and pillows. Hercules loves it, but it all needs clearing up.'

'Oh, let them have fun,' she said. 'I'm happy to deal with the mess.'

I took the pan off the hob. The sauce was practically boiling.

'Perhaps you'd like to call them through for supper,' I said. 'Also Lou and May.'

'How have they been with Hercules?'

'Lou has turned into the damn dog's personal paparazzi. She won't leave him alone. Even when I managed to crate him for a sleep, she woke him up taking pictures for her Facebook page. As for May . . .' I paused there for a moment. 'Let's just say she just doesn't like change.'

I turned to the worktop in order to serve the pasta into bowls. From behind me, Emma placed a hand on my shoulder.

'Why don't you get some fresh air with Sesi?' she suggested. 'Hercules is my responsibility. I can take over now.'

There is a path through the woods behind our house that forms a circuit. Strictly speaking, one section is out of bounds to the general public. It belonged to a man with an unpredictable temperament and a penchant for massive campfires. He wasn't local, however, and in fact looked like he might be more at home in the backwaters of the Appalachian Mountains. He had allowed me to walk his section of the path a long time ago. The trouble was he kept repeating the invitation whenever I saw him out on the lane. It was as if he had no memory of already granting me permission, which made me worry how he'd react if he actually found me on his land. Once, on a family walk, the little ones had scampered ahead. We found him chatting merrily to them just in front of the little cabin he had in a clearing. He seemed fine, but for the chainsaw idling in his hands. I'm sure he meant no harm, but it was worth keeping a keen eye open on a full loop through the woods.

Looking out for the man as I walked served to take my mind off Hercules. I really couldn't afford to take out more time for another pet, even a fortnight would have an impact on my work, but I genuinely believed Emma knew that. She certainly pulled her weight while I was away. By the time I returned to the house, I found she had served tea, washed up and was even beginning to steer Frank towards bed. In practice, this meant Emma read a story to our son while Hercules vigorously humped Frank's favourite teddy on the carpet in front of him. She was doing a great job of bringing the story to life, using different voices for each character. Throughout, Frank watched the puppy intently, and continued to do so when Emma reached the last page and closed the book.

'Oh!' she said, on realising what had dominated his attention. 'We can wash him,' she added, and lifted the puppy from the bear. 'Do you want a goodnight kiss from Hercules?'

Frank shook his head more than was necessary, responding as if his mother had just levelled a threat at him.

'We need to get that behaviour under control,' I observed, as Frank climbed into bed. 'Even if it is just natural, Hercules needs to know it's wrong.'

'I'm sure it's only a phase,' she said, carrying the puppy with her as we retreated from the bedroom. 'Sesi was hard work when we first got her, but she calmed down. I still can't believe she played so nicely with Hercules.'

I switched off the light in Frank's bedroom and bid him goodnight.

'She didn't play with him as such. She just put up with a lot of pestering.'

'Well, at least she didn't attack, which was my main concern.' Emma led the way downstairs with Hercules nestled in the crook of one arm. 'I guess that proves it's safe for them to be together.'

'Hercules looked hellbent on provoking her, though. After this afternoon, I'd say Sesi needs protecting from *him*.'

'Don't be ridiculous.' Emma turned with an expression of scorn and amusement. I couldn't help but think the puppy in her possession was giving me exactly the same look. 'How could something this cute be a threat to your dog?'

'Given how many times he's lost control of his bladder today, I'd say the most immediate threat would be to your work clothes. It's been a long while, after all.'

Emma regarded the puppy, and immediately held him away from her.

'What shall I do?'

'Pop him out the front door,' I suggested. 'It's fenced off from the lane, so he can't come to any harm. I've done it a couple of times this afternoon.'

Emma brought the puppy back into her full embrace.

'You left him out there? On his own?'

We were talking about a small strip of garden and a path with a gate onto the drive. It was the only section of grass that hadn't been destroyed by minipig or poultry, and I intended to keep it that way. What's more, the entire section was completely secure. I had checked it myself.

'Hercules has to learn to go somewhere other than the carpets,' I pointed out. 'Plus he's safe from the chickens there.'

Emma looked to the front door. It had been dark for some time.

'I'll take him outside,' she agreed finally. 'But I'm staying there until he's finished.'

After the downpour we'd had at the weekend, a cold front had begun to creep in. It was too early to switch on the central heating. I was alone in this view, but also the only one who knew how to operate the system. Playing by my rules, the family were welcome to bask before the wood burner in the front room, which was cheaper to run than the boiler, while bed time was a question of calling upon Arctic survival methods. One upside of this regime was that the little ones didn't tend to drift downstairs three hours later claiming that they couldn't sleep. Once they were both tucked in, even Frank and Honey knew that they probably couldn't make it back out to the top of the stairs without hypothermia setting in. With no desire to return to my desk after the day I'd had, I settled down on the sofa and waited for Emma to return. May and Lou soon joined me. They tuned into their regular soap opera while I found a magazine and tuned out until it was over.

Half an hour later, with the credits rolling, I thought I had better check that everything was OK outside.

I opened the front door, blinked at the cold air that rushed in, and found Emma shivering on the path. In front of her, on grass that was beginning to form a frost, Hercules was sniffing around with great interest.

'He still hasn't cocked his leg,' she said, through chattering teeth. 'How long does it take?'

I looked at the puppy.

'Hercules doesn't do that thing,' I said, and half-heartedly acted out what she'd been hoping to see from him. 'I noticed that earlier when he peed on the carpet. He's either too young or his body is so long he can't support himself on three legs.'

'So how can you tell if he's done it?'

'Oh, that's easy.' I stepped out and scooped up the puppy. Holding him out with both hands, I invited Emma to inspect his undercarriage. 'You see these long strands of hair? If they're wet that means he's good to come inside.'

'So, that's his tinkle hair?'

I brought Hercules down to chest level and flattened my lips at my wife.

'Shall we go in?' I suggested, and hoped she would leave such a less-than-technical term out in the cold.

We didn't keep Sesi confined to the boot room day and night. As much as she felt comfortable in what was effectively her lair, we always invited her to join us in the front room each evening. By then she was tired, less boisterous and unlikely to knock things over. As a rule, she would trot in just as soon as I opened the gate, and quickly arrange herself at our feet in front of the sofa. I saw no reason why Hercules should take away this treat. What I should've considered was how he had reacted in her presence out in the yard. As soon as the puppy caught sight of the Shepherd coming through the kitchen, he scrambled into her path. I moved to intervene, only for Emma to step in before me.

'I'll handle this,' she said, and hauled the sausage dog from harm's way. 'He'll calm down.'

Over the course of the next hour, Hercules maintained a level of hyperactivity that you might expect from a child on a diet of fries washed down with cheap cola. Sesi was the focus of his attention. Not that she enjoyed it one bit. Yet again, the puppy devoted himself to winding her up. He would slide off Emma's lap just as soon as she had settled him. Within seconds, Sesi would be up on her forelegs snarling wildly, with her head craned as far back from Hercules as possible. Keeping the peace was exhausting. For Emma, at any rate. Every time I offered to help, she remained determined to stick to the terms of the agreement.

When bed time beckoned, all Emma could do was return the puppy to his crate and leave him to howl. Sesi took herself into my office at once, leaving me with a look of utter betrayal. I felt sorry for her, but figured Hercules would have to conk out at some point. Which indeed he did, around dawn the next morning, when I woke up to the familiar squeals from the minipigs.

Snapping open my eyes, as if dragged from one nightmare into another, I turned my head to find Emma staring at the ceiling. Even in the breaking light, I could see that she was wide awake.

'Everything OK?' I asked, noting groggily that she looked a little tense.

'Just fine,' said Emma. 'You slept well.'

With Roxi's honking on the rise, I turned and reached down beside the bed. Such was the daily scramble to get to the bottom of the garden that I kept my clothes close to hand. Grabbing my gown was just not an option when it was this cold. I needed to be dressed, and fast, which is why I had taken to arranging what I needed on the carpet in the order that I should put things on. By placing my socks at the bottom, followed by my jeans and a pair of pants on top, then a jumper overlaid with a T-shirt, I could haul my clothes on correctly without turning on the light and blinding us both. Emma always objected that if she got up in the middle of the night it looked like some kind of ghastly intruder pervert lying on the floor, but in general she slept through. In fact, it was unusual to find Emma awake before me. Normally, she would get up a minute or so after I left the bedroom and make two cups of tea, so we could at least come alive before the kids. As I struggled into one sock after another, it struck me that she may have been like this for some time.

'How was your night?' I asked with some hesitation.

'Well,' she said, and paused to yawn, 'the last hour has been quiet.'

I grabbed my jeans without looking down at them.

'Did Hercules keep you up again?'

'Pretty much since we went to bed,' she confirmed.

I buttoned myself up, before hooking my jumper and T-shirt with my foot.

'I do think you should reconsider this tough love position,' I said, as Butch and Roxi escalated the volume. 'Caving in worked for me.'

'No way,' declared Emma. 'I'm not going to be defeated by a sausage dog. I don't care how many sleepless nights it takes, at some point Hercules will have to recognise this family does not revolve around him.'

# 18

## Last Legs

As the week went on, it became quite clear that we had taken on a creature of habit. Hercules liked to sleep all morning, while I was at work, and then slowly crank up his level of activity until it peaked when we went to bed.

In terms of my roles and responsibilities, he didn't really get under my feet. The kids played with the puppy after school, and then let him doze when he became a bit scratchy.

It was when Emma came home that Hercules went haywire. He learned to pick up on the sound of her car on the drive, and would be first to greet her when she opened the door. From that moment on, however, he wouldn't leave her alone. That Emma indulged him in this didn't help. Despite the installation of a child gate, she'd allow him upstairs when she changed out of her work clothes, and when they both vanished one evening I discovered she had taken him into the bathroom with her.

'He needs to learn some boundaries,' I suggested, when she reappeared. 'You're spoiling him.'

'Rubbish. It's just that Dachshunds are known to bond with one person only,' she told me. 'It's important that he considers me to be his number one.'

I might've disapproved of the way that Emma was forging this connection. Then again, if it worked that was fine by me.

Everyone considered Hercules to be the last word in cute. I just saw him as a low-lying hassle. When he was up and running, his ability to get under my feet knew no bounds. I only had to cross the kitchen, usually carrying a pan of boiling water, for him to dart across my path. It took so long for his body to clear out of the way that I would be forced to execute a kind of folk jig to prevent the water from slopping over. As for his toilet-training, I was putting him out onto the grass at the front on a regular basis. I even waited in the cold with him, but he still wasn't truly watertight. I had hoped that Hercules would be housetrained by the time Emma took him to work. Sesi had been a dream for me in that department, after all, despite being a nightmare in others.

As the days ticked by, I began to doubt that Hercules would be safe on office carpets. Still, that wasn't my problem. Where I did feel uncomfortable was in Emma's determination to deal with the sausage dog herself outside of working hours. Hercules was just so manic in her presence that he took up all her time. She politely refused all help from me, but I could see it was taking its toll. Mostly this was down to the fact that she couldn't sleep through his nightly howling. Sesi looked equally frazzled, and yet my dog didn't have to hold down a day job.

'*Please* will you think about giving up with the sleep-training,' I said one morning, after waking to find that Emma had endured another dreadful night. She had slept a bit, so she said. It's just Hercules's persistent yelping continued to stir her.

'I'm not backing down,' she stressed, as the minipigs summoned me out of bed. 'But I have to say he's a determined little thing.'

I was clambering into my laid-out clothes as she said this. What came into my head prompted me to pause for a moment and think hard about whether I should express it. Had Ossie the assistance dog been present, he could've simply taken over the task of dressing me.

'You know what?' I said quietly. 'I could always keep him up this morning. It might tire him out later on.'

Emma seemed slow to process my offer. Then her expression brightened considerably and I realised I had just sacrificed any chance of getting some work done.

At breakfast time, Hercules was so happy to be in our company that he'd pelt around looking for anyone who would pay him attention. This wasn't hard to find, apart from when he turned to me. On the upside, after a night without sleep he would soon start slowing down. By the time the kids were ready to leave for school, Hercules was so tired he could barely stand. Normally, if I was doing the school run, I'd take the opportunity to pop him inside his crate first. He'd be fast asleep by the time I came home. I could then forget about him until the early afternoon. On this occasion, with Sesi watching me from her bed, I opened up the crate on my return and lifted the slumbering puppy from his cushion. Hercules stretched in my hands, but made no effort to wake.

'Rise and shine,' I said, and placed him on the floor. 'Look lively, little one.'

Hercules simply flopped where I left him. I stood up, hoping that would encourage him onto his paws. Instead, he opened one eye, looked at me accusingly, and then hauled himself onto the corner of Sesi's bed. My dog looked appalled. Hercules ignored her growls completely and curled up with his head resting midway up his back.

'What now?' I asked myself. I couldn't just leave him there. Not only was I supposed to be occupying him all morning, I still didn't trust Sesi not to chew him up and spit out the bones. It left me with no option but to lift him out of harm's way.

Hercules reacted like a puppy who had ingested horse tranquilliser. He just flopped over my shoulder, while I supported his back with one hand and his bottom with the other. 'Wake up, big guy, come on!' I took to walking around the house with him, at a loss as to what else to do. I even opened the front door, sure that the sudden drop in temperature would serve as the equivalent of a cold shower. Instead, when I took him outside, Hercules sagged onto the grass with his back legs buckled uselessly and his head hanging low. Then he started to shiver.

It was no good. Unwilling to risk him catching a chill, I scooped him up once more and carried him into my office. I settled in my chair with the puppy on my lap. For a moment, Hercules looked vaguely interested in the landscape of my desk, only to sigh and rest his head on my leg.

'Fine,' I muttered, aware that I had used up about half an hour of my precious work time. 'You sleep on the job.'

I began to work, thinking at the same time that Hercules would soon get fed up with the clatter of the keyboard. He seemed quite content, however. Unlike me. The puppy didn't make it any easier when he began to turn and stretch out in his sleep. This was fine when he was positioned along the length of my thighs. When he hauled himself around to lie across my lap, however, there simply wasn't enough of me to support him. He just sort of draped himself, with his head dangling freely on one side and his back legs on the other. It looked really uncomfortable, plus he was proving to be a bit windy, but as I was on a roll with my work I just left him like that. He only stirred, in fact, when my phone rang. As soon as I grabbed the handset, however, he flopped back into position.

'Hi,' said Emma, when I answered the call. 'I just wanted to thank you for keeping Hercules awake for me. It was kind of you to offer. I can't tell you how tired I feel right now.'

'Hopefully he'll sleep soundly tonight,' I said, and grimaced to myself. Somehow, I just couldn't admit that he was currently arranged like a towel across my lap.

'I hope he's not proving too much of a distraction,' said Emma. I could hear her rattling away at her keyboard as she spoke to me, answering emails most probably, which was always the way with her. I considered tapping away myself, just to sound busy.

'Hercules is fine,' I said, which wasn't untrue and made up for the outright lie that followed. 'He's playing in the kitchen.'

As I drew breath to move away from the subject, Hercules emitted a long and squeaky fart. I knew that it was loud enough to have been picked up down the line because all of a sudden Emma stopped typing. I didn't know what to say. Did I blame it on Hercules, which was effectively an admission of lying, or take responsibility and come across like a bit of an animal myself?

'Is Sesi with you?' she asked finally.

'Yes!' I said, perhaps a little too quickly, and revolved in my chair to face my dog. She was asleep on her bed in the boot room. 'Bad dog! That kind of behaviour belongs outside.'

Sesi lifted her head from her paws and looked a little puzzled. I mouthed an apology at her and turned to face my desk once more. As I focused on finishing the call, I also had to endure the stink created by the puppy. It was awful, and once Emma rang off to get back to work I woke Hercules with a few choice words.

'What's wrong with you?' Rising to my feet, I deposited the dog on the chair just to create some distance between us. 'Is this the result of having long guts or something? How long does it take for a meal to pass through you? Weeks? *Months*?'

Hercules's only answer was to curl up on my chair and

close his eyes. I had to do something. I just wasn't quite sure what. The puppy was clearly fit for nothing but snoring. I could continue to try and wake him, but then I worried that it might be damaging for him at such a young age. Hercules looked perfectly content, there on my chair. I figured perhaps he was at that stage of the sleep cycle where nothing could rouse him. It reminded me of May, who had lately taken to signalling that she was in this phase at night by snoring in the most chilling manner. It had something to do with the way she inhaled. Every breath sounded like a wraith repeatedly calling '*M-u-m*' in the most drawn out of ways. The first time it happened, late one evening, Emma and I were in the front room watching television. I had to mute the sound to hear it clearly. As soon as I did so, we both looked at one another without blinking.

'Is that May?' asked Emma.

'She's summoning you,' I said. 'Go to her.'

'What? She sounds possessed!'

This wasn't far from the truth. I imagined my daughter was standing at the foot of the stairs in a nightgown, possibly hovering several inches in the air.

'*M-u-m . . . m-u-m . . .*'

Aware of my responsibilities as a parent, but not before pointedly making a big deal out of being the one to leave the sofa, I made my way upstairs to investigate. With no sign of May where I had feared I might find her, I called back for Emma to join me.

'It's coming from her bedroom,' I said. 'There's no way I'm going in there alone.'

'*M-u-m . . . m-u-m . . . m-u-m . . .*'

'For goodness sake, Matt.'

Joining me outside May's bedroom, Emma pushed open the

door. Neither of us stepped inside. We just waited for the light from the landing to spread across the bed.

'May?'

*'M-u-m . . . m-u-m . . .'*

She was lying on her back, tucked up tightly, fast asleep with her mouth wide open. With a visual reference, it was clear that May was just snoring. When I shook her gently by the shoulder, hoping to wake her briefly so she'd roll onto her side, it also became apparent that we might have to live with the noise all night.

In short, our daughter would not be woken. So soundly was she sleeping that nothing could rouse her – and the same applied to the puppy. Curled up on my office chair that morning, Hercules was effectively dead to the world. It left me with no choice but to wheel my chair to one side, find a stool from the kitchen and put in an uncomfortable work session until the kids came home from school. Hercules was such a creature of habit that he didn't stir until they piled home. That he went on to play with the little ones through much of the afternoon didn't leave me feeling confident he'd be tired out by the time Emma finished work. As I prepared tea for the children, I felt bad about letting him sleep again. There hadn't been much I could've done about it, but Emma would pay the price later on. It was a feeling also tinged with guilt. Not only had I failed to keep my promise, my wife had sounded so grateful to me when she called.

About half an hour before Emma was due back from work, I decided there was only one way to clear my conscience. I would prepare a nice, romantic meal for two. That way, even if Hercules proved to be a nightmare, I could lull her into feeling relaxed. I spent the time consulting cookery books until I found something we actually had in the fridge, cleared the kids' tea once they'd finished and then set the table again. For once we would not be eating from trays on our laps in front of the TV. It was a small gesture, but served to make me feel much better about the fact that when Emma got home she was greeted by a puppy so brimming with energy that he started running circles around her feet.

'You don't look very tired, Hercules,' she said, on shrugging off her coat and unzipping her boots. 'Or are you just pleased to see me?'

Ignoring the silly voice Emma had adopted to address the dog, I suggested that he wasn't the only one who looked forward to her return.

'I'm cooking,' I said, in case the apron I had strapped on didn't speak for itself.

'What? Properly?' Emma brightened when I drew her attention to the place mats on the table. She looked wiped out, but clearly happy to be home. 'Ah, that's sweet. We never eat properly.'

'I'll serve up once the little ones are in bed,' I told her.

'May and Lou can make the most of the front room,' she added, and then scooped Hercules into her arms. 'With this little man out for the count, it'll be just the two of us.'

It was a rare thing for Emma and me to spend time alone together. The demands from children and animals put paid to that. Technically, we weren't going to be entirely alone that evening. Hercules showed no sign of winding down, as Emma had been hoping. Given that his day had been no different to any other, this came as no surprise to me whatsoever.

'I'm really surprised,' I told Emma nonetheless, as I finished cooking supper. 'I'd have thought he'd be on his last legs by now.'

Hercules was tearing after a tennis ball that Emma had just

bounced off the skirting board for him. With no grip on the floor, when he tried to switch back in the opposite direction he just swept onwards like an out-of-control broom.

'Never mind,' she said, to my genuine astonishment. 'Are we ready to serve?'

'Almost,' I said, and began to assemble the food on two plates. 'I think you're going to like this.'

'It looks delicious,' she said. 'This is almost quite romantic.'

'Almost?' I caught her eye and chuckled. This was going much better than I had expected. Hercules was still snaking around, but Emma didn't seem to mind one bit. 'I'll open a bottle of wine and we're good to go.'

'Aren't you forgetting something?' she asked.

I looked around, sure that I had covered every base.

'I don't think so,' I said.

'Some romantic you turned out to be,' she said playfully, and headed in the direction of my office.

I went back to serving the supper. Then I uncorked the wine and poured a glass for Emma. When the ceiling lights dimmed all of a sudden, I glanced up and saw her with one hand on the switch and the other clutching something that caused a catch in my breath.

'Grab a candle and a lighter from the drawer,' she said, and crossed to the table. 'We haven't used this in years.'

The last time I had paid that holder any attention whatsoever, I had been urinating disastrously into it. After that, I had put it back on the shelf. To my great shame, but given that a puppy took up all my attention, I had just forgotten about it altogether. Emma placed the holder on the table. As she did so, a bead of liquid snaked over the rim and down the length to the base. Unlike me, Emma didn't notice. She was too busy looking at me quizzically.

'Matt,' she said gently, as if to stir me from a dream – or, as it felt at that time, a horrific nightmare, 'the candle and the lighter?'

'Oh, right. Of course.' I turned my back on Emma, heading for the drawer, and swore in silence. I was appalled at myself for leaving it on the ledge like that, and barely able to imagine how my wife would respond should she witness what it contained. For a second I considered coming clean, but by now my head was spinning with shock and sheer dread. Instead, practically on autopilot, I opened the drawer and began to rummage. I spotted what I was looking for straight away, but that didn't stop me from taking several seconds to think of a get-out clause. I could come up with nothing, however. Supper was served, and cooling on the table. The lights were set for an intimate meal for two, and for all the wrong reasons here was I set to make it an evening Emma would never forget. Aware that I was stalling badly, I picked out the candle and the lighter. Then, like a soldier before the firing squad, I faced my wife once more.

'Found them.' I smiled weakly. 'Hope the lighter hasn't run out of gas.'

'It's new,' she said, as if to remind me. 'What's wrong?'

'Nothing!' I said, a little too quickly, and promptly side-stepped the puppy.

Emma watched him skittering after the tennis ball. She seemed delighted by his presence still, and dipped down to stroke him.

That's when I seized the moment. It was the only course of action I could think to take. Without pause for thought, I reached for the candle holder and tipped the contents into my empty wine glass. Emma was still focused on the puppy while I slotted the candle cleanly into the holder and lit the wick. Finally she stood up, and looked admiringly at the set-up in front of her. Feeling only relief, I pulled back her chair so she could sit.

'This is so nice,' said Emma, and took her place. As I moved around to my seat, feeling hugely pleased with myself, she reached for the glass of red wine I had poured for her. 'Here's to us!' she proposed, and then followed my gaze to the glass in front of me. While my expression froze, Emma's turned to surprise. 'I didn't realise white was an option,' she said. 'What is that? A Chardonnay?'

* * *

Under the circumstances, supper went better than expected. Hercules hurtled about on tiny legs that looked unfit to support him, but Emma didn't seem to mind. I chose to leave my wine untouched that night, for understandable reasons, and though Emma only had the one glass it just combined with her lack of sleep and left her yawning. It was still good to spend time together, without constant interruption from the kids, but I could see we weren't going to make it a late one. For one thing, it was quite chilly. I could've suggested that we regroup in the front room, where the wood burner was keeping Lou and May nice and warm. Looking at Emma, I figured she'd just collapse into a doze on the sofa.

'Why don't you go to bed?' I suggested, once we'd eaten. 'Hercules can hang out with me while I clear up the kitchen.'

'He's my responsibility,' said Emma, yawning into the back of her hand.

'And you're going to make yourself ill if you keep saying that.' I glanced at the floor. Hercules was hunting titbits under the table. 'He'll be fine,' I insisted. 'And you'll feel better for a good night's sleep. Who knows? You might even make it through the night if you get a head start on him now.'

Emma thought about this for a second.

'This is a one-off, right? I'm absolutely not trying to slide out of looking after him.'

'Emma. You're exhausted. Take yourself to bed!'

Reluctantly, Emma rose from the table.

'Just promise me one thing,' she said. 'If he cries in the night, and I happen to sleep through, you won't go downstairs to him.'

'Of course not,' I assured her. 'This sausage dog lives by your rules.'

I had things to do before I turned in. Hercules was happy pottering while I did the dishes. He followed me into the front room when I popped in and reminded May and Lou that it was way beyond their bed time. Then all I had to do was let out each dog in turn so that they could relieve themselves before bed. Leaving Sesi to bask in front of the wood burner, I picked up Hercules and carried him to the front door. I think both of us were taken by surprise at how cold it was outside. Still, it had to be done, and so I set the puppy on the frosted grass and waited. To give Hercules credit, he hadn't had an accident all evening. Surely, I thought, he must be bursting. The puppy examined the ground with his tail wagging.

'Come on, Hercules,' I whispered, and hugged myself against the chill. 'Let's make this easy on us both.'

Fifteen minutes later, the puppy bounded back over the threshold and into the hallway. Following close behind, I shut the door and wondered how long it would take me before I regained feeling in my fingers. I was utterly freezing. My teeth chattered and it felt like every muscle in my body was trembling. Hercules looked absolutely fine. Unlike me, he had a coat, which is why I guess he'd taken his time. Aware that I still had to take Sesi outside, I placed Hercules in his crate and returned for my dog. She took one look outside before glancing at me and heading directly for her bed. I couldn't blame her. I also knew she possessed a cast-iron bladder, and so I closed the child gate into the boot room and switched off the lights. Hercules squeaked in response, only to stop when I peered into his crate.

'Don't go thinking I'm a soft touch,' I said, still feeling chilled to the core. 'Just give it up and go to sleep.'

I left the door ajar, and turned the kitchen lights down low. Hercules had no reason to be scared. Unless, of course, he upset Sesi. As she had taken herself off into my office, I figured she was simply preparing for another long night of noise. Sure enough, as soon as I reached the staircase the puppy began to cry. I crept onwards, but every step only served to increase the urgency and volume of his yelping. On reaching the landing, Hercules was howling so loudly I figured someone would soon drift out of their bedroom and make a formal complaint. I was cold. I wanted to tuck in under the duvet and sleep. With that in mind, I turned and headed downstairs again. If I reached Hercules quick enough, I thought to myself, Emma wouldn't even know that I had gone against her wishes. I felt sure that she was wrong in her approach to sleep-training. We didn't just abandon the kids to the night when they were little. It was a question of slowly reducing the number of visits.

Sure enough, as soon as I eased open the door to the boot room, Hercules switched his focus from weeping to wagging his tail.

'Hush now,' I told him, crouching for a moment. 'It's OK for you, on a nice warm blanket. I'm so cold I could be close to flat-lining.'

The puppy looked a little crestfallen when I didn't let him out. Crucially, he did so without a whimper. I stood up once more, and took a step backwards, which was enough to draw a squeak from him. I paused, thinking things through. Hercules would undoubtedly kick off if I just left him again, but he did at least look tired to me. If I just hung around in the kitchen, I thought to myself, surely he would nod off and earn us all an undisturbed night. Despite the fact that I longed to snuggle up to Emma and leach some of her body warmth, waiting for five minutes seemed like a price worth paying. As Hercules settled on his blanket once more, I thought I'd make full use of the time, and do something nice for Emma as much as for myself. Without making eye contact with the puppy, or Sesi who was holed up in my office, I crept through to the utility room. There, among the stuff in the cupboards that we rarely used, I found a hot-water bottle. I hadn't made one of these for ages. On this, the first truly cold night of the winter season, it felt like one smart move indeed. Not only would it bring me back to room temperature, I thought to myself, on heading back to switch on the kettle, it would keep us snug throughout the night.

Waiting in the kitchen. I pretended not to pay any attention to the puppy. I didn't want to fire him up in any way. If anything, having me close by seemed to help him relax. From the corner of my eye, I watched Hercules rest his head on his paws. A moment later, with a flick that travelled the length of his body, he turned onto his side and shut his eyes. As the kettle came to the boil and then clicked itself off, I unscrewed the lid from the bottle feeling as if I had done the right thing. I had been delayed in going to bed, but at least we'd all get a good night's sleep at last.

# 19

## Nothing to Fuss About

The next morning was the usual nightmare. The minipigs kicked off proceedings. When I crashed downstairs and into the boot room, wearing my pre-positioned jumper the wrong way round, Sesi simply watched me in the knowledge that I would be back within minutes to walk her. Since Hercules arrived, Emma had taken to following me down in order to deal with him. If the puppy hadn't wet his blanket overnight, he would do so out of sheer excitement on seeing me. I figured that couldn't last much longer. Given that I basically ignored him in my hurry to deal with Butch and Roxi, it would only be a matter of time before he considered me with the same indifference that I showed him. Emma would surely become the sole focus for his affections, and that would really take off once he joined her in the office.

On this occasion, once I'd fed Butch and Roxi, I came back to find no sign of Emma. Usually she was busy hauling out a soggy blanket from the crate and replacing it with a dry one. Hercules peered up at me from his confines. He appeared puzzled, as did I. Given that he looked like he had yet to unleash the floodgates, I released him from the crate and carried him out to the front garden.

Ten minutes later, as cold as I had been the night before, I returned to the bedroom. Emma was sitting on the edge of the bed, inspecting the back of one leg. Ignoring her for a moment, I faced the mirror and tutted.

'Look what your puppy has done,' I said, and turned to show her the dark, wet circle he had left on my jumper. 'I wait for ages for him to do his thing. When I finally pick him up, he decides to make a start.'

Emma seemed deaf to my complaint. I had expected her to come back in the puppy's defence by acknowledging that he'd slept through the night. Instead, clutching her ankle, she continued to inspect the calf.

'What do you think this is?' she asked finally. 'It wasn't there when I went to bed.'

I crouched to take a look. Three little blisters studded the back of her leg. A vertical, fine red line joined them together.

'No idea,' I said in all honesty. 'Does it hurt?'

'*Yes*, it hurts.'

It was unusual for Emma to handle pain badly. She'd given birth to four children drawing upon nothing but gas, air and curses. To reply this abruptly told me it was bothering her.

'Is it a bite?' I suggested. 'Or a boot rub, perhaps? You were wearing boots all day yesterday.'

'It's what I'm thinking,' she said. 'I hadn't worn them in ages, and I was on my feet all afternoon.'

From downstairs came the sound of a plaintive bark. Sesi was awaiting her walk. I glanced at the clock. I was at least fifteen minutes behind schedule here. If I didn't get a move on, the little ones would be going to school without breakfast.

'Why don't you stick a plaster on it?' I suggested. 'And stay away from those boots for a while.'

My success in sleep-training Hercules went unnoticed by Emma, but not by me. I had to deal with the consequences that morning, which took the form of a puppy with boundless energy. Instead of lying curled up and out for the count in his crate, Hercules made it his mission to disturb both me and Sesi. It wasn't hard to upset my dog. Every time he invaded her personal space, she would rise up and snarl at him. The problem was her space covered every square inch of my office. As soon as Hercules placed one paw over the threshold, she would sound a warning. When he ignored her completely, it would all kick off. Sesi didn't once attack the puppy. If anything, she would try to avoid contact with him as he bounced underneath her head. But eventually, as the noise she made became increasingly aggressive, I would have to step in and put a stop to it. As a result, I did very little work. Instead, with my concentration in ruins, I ordered a zombie DVD online and illustrated my To-Do list with the sort of chart you'd find on the wall of a cell. Mine simply counted down the days before I was free from the sausage dog during office hours.

Towards lunchtime, while standing outside the front door waiting for Hercules to relieve himself, I decided I would introduce him to the minipigs. The hens were out on the garden, scratching through the frost, and so I opted to place the puppy on a leash. If any of them closed in, I could winch him to safety in an instant.

Butch and Roxi were sensibly tucked up in their sleeping quarters when we approached. Hercules happily trotted in front of me. He didn't seem to care that several hens were stalking him, though they backed away when the minipigs appeared. This was down to the fact that the pair crashed out into the open like bulls. As the entrance in the side of the shed wasn't quite big enough for them both, there would always be a bit of a tussle between them to be the first through. I had never seen Roxi lose this battle. Butch was no micro pet. It's just she was so much bigger than him. Having grown beyond all expectations, they had at least found a happy place here under the eaves of an oak. Despite the workload involved in their upkeep, we could be proud of the fact that we had never crumbled and discussed rehousing them. Privately, it had crossed my mind on many occasions, of course – often when someone left the gate open and they'd set about trashing the borders.

'Heads up, fellas,' I announced as our two honking porkers shook themselves down before sauntering across to greet me. 'I want to introduce you to a little guy who wouldn't be here if you'd both stayed small and cute. Butch and Roxi? Meet Hercules.'

Unlike my hens, the puppy seemed totally unfazed by the two beasts behind the picket fence. From his perspective, I imagined all he could see between the slats were two huge floating snouts. Without any sense of hesitation, Hercules lifted his head high and sniffed. Butch was first to meet him. The minipig's nostrils expanded and contracted, before the sausage dog moved across to the next snout. Roxi also took a moment to breathe in the new smells afforded by the Dachshund. I'm not entirely sure what she made of it, but she responded with a snort that was strong enough to blow Hercules off his paws.

'Go easy!' I told her, as Hercules picked himself off the ground. This time, he showed some caution in returning to the fence. Instead of padding closer, he just stretched himself forward to his full extent. I stood over him with my arms folded, shaking my head at the sight. He might've been trying to make himself even longer than he was, but it wasn't going to impress a pair of weighty pigs. It was only when I heard the sound of a horse on the lane that I decided to call time on this meet and greet. Riders regularly passed the house. I also knew they could see over the top of the fence. I often spotted them from the front room window. Generally, they looked amused at the excavation site that Butch and Roxi had created. It would barely be worthy of a glance if we lived on a farm. As the pigs occupied a domestic back garden, however, I imagine most people looked upon the mess and wondered what on earth we were thinking. Unwilling to be spotted with another ridiculous pet, I hurried inside with Hercules under my arm. He belonged to my wife, after all. In due course, she could face the world with him.

\* \* \*

I was relieved to see Emma at the end of that day. Hercules might've been falling into a decent sleep routine, but it had cost me in terms of working hours. The kids were at the table, eating fish fingers and chips, both of which I had cooked for too long while standing in the cold waiting for the puppy to finally take a leak.

'Mum,' called May, before Emma had stepped into the kitchen, 'I'm worried that Hercules will get frostbite if Dad keeps forcing him outside.'

'I'm not forcing him,' I said from the sink. 'It's called toilet-training.'

'More like torture.' May stabbed at a chip with her fork, which was so crisp it shattered on the plate. She used her fingers to pick up another one. 'If you don't like the dog, just say so.'

I waited for her to take a bite, just so I knew that I wouldn't be interrupted.

'Hercules has to learn. He's a dog. His coat will keep him nice and warm. If anyone is going to suffer from standing out in the cold, it's me.'

'Tell him, Mum!'

Usually, when one of the children had saved up a complaint for Emma, she would handle it as if in work mode. Having spent the day dealing with staff, her first response would be to negotiate some kind of peace deal. Even when I was in the right, which in my opinion was one hundred percent of the time, Emma would still aim to appease the kids as much as me. On this occasion, however, she didn't even look like she had heard a word of our exchange.

'Everything OK?' I asked, as she drifted past Sesi and closed the gate behind her. Hercules rushed out from under the table to greet her. Grimacing just a little, Emma reached down and ruffled his head. What she didn't do was scoop him up as he was clearly hoping. 'You look kind of pale,' I added.

'Oh, I'm fine,' she said. 'I might've picked up a bit of a bug, but nothing to fuss about.'

'Mum, will you please talk to Dad about being mean to Hercules.'

May seemed not to notice that her mother was off colour. When I turned to face the table, I found that Lou and the little ones were equally oblivious.

'Frank and Honey, I think Mario needs a break as much as you. Put those DS's away right now. We don't play video games at the table.'

Lou looked up from her phone and sniggered. Then she caught my eye and realised that perhaps she had compromised herself.

'Same thing applies to phones,' I told her. 'Now is not the time to text.'

'Text?' Lou raised one eyebrow. 'Nobody texts any more, Dad.'

'Really?' I looked to Emma, but she was rummaging through her bag. 'I text all the time.'

'It's for losers,' Lou told me flatly. 'Instant messaging is what everyone uses.'

'Maybe so,' I said, 'but we're not planning a riot here. We're eating tea.'

Lou prepared to protest, but once again her mother wasn't listening.

'Do we have any painkillers?' asked Emma, and stopped rooting through her bag. 'I think I've left mine at the office.'

'Only the kids' stuff,' I said.

Emma tutted to herself.

'Do you mind if I run a bath?' she asked. 'I'm sure I'll feel better afterwards.'

For a puppy that had not been with us long, Hercules was quick to find his place in the family. Having worked out that Sesi wasn't going to risk my displeasure by ripping his throat out, he continued to test her patience by throwing himself at her at every opportunity. This wasn't such an issue with the child gate in place. It just meant that Sesi was bound to simmer with resentment at the fact that the new arrival was allowed the run of the house. The other problem I had concerned the way that Hercules related to the children. While Lou regarded him as a poster boy for her Facebook page, and May found new ways to worry about his welfare, the little ones didn't quite know how to handle him. If anything, they behaved more like puppies than little people, and I foresaw trouble ahead.

'Please stop yelping at Hercules,' I said at one point. 'Especially on all fours like that. It's only going to confuse him.'

Frank and Honey climbed back onto their feet, for about a minute at most. As soon as I turned my attention elsewhere, they were back on the carpet, scampering around. Hercules loved every moment. I could only hope that this increase in activity would exhaust him later on. If Emma was unwell then the last thing we needed was an insomniac puppy. Leaving the little ones to bark at will, I decided to head upstairs to check on her. The bathroom door was ajar. When she didn't answer, I eased it open. The room was steamed up, with the last of the water draining from the bath. Knowing how Emma liked to soak, it seemed odd to me that she'd climb out so soon. I turned for the bedroom, and found her lying on the bed with her eyes closed. She was wearing a dressing gown, with a towel around her head, and a flushed look as if she'd just stepped out of a sauna.

'How are you feeling?' I asked when she opened her eyes. 'You look a bit hot.'

'The bath was too much for me,' she said. 'It made me feel sick.'

I felt her forehead. It was hard to tell whether she was showing a temperature or had simply cooked herself as she often liked to do. Her tolerance to very hot water was far greater than mine, so it was a surprise to hear her complain.

'Is it a bug, do you think? A virus doing the rounds?'

'Could be,' she said. 'Let's just hope nobody else picks it up.'

Emma crooked one leg at the knee. It was then the plaster on the back of her calf caught my attention.

'Ouch,' I said, noting how the skin around it had become inflamed.

'That doesn't help,' said Emma. 'It's so sore.'

Just then, a squabble broke out downstairs between Frank and Honey.

'It's bound to be about the puppy,' I said with a sigh. 'Somehow, I need to encourage them back under Mario's watchful eye.'

Pulling the air between her teeth, Emma swung herself onto the edge of the bed.

'I'll sort it,' she said. 'They're just tired. It's past their bed time.'

'Let me handle that,' I said, as she climbed to her feet.

'But I haven't seen them all day,' she insisted, and shuffled out to find them.

Even when she was suffering, Emma didn't believe in getting ill. She never had done. In all our years together, she hadn't once holed up in bed or the bathroom like anyone else with flu or a stomach bug. Her sick leave went unclaimed at work, and though she was sympathetic to the unwell, I knew deep down she found it hard to understand how anyone couldn't just soldier on. Watching her gather the little ones, which basically involved extracting the puppy so she had their full attention, I felt sure that she would ride out any fever without complaint.

# 20

## A Casualty

'I feel dreadful,' said Emma the next day after work. 'My head won't stop spinning.'

As usual, she had returned around tea time. I was just serving up plates of sausages and mash when she appeared in the kitchen, and had my back to her. The little ones had already started eating, only to freeze on looking at their mother.

'Oh my God,' Lou declared, while May's eyes widened in shock.

'What's wrong?' I asked, turning to face her. 'Good grief!'

At first glance, Emma looked as if all the blood had been drained from her face. I had never seen anyone look so pale, and nor had the kids. With dark shadows slung under her eyes, and a slight slump in her posture, she really did look like she would topple at any moment.

'I'll be fine,' she insisted, and set her bag on the floor. I noticed that even Hercules and Sesi had kept their distance from her, as if picking up on something beyond our senses. 'Let me get changed, Matt, and you can go back to your office.'

'Work can wait,' I said, despite the fact that Hercules had distracted me all morning. 'I'm worried about you. We all are.'

'Mum,' said May, who had yet to lift her knife and fork. 'You're not about to die, are you?'

'Of course not!' Emma laughed, and picked up the post on

the kitchen counter. 'I don't feel too great but the weekend is here. If that doesn't sort me out, nothing will.' She stopped there and picked out a thin cardboard package from the sheaf of bills and junk mail. 'What's this?'

'The DVD I ordered,' I said, and invited her to open it up. 'The zombie one we wanted to watch.'

Horror films were a guilty pleasure that Emma and I had enjoyed for years. Every now and then we'd hope to scare ourselves as a way of winding down from the week. That Lou and May were too frightened to read the blurb on the back of the movie that had just arrived was a bonus. As much as we liked their company at the end of the day, I was keen to grab more time for ourselves, which is exactly what my latest purchase represented.

'Looks good,' said Emma, having inspected the box.

'That's if you're up for it,' I pointed out. 'I have to say you look like you're about to collapse.'

Smiling weakly, Emma tossed the post back on the worktop.

'If everyone stops fussing,' she said, 'I can focus on feeling better.'

In Emma's shoes, I'd have holed up in the bedroom, closed the curtains and crawled under the duvet. I wasn't quick to complain about feeling under the weather, but I was in full agreement with the children. Their mother looked terrible, and was clearly in denial about it. Despite the fact that I had work to do, I couldn't bring myself to leave her to look after the kids. There was no way that I could insist that she take a break, and so I simply worked with her towards reaching that point in the evening where we could flop together on the sofa. I had stoked the wood burner to keep the chill at bay. As it was producing more heat than normal, Sesi kept her distance and lay at the foot of the sofa. Hercules showed no such caution. He stretched out on the hearth to such an extent that I'd been unable to resist summoning Lou for a picture opportunity. She had reeled off several shots, before taking herself upstairs with May to update her friends and followers.

'Alone at last,' I said, and clapped my hands together. 'What do you think about a film?'

I turned to face Emma. It was then I realised she looked no better than when she had arrived home.

'A film would be good,' she said. 'Though I might not make it to the end.'

I was set to check she didn't mean that in a terminal way, but thought better of it. Instead, on firing up the DVD player, I settled back and prepared to scare myself so acutely that I would be prepared to let Hercules pee on the carpet rather than stand outside in the dark with him. The movie was about a small band of survivors from a zombie apocalypse. It was the kind of film that was low on gore, but high on creeps due to the fact that one of the survivors feared he had been scratched during an escape from the living dead. Over the course of an hour and a half, we watched his slow decline and rising suspicions among those around him. I was gripped. Emma just seemed distracted. She kept changing her position and muttering to herself from time to time.

'Everything alright?' I asked eventually.

'The plaster is really itching me,' she said, rubbing at her calf through the fabric of her jeans. 'It's probably about time it came off.'

As the film moved towards a climax, I was faintly aware that Emma had eased off one sock and was preparing to investigate the cause of her discomfort. On the screen, the poor guy with the zombie scratch had accepted his fate. While a debate about what to do with him raged outside the room in which he'd been locked, he calmly removed his belt and fashioned it into a noose. I didn't watch him take matters into his own hands. Instead, I found myself looking aghast at what Emma had just revealed as she scrunched up the hem of her jeans.

'I don't think you should peel that plaster off,' I said after a moment to compose myself. 'Otherwise a chunk of your leg might come with it.'

The day before, the surrounding skin looked a little inflamed. Now, the affected area had doubled in size, and turned black.

'Oh,' said Emma simply.

'What's that smell?' I asked, and sniffed the air. With great effort, I managed not to retch on realising it was coming from the discoloured slab of flesh. 'OK, we should probably get this seen to. If we leave Lou in charge, I can take you to A&E.'

'Let's not overreact,' said Emma, without much conviction. 'I think we should see how it looks in the morning.'

On the screen, the poor guy swinging from the rafter was in the process of coming alive once more, but not in a good way.

'The morning might be too late,' I said, and gestured at the television. 'Have you not been paying attention?'

Emma glanced at the screen. She then shook her head, as if dismissing a thought she had admittedly entertained herself.

'I'm not about to become a zombie,' she said. 'That's just silly. It's a boot rub. One that's gone a bit manky.'

'A *bit*! That's an understatement.'

Clasping her foot at the heel, Emma rotated her leg.

'I just can't believe a boot would do this.'

'It's the only explanation. Unless you've picked up a scratch that's become infected . . . or a bite,' I added with some hesitation.

This time Emma frowned at me.

'I think I've seen enough of this film for now,' she said. 'Hopefully, a good night's sleep will sort me out.'

I followed Emma to bed some time later. Once again, Hercules kicked up a fuss from his crate as soon as I climbed the staircase. This time, I knew just how to handle him, and crept back down to soothe the puppy with my presence. Waiting for him to settle, and feeling the cold as I had two nights earlier, I flicked on the kettle to fill a hot-water bottle.

A moment later, I flicked it off again and stared at my reflection in the window. As it was pitch black outside, and the overhead lights were shining bright, the expression on my face showed the awful realisation that had just sprung into my mind.

Hercules went on to sleep like a dream until dawn. I woke some time before the minipigs, feeling suffocated by my conscience. Beside me, Emma dozed fitfully. Her eyes flitted under heavy lids, while her brow was needled in sweat. I felt awful, just not in the same way as my wife. Once I'd finished buying Butch and Roxi's silence with breakfast, I returned to the bedroom with the puppy in my arms. I needed to soften what I had to say, and this seemed the most immediate way.

'Morning' croaked Emma, and held out her arms for Hercules. 'The way I'm still feeling, a cuddle beats a cup of tea.'

'I'd happily make you one,' I said, and rested on the edge of the bed. 'I'm just not sure I can trust myself with scalding water.'

Emma looked puzzled. She stroked Hercules, who had already settled in her lap.

'What's on your mind?' she asked.

Solemnly, I fished under the bed for the hot-water bottle.

'I think I know what caused those blisters,' I admitted. 'You were asleep when I slipped the bottle under the duvet. It must've touched your leg.'

Emma considered this for a second, before dismissing it out of hand.

'I'd have felt the heat straight away and moved. It wasn't the bottle.'

'You were quite tired,' I pointed out. 'And you'd had a glass of wine.'

'What are you suggesting?' asked Emma, bristling visibly now. 'That I was so senselessly drunk I couldn't feel it burning? That kind of thing happens to gin-addled old ladies, not me. It's a boot rub gone bad. End of story.'

An awkward pause opened up between us.

'Does it look any better this morning?' I asked, if only to break the silence.

Hercules was quite happily snuggled in beside Emma by now. With his chin resting on her thigh, he looked at me in a way that suggested he had just taken sides.

'Let's see.' Emma folded back the duvet, gasped and promptly folded it back over her leg again. It was just enough time for us both to see that the injury hadn't improved one bit. If anything, the area of blackened flesh had only increased. It left the plaster looking totally insignificant, and worried me hugely.

'I think it's hospital time, don't you?'

Emma didn't disagree. Instead, she pointed out that Honey had a swimming lesson an hour from now.

'She can't afford to miss it. It's really important.'

'You can't put it off any more.' I rose to my feet, and reached forward so that she could hand me the puppy. 'Consider this an intervention.'

'We can't all go,' she said, clinging onto him. 'Who's going to look after Hercules?'

Even though Emma remained convinced that her boots were to blame, I still felt really bad about the situation. I might've persuaded her to seek medical attention, but the fact that she insisted on driving herself to hospital didn't seem right at all. I wanted to look after her. She just refused outright, and insisted that my time was better spent making sure the day ran as normal for the family. I figured she would be gone for a couple of hours, and home in time for a late lunch. By mid afternoon, with every call I made going straight to her answer machine, I began to fret.

'Is Mum going to be OK?' asked May, again.

'You don't need to worry yourself about it,' I assured her. 'It can take a long time to be seen by a doctor.'

May nodded, but seemed unconvinced.

'Do you really think she's been bitten by a zombie?' she asked.

'Of course not,' I said, and promptly stepped aside as Frank, Honey and then Hercules scampered past. 'She'd have died and come alive again by now,' I added, though May was in no mood for laughter.

Just then, my mobile phone began to ring. Hurriedly, I grabbed it from my pocket and took the call.

'Hi,' I said, expecting to hear Emma.

'It's Lou,' came the voice down the line, so clearly that I realised I could also hear her upstairs. 'Can I take Hercules to see a friend?'

I tilted the phone away from my ear, and looked up at the ceiling.

'Are you in your bedroom?' I asked out loud.

A moment later, following the sound of padding footsteps, my eldest daughter appeared at the banisters. She had her phone pressed to her ear.

'So, what do you think? Can I take him out?'

I ended the call on my phone, before suggesting that Lou did likewise.

'I can't believe you just used your mobile to speak to me,' I said. 'Here's a new rule for you. If we're under the same roof, come and talk to me face to face.'

Lou shrugged, clutching her phone with both hands as she peered down at me. 'So, can I take Hercules?'

'He's not allowed to leave the house yet,' I reminded her.

'Then how about my friends come here? Everyone is busting to meet him, and he's such a sweetheart at the moment.'

Throughout this exchange, Frank and Honey continued to charge about with Hercules. They whooped and squealed as he nipped at their socks, which really wasn't something I wanted to encourage.

'Now is not a great time,' I said. 'And I know what you're like, Lou. If I say yes, one hundred and twenty seven teenage girls will descend upon the house. You'll spoil the puppy and then . . . I don't know. Do baking or something.'

'I won't do that.'

'You always do baking,' May said, to back me up. 'Your Facebook page is full of pictures of your cupcakes. Cupcakes and Hercules.'

'Plus you never wash up properly afterwards,' I added. My eldest looked crestfallen. She toyed with the phone in her hands, eyes down as if this wasn't a chat with her dad but an interview with Martin Bashir. 'At least can't it wait until Mum is better?' I suggested. 'It would just be easier to manage if we're both here.'

On weekdays, school was the reason that I managed to work and keep the household afloat. At weekends, with everyone at home, Emma's presence was vital. Between us, things got done. It meant one parent could be out and about, from doing the grocery shopping or ferrying children to friends and clubs, while the other ticked off the tasks at home. Alone, I felt as stressed as a stranded space marine under siege from alien hoards. Hercules hardly helped, though it wasn't his fault that he'd just caused a disagreement between my eldest and me.

'Mum would've let me have friends round,' she muttered, and withdrew from the banisters.

I turned to face May. Behind her, Frank and Honey had jumped onto the sofa, giggling as Hercules tried to follow them. My efforts to encourage them to behave themselves around the puppy was officially a lost cause.

'What's up with Lou?' I asked. 'She's not normally this moody.'

'Probably has issues with her boyfriend,' said May, matter-of-factly.

This was news to me. Not that Lou had issues with a boyfriend, but that she had a boyfriend at all.

'She's dating? I didn't know that. She's never had a boyfriend. Why didn't I know she had a boyfriend?'

May regarded me like I should know the answer already.

'Why would she tell you? You're her dad.'

'Which is precisely why I *should* know.'

'You don't need to worry,' said May. 'Alfie is cool.'

I took a second to digest this.

'*Alfie?* She's dating a boy called Alfie?'

May studied my expression closely.

'What's the problem? Why are you frowning?'

As a father, I had never been in this position before. In

grappling with the fact that my eldest daughter was old enough to date, I also had to deal with the realisation that I was one of those dads who feared the very worst about a boy. That my alarm was based on little more than a fear that he'd been named after the film probably told me more about myself than him.

'Lou!' I called out, almost instinctively, as her sister left the room. 'Can you pop downstairs? I need a word.'

*'A word about what?'*

The voice, whisper-quiet, came from the boot room. There stood Emma. Back from the hospital. She looked pale, tired and detached.

'Hey!' I said brightly. 'You should've called. How are you? What did the doctors say?'

Earlier, Emma had set out wearing a loose pair of jogging bottoms. It was the only item of clothing she could bear to wear that didn't leave her wincing in pain. Reaching down, she showed off a bandage that ran from her ankle to her knee.

'It wasn't a boot rub,' she said, and covered the bandage again. 'You were right.'

'A burn?' I walked across the kitchen towards her, stepping over Hercules as he pelted across my path. The little ones were close behind. I paid them no attention whatsoever. Instead my focus was locked entirely on my wife.

'A third-degree burn,' she said next.

*'What?'* I wasn't surprised by the diagnosis, but the severity took my breath away. 'I'm sorry,' I said next. 'That's all my fault.'

'They just think I was really unlucky. When you slipped the bottle into bed, I was fast asleep. It didn't touch my leg. The edge just came very close indeed, and slow-cooked me through the night.'

'I suppose it explains the three little blisters in a line,' I said. 'But not the zombie flesh you ended up with.'

Emma pressed her lips together.

'The reason it went bad is on account of a slight tissue infection, but it's all in hand now. I've been prescribed painkillers and antibiotics for the next seven days, and have to rest my leg. After that, it's business as usual.'

'So what will you do?' I asked, mindful of the puppy. 'Take next week off work?'

'Of course not,' she said. 'That would just be skiving. I'm only going to be sitting at my desk all day. I'll cope just fine.'

Frank, Honey and Hercules had taken their chase elsewhere in the house. I could hear things toppling in the front room. Feeling entirely responsible for Emma's accident, I knew what had to be done to ensure her swift recovery.

'Maybe Hercules should stay here,' I suggested. 'Just until you're back up to speed.'

'I'm sure he'll be settled with me at work,' she said, as Frank careered into the kitchen with his sister close behind. As Hercules gave chase, his paws scrambled uselessly for grip on the tiles. With a thud, he crashed into the kickboard under the cooker.

'I insist,' I said, forcing each word out. 'One more week at home won't hurt.'

# 21

# All About Flour Babies

When it came to dealing with very small children, I had ample experience. I'd changed nappies many more times than I'd ever knotted a tie, and though I'd never been inside a boardroom my negotiation tactics were second to none. I wasn't skilled in honing contracts, but if someone threw a meltdown because we'd run out of ketchup, I could have them smiling in seconds.

On paper, at least, I was prepared for the teenage years. Thanks to my monthly problem page, I was comfortable tackling sensitive issues faced by young people. I didn't bluster and blush when it came to discussing sex and relationships. In fact, I firmly believed that parents should be equipped to provide balanced information and advice to their growing kids in order to prepare them for adulthood. It wasn't a question of sitting them down and providing a lecture. You simply had to make them aware that they could talk to you about anything, in their own time, without fear of being judged or getting into trouble.

Then Lou got herself a boyfriend called Alfie and I freaked out completely.

In a way, it was fortunate that Emma was on hand to calm me down. I repeated exactly what May had told me, but she didn't feel the need to summon Lou as I had. First she took me to task for making assumptions about a boy we knew nothing about. Then she promised to have a chat with Lou in a way that didn't alienate her completely. Frankly, I didn't think it could come soon enough.

'You're her father,' Emma reminded me. 'Why on earth would she want to talk about stuff like this with you?'

It left me with no choice. All I could do was back off from the issue and hope that Emma would find a good time to speak to our eldest. Had I thought things through, of course, I might have reminded myself that Emma was in pain and preoccupied by her leg injury. A heart-to-heart with her daughter was unlikely to be at the top of her list of priorities.

Sure enough, that weekend Emma generally operated at half speed. Against my advice, she took herself to work on the Monday, leaving me in charge of Hercules once more. He still drove me to distraction whenever I sat down to write, but it was Lou and her love life that nagged at the fringes of my concentration.

On her return from school, I realised that I might just have found the perfect opportunity to open up a conversation.

'What's that?' I asked as she dumped a plastic carrier bag on the kitchen surface.

'My homework.' Lou headed straight for the bread bin. 'Do we have any peanut butter?'

Curious, I hooked a finger into the bag's handle so I could look inside. 'Is this a cooking assignment, then?' I asked. 'What are you making? Pancakes?'

Lou was searching through the cupboard now. 'It's my sex education assignment?' she said in the form of a question designed to kickstart my failing memory. 'The flour baby thing?'

I glanced back inside the bag. It contained a one kilogram pack of self-raising flour and another pack of plain.

'Is this it?' I asked. 'I was expecting a doll or something.'

With the jar or peanut butter located, Lou swung around to face me.

'You know what's really unfair?' she said. 'Everyone else only has to look after one baby. Miss picked on me to have the twins.'

'Twins? Right!' I peered back in at the two packs of flour. 'Shouldn't you be doing something with them? As a rule, babies don't really enjoy being kept in carrier bags.'

'Justin and Beyoncé are fine,' said Lou, and appeared to remind herself of the jar in her hand. 'They can wait until I've eaten.'

As tempted as I was to encourage my daughter to think a little more long-term, and choose names with meaning rather than current celebrity status, I decided this was an opportunity that I couldn't ignore. As her mother had failed to raise the issue over the weekend, I would step up to the plate and swing for that special chat. Since Lou had a boyfriend, I wanted to be assured that there would be no real offspring to name for many years to come.

'These flour babies,' I said hesitantly, and waited for Lou to finish trowelling enough peanut butter on her bread to fix a house brick. 'Do we know where they come from?'

'Tesco, I should think. There's a store near the school.'

'I mean for real,' I followed up quickly. 'Lou, I know you have a boyfriend now. It's vital that you're informed about—'

'*Who* told you?' Lou wheeled around, toast in hand. 'Was it May? It must've been May. I can't believe May blabbed about that!'

'She didn't say anything bad,' I assured her. 'In fact, she seemed very supportive of young Alfred.'

Lou froze. Then, with a steely glare, she raised her toast to her mouth and ripped a section away as if it was raw meat.

'His name is Alfie,' she said before chewing. 'And that's it.'

'OK. Whatever,' I replied. 'My point is that as your father I have to be responsible and make sure—'

'I have homework.' Lou broke away from the conversation and headed for the stairs. 'I need to learn about oxbow lakes. You know? *Important* stuff!'

I watched her go, and breathed out not so much with a sigh but an air of deflation. Just then a rhythmic squeaking drew my attention to a spot underneath the kitchen table. There, with his eyes tight in concentration, Hercules was busy making puppy love to one of Frank's soft toys. I pinched the bridge of my nose, anxious not to let this moment get any further out of hand. Already Lou had begun stomping her way up the stairs.

'What about your flour babies?' I called after her. 'Justin and Beyoncé are in danger of being neglected here.'

A moment later, with her lips pressed firmly together, Lou returned and snatched the bag from the worktop. She then marched off with such force that the contents clipped the doorframe on her way out of the kitchen.

I had no intention of giving up. As a father, that would be a dereliction of duty. Instead, I decided that if I was going to speak openly with Lou then she would need to have no escape route. That moment arrived the next day, late in the afternoon, when Sesi had an appointment at the vet for her annual boosters. All I had to do was arrange for May and the little ones to spend time with friends after school. Then, instead of leaving Lou in front of her laptop, I asked if she would like to join me.

'Why?' she asked, still working at the keyboard.

Having grown up with the internet, Lou had the amazing ability of being able to conduct a conversation online and another one face to face.

'Sesi can be a bit excitable when it comes to going anywhere other than the woods,' I told her, having prepared for this question beforehand. 'She pulls on her lead like crazy. If you can come with me just to open the doors and stuff it would make my life a whole lot easier.'

Lou responded by tapping at the keyboard again. For a moment, I wondered whether I needed to go online for my answer.

'That's cool,' she said finally, and closed the lid of her laptop. 'And I'm sorry if I was snappy with you yesterday. Someone told me that Alfie had deleted me from his address book, but it turned out to be lies.'

I was surprised that Lou had just been so open with me about her boyfriend. I also knew that I should bide my time. As she left her chair to follow me, I couldn't help noticing the carrier bag dumped beside her wastepaper bin.

'What about the twins?' I said. 'Shouldn't they come too?'

Lou took a moment to work out what I was talking about. When the flour babies returned to her attention, her shoulders sagged so noticeably that her arms seemed to lengthen by several inches.

'Dad, it's just two packs of flour.'

'Called Justin and Beyoncé,' I reminded her.

'We're going to pop Hercules in a crate before we go so he's safe and sound. Can't we do the same thing with the twins?'

'Lou, it's important that you take this assignment seriously. It might just show you that babies are a big responsibility.'

Lou's expression tightened. She glanced at the door, clearly considering whether to flounce out. I told myself not to push the underlying issue. Very shortly she would have no choice but to hear out what I had to say. At the same time, it was important that my daughter didn't neglect her homework. Calmly, I repeated the suggestion that the twins should come with us.

'OK,' she said with a sigh, and collected the bag. 'But they're staying in the car when we get there.'

Lou caught my eye as we turned to leave the room. She grinned, despite herself, which I took to be a promising sign.

With Sesi in the back of the car, safely behind a mesh guard, I set off with Lou in the passenger seat. As we no longer owned any booster seats, she had stowed Justin and Beyoncé in the footwell behind me. They were out of her sight, but certainly not out of my mind. For this was the moment I had been working towards.

'Sweetheart,' I began, on turning out of the village, 'this boy, Alfred . . .'

'Dad! Not again. And stop calling him that! You're making him sound lame.'

Back home, this would've prompted her to march off and slam a door behind her. Out here she had the option of throwing herself from a moving vehicle, but I was pretty sure that wouldn't happen.

'I'm sure he's a lovely lad,' I pressed on. In response, Lou touched two fingers to her temple, like I was giving her a headache. I had tried to sound upbeat and engaged. This wasn't an interrogation, after all. 'How old is he, out of interest?'

'OK. I think I know where this is going, so let me spell it out to you. We're not sleeping with each other.'

For a split second, the car felt like it was about to leave the road.

'Well, that's good to hear,' I said, struggling to sound casual and relaxed. 'So, what is he? Sixteen? *Seven*teen?'

'Fifteen,' she said, matter-of-factly. 'A month younger than me. And it's just a date thing, Dad. Nothing serious. You don't have to worry.'

'Well, it doesn't sound like Alfie is the kind of boy who would try it on,' I added, fishing manically now. 'What do his previous string of girlfriends have to say about him?'

'That's enough! Stop the car!'

I lifted my hands from the steering wheel in submission, only to clasp it in a hurry once again.

'Lou, this is really difficult for me. I'm your dad. I'm just concerned.'

'For your information, Alfie is really smart. He's in the top set for maths.'

'Is he really?' I couldn't help but sound surprised, which was hardly likely to make things any better between my daughter and me. 'Well, that's good to hear.'

Lou sighed and folded her arms, while I focused on pulling up at the junction.

'He's coming over after school on Wednesday,' she said quietly. 'If that's alright with you.'

I pulled out onto the main road, thinking I could at least get the measure of this kid by meeting him face to face. 'That's fine by me,' I said after a moment. 'I'll cook something special for tea.'

'Please don't do that, Dad. Just treat him like any other friend of mine.'

*One who plans to get his wicked way with my daughter*, I thought to myself, and assured Lou that I wouldn't embarrass her in any way.

\* \* \*

We drove the last stretch of the journey in awkward silence. As a way to make peace, I switched on the radio and selected a station I knew Lou would like. It was playing a song by a woman boasting about how the boys were drawn to her milk-shake or something. Lou reached forward and chose another station. As a result, it was a relief to arrive outside the vet and climb out of the car. We did at least have Sesi to focus on. For some reason, she adored coming here. I suspected it had something to do with the treat the vet fed her after receiving her jabs. Whatever the case, it meant I had thirty-five pounds of overexcited Shepherd to handle. Just getting her out of the car was a test. From experience, she'd jump out just as soon as I opened the boot. To stop her from doing this, and poten-tially racing off, I had to wag my finger at her through the glass and order her to stay put. Lou watched as I crouched down, cracked open the boot and then reached in blindly for her leash.

'Why can't she be normal?' she asked. 'Like any other dog?'

With the leash in my hand, Sesi made a controlled exit from the vehicle.

'Do you mean normal like Hercules?' I asked. 'I'd say he quite literally stretches the definition somewhat.'

Lou smiled, which was good to see. Behind us, another car had just parked up. With the aid of a walking stick, an elderly man climbed out of the driving seat. He was wearing a cagoule, which struck me as being a bit unsuitable for the cold weather. I watched him open up the rear door and help a dog out that looked as if it had lived about the same number of years as its owner. Both appeared quite plodding and ponderous in the way they moved, though I didn't pay them that much attention. I was focused instead on finding the keys so that I could lock up. Sesi was wired, which meant she pulled on the leash as I fumbled to free the fob from a thread in my pocket.

'Can you take the dog for a second?' I asked Lou, who reached out to grasp the leash. As she did so, the old man and his geriatric dog shuffled across the tarmac towards the main door. He hadn't even bothered with a leash. The dog just wobbled along by his side. It was all too much for Sesi, who jerked free from Lou's grip and barrelled towards what was possibly the most unlikely threat to her safety. '*Sesi!* Don't do it!'

With the keys still stuck in my pocket, I threw myself at the snaking leash; grabbing it from the floor just as Sesi smothered her poor victim. The old man wheeled around as his dog yelped in shock. I knew that Sesi was all snarl and no bite. Even so, it was totally unforgivable and basically the canine equivalent of mugging a granny for the pennies in her purse. Mortified, I hauled my Shepherd from the poor dog she had floored. Dragging her away, I jabbered an apology and pleaded weakly that it was really quite out of character.

'It's just her way of saying hello,' I said, searching for a way to make amends.

The man before me looked speechless, as if unsure whether this was all a bad dream. As the old dog picked itself up, he stooped to check her over.

'Is everything OK?' asked Lou.

The man whispered some words to the dog, stroking its head as he did so, but seemed entirely tuned out from everything else. Even when the pair continued on their way towards the door, he ignored us completely.

'On the upside,' I called after him, 'if your dog is hurt in any way then we've come to the right place.'

Lou shook her head and glared at Sesi.

'Unbelievable. What is it with her and other dogs?'

'It's just the way she's made,' I said, and finally freed the key from my pocket. 'Until he goes to work with your mother, Hercules really should watch his back with her around. And let's face it, there's a lot of that to cover.'

Inside, I found the waiting room was almost full. The old man had taken one of the last chairs near to the vet's examination room. His dog remained standing, trembling quietly. I really hoped this was down to age and not the result of Sesi's ambush. The only free places were right beside them. Given what had just happened, I decided we should just hang back. It was a surprise when the vet appeared at her door and called the old man in. At least a dozen people and their pets had been here before him. Still, it meant I didn't have to feel quite so awkward, and also gave us a chance to sit. As he rose to his feet, the vet offered him a distinctly brave kind of smile. Then she stepped aside and held the door open for them both. I followed Lou to the vacated chairs, shortening Sesi's leash so she couldn't lunge at any of the dogs waiting with their owners. The vet could be heard talking inside the examination room, but it was too muffled to understand. Then the old man began to speak. His tone sounded considered, like he'd thought about what he was going to say for quite some time. I gazed at my dog, wondering how long we would have to wait. When the man's words gave way to an anguished sob, I looked up smartly, as did Lou beside me.

'Is he crying?' she whispered.

An awkward silence gripped the waiting room when the vet opened the door once more. Lou had her answer when the old man stepped out. He was clutching the dog's lead and collar like a priest might hold a prayer book. He stopped and offered his hand to the vet, only for her to wrap her arms around him in a brief but comforting hug.

'He didn't feel a thing,' she told him. 'It was really very quick and peaceful.'

The poor man's tears might have run freely as he thanked the vet for her kindness and made his way to the main door. I really don't know. Like Lou, I was too busy staring at the floor.

*   *   *

'Can you believe it?' I reported to Emma that evening. 'It's probably the most difficult moment in any pet owner's life, and Sesi had to make it even worse. The dog was probably his only companion. A faithful friend to see him through the winter of his years. It was totally clapped out, posed no danger whatsoever, and yet its final memory before being put to sleep involved getting flattened for no reason by a deranged Canadian Shepherd. Lou and I were totally ashamed of ourselves.'

'That's nice.' Emma was sitting at the kitchen table with her bad leg up on a chair. Throughout my account of our shaming at the vet, she had been running a finger over the bandage. I wondered whether she had taken in a word I'd just said.

'We also had a talk,' I said, pushing on regardless. 'At least I tried to have a talk. Lou just shut down and told me I was fussing. Still, at least I get to meet her boyfriend soon. Alfie is coming here for tea.'

'Great,' she said, which only served to convince me that she really wasn't listening.

'Emma.' I waited for her to look up. 'Is everything OK?'

She seemed set to assure me that everything was fine, but the look on my face must've told her I wasn't going to accept that any longer. Despite telling her colleagues it was nothing to fuss about, I could see that her leg was an issue.

'It just doesn't feel right,' she said eventually.

'Then go back to the burns unit,' I told her. 'Don't try to be such a tough guy.'

Emma appeared to think about this for a moment, only to be distracted by the appearance of the Dachshund dragging one of his toys into the kitchen. The string of plastic sausages had been chosen for him by Emma, and the irony wasn't lost on either of us. It was also unusual to see Hercules pay attention to it. Generally, a toy had to be sexually attractive to him before he showed any interest. As he whipped the sausage string from side to side, Sesi watched closely from behind the child gate. Given what had happened that morning, I was in no mood to bring them together again just yet. Instead, I just laughed at the puppy, as did Emma.

'I know having Hercules is a pain,' she said next. 'But he does bring joy into the house.'

'So does a bottle of wine,' I told her. 'Only that's not going to happen while you're on medication. The sooner we get you sorted out the better. You can take Hercules to the office and I can actually get some work done for a change.'

Emma nodded, smiling still as Hercules dropped the string of sausages to chase his own tail. It was so far away that I wondered if he even recognised it as something attached to him.

'Let's see how my leg feels in the morning,' she said. 'We'll make a decision then.'

Overnight, the cold weather was swept aside by an utterly freezing front. Like everyone, I had seen the forecast. I just didn't really believe such Siberian conditions could happen to us here. It was so brutal I had difficulty getting to sleep. While Emma dozed, I had to fight the temptation to creep downstairs and fill the hot-water bottle. When I finally dropped off, I dreamed that we threw out all the bottles in the house and started using the minipigs to warm our beds before we climbed in. Inevitably, this turned into a nightmare when the combined weight of Butch and Roxi caused the upper floor to collapse to the ground. When I finally surfaced from the imaginary ruins, roused by real-life honking from the garden, I found the curtains open on a landscape that looked like it had suffered a massive fright. Everything from the trees to the fields was frosted white. Emma stood in front of the window, taking in the view. She was already half-dressed for work.

'So,' I said blearily, 'I take it your leg has improved.'

'Not really,' she said, buttoning up her blouse, 'but I've got back-to-back meetings all day.'

'Then cancel them,' I told her, sitting up now.

'It'll be fine,' she said. 'I can always go back to the hospital tomorrow.'

'But I know that you won't.' I rarely got cross with Emma. Generally, if I had an issue with my wife then I would expect her to read my mind. I always took the view that whatever problem I had was blindingly obvious, and if she couldn't see it for herself then I had no option but to brood about it. On this occasion, however, Emma's stubborn streak left me with no choice but to spell out my feelings. 'You have to get it seen again,' I told her. 'It's no good just hoping it'll get better.'

'Really, Matt. Today is just too important.'

Emma still looked as washed out and feverish as she had the day before. She was in no fit state to go to work. That was clear to me. Short of confiscating her car keys, however, I couldn't force her to phone in sick. As Butch and Roxi had started bellowing for breakfast, now was not the time for me to focus on persuading her to change her mind.

'This evening,' I said, by way of compromise. 'If there's no improvement by the time you get back, I'll drive you to the hospital myself.'

## 22

# Branded by Love

In the office, my colleagues for the day took the shape of two packs of flour and a young sausage dog.

It was my hardline stance on parenting that explained why Lou had left me with Justin and Beyoncé. Having insisted that my eldest treat her assignment seriously, Lou took every opportunity to foist them onto me whenever she left the house. Naturally, I made sure that the twins were safe and well. They just weren't particularly stimulated because I had work to do. Having Hercules with me didn't help in any way. Now that he was wide awake during the day, he competed with the keyboard for my attention.

Quite literally, I couldn't tap out a sentence without being drawn from my desk to stop him from chewing up stuff. Ideally, I'd have fenced him into the boot room, where all the footwear was on a rack too high for him to reach. What stopped me initially was Sesi. I just couldn't risk placing the puppy in her company – not without intensive monitoring, and I just didn't have the time. At one stage that morning I did try to swap them over, but Hercules took exception to being behind bars. Eventually, worn down by the constant interruption, I decided he would just have to take his chances with my dog. To be fair to Sesi, she had stopped paying such intense interest in the puppy. She still followed his every move with her eyes, but did so with her head resting on her paws. In a bid to get more than a page written before the kids finished school, I opened up the gate into the boot room and invited her to share the space with Hercules.

'I really need your help here,' I told her. 'Consider yourself a kind of canine babysitter.'

If Sesi showed some reluctance, Hercules more than made up for it by rushing at her in excitement. At once she was up on her feet, growling madly as the puppy repeated his trick of jumping at her head. Such was his length that his balance was all over the place. He'd launch himself upwards and then swing over with a twist in the manner of a performing seal. After a couple of attempts, Sesi moved into my office, but it was only in a bid to get away from him. When Hercules scampered after her, eager to continue the game, it became quite clear to me that I had just made matters worse for myself. In order to restore order, I decided we all needed a break. Leaving Sesi to settle, I took Hercules into the kitchen with me and switched on the kettle. I was feeling tense. Not just about my work output but the fact that Emma's dog was here at all. I recognised it was entirely my fault, of course. Had I left my wife to freeze through the night instead of slipping a scalding bottle into bed then Hercules wouldn't be here with me at all. The only thing I could do was hope he calmed down sooner rather than later.

The sound of the front gate creaking open didn't help matters. Every time it served to fire up Sesi. In a way, it was quite reassuring. It meant nobody came to our door selling dodgy dishcloths or fish from the back of a van. I turned to face the window, just as the postman crunched through the frost on the path outside. Understandably, on account of the ferocious barking from behind me, he looked a little nervous. He was also carrying a package too big for the letter box, and so I headed for the front door. Hercules dashed to follow me, snaking through each child gate as I opened them for myself. The last thing I wanted was for him to slip out of the house in case the front gate was open. And so, as I reached for the door, I dipped down and scooped the puppy into the crook of my elbow.

'Hi,' I said brightly. 'Sorry about the racket.'

I couldn't help noticing how the postman had retreated from the porch as I opened up the door. He was clutching the package to his chest, as if preparing to defend himself with it. Standing before him, I noted a puzzled expression cross his face.

'Your dog makes a lot of noise,' he said. 'For something so weenie.'

A moment passed before I connected the postman's comment with the barking that had started when he opened the gate.

'Oh, that wasn't *this* dog,' I explained, and then thought some more about his description of the puppy I was clutching. I cleared my throat, hoping to find some depth to my voice. 'This one belongs to my wife,' I added. 'My dog is a Shepherd. A big one, as I'm sure you can tell.'

The postman smiled to himself, and then appeared to remember the package in his hands.

'Here you go, Paris. Have a good day now.'

Later, with the kids home from school, it was Lou who explained to me just what the postman had meant.

'Paris as in Hilton,' she said. 'The American socialite with a taste for little lapdogs.'

Once again, Hercules had mounted his toy pheasant. I watched him humping it earnestly for a moment.

'But Hercules isn't a lapdog,' I said. 'For one thing, he doesn't fit. He sort of hangs on for about a minute before slipping off.'

'So he's not a lapdog,' said Lou. 'But sometimes the way you hold him is a little . . . girly.'

'A *little* girly?' May was at the table, flicking through the latest issue of the teen magazine with my agony column in it. I received a copy every month. Lately, I never got beyond the cover page before it made its way into her hands. 'It's girly alright.'

'But I'm not supposed to have anything to do with him!' I said in protest. 'It was agreed that he would spend his entire time with your mother, at work and home.'

May continued leafing through the magazine, skipping the page with my column.

'Then maybe you shouldn't have branded her,' she said casually.

Her comment left me lost for words for a second.

'It was an accident. I didn't do it on purpose. It was just one of those things.'

May nodded without looking up. I faced her sister, who averted her gaze.

'Let's hope she gets better soon,' said Lou, before heading for the stairs. 'At least then you can answer the door with your head held high.'

I exchanged a glance with May. She looked at me like her view was universal, and then appeared to remind herself of something.

'Lou,' she bellowed next. 'Don't forget Justin and Beyoncé. You don't want Dad branding them, too.'

\* \* \*

That afternoon saw snowflakes tumbling from the sky. They also settled on the ground. Looking up, the clouds appeared set to unleash a lot more, and so I headed for the back garden to check on the chickens, Butch and Roxi. At the weekend, May had decided that what the minipigs needed in their sleeping quarters, as well as extra straw, was a blanket. Not the worn-out, threadbare one that she carefully removed from the airing cupboard, but the nice woollen one underneath it that we used to sit on for picnics. When I found it, ejected from the shed by the minipigs and ripped in several places, I had to remind myself that May only had their best interests at heart.

'Winter just got serious,' I told them when they bundled out to greet me. As I scratched Butch behind one ear, Roxi turned to her water trough, which had frozen over, and pushed her snout through the ice with ease. 'Something tells me you'll survive.'

The chickens had gathered behind me, also holding out hope for a treat. All four ex-battery hens eyeballed me in a way that suggested I should probably pop into the shed and see what I could find. Inside, my worktop supported nothing more than a Frisbee and one broken swing-ball racket. Tom had built the worktop for me when he converted the shed to accommodate the minipigs' sleeping quarters. I had even gone out and bought a vice, but it was yet to be used. For one thing, even if I had any talent to build stuff, I couldn't move freely inside the shed on account of the straw bale. We got through one a week. Short of keeping it in the hallway, this was the only place where I could store it. Fishing about in a plastic tub stationed just inside the door, I plucked out two windfall apples donated to us by our neighbour, stepped out into the cold once more and gave one each to the livestock and poultry.

Our garden was no place for a small farm, but that is what it had become. I had even been forced to build a muck heap to cope with all the dung. Butch and Roxi were producing a bucket a day. Leaving it on the ground stopped being an option the summer before, when the flies it attracted practically kept us imprisoned in the house. So, binding together four wooden pallets that Tom had kindly dropped off for me, I constructed a wonky-looking box in the corner between the fence and their enclosure. Unusually for me, it hadn't fallen apart. In fact, with a sheet of tarpaulin slung over the heap, it actually served a purpose. The contents began to rot down, at a rate that allowed me to continually fill it. I should've been proud of my achievements. Instead, I just saw it as yet another garden sacrifice to the upkeep of two pigs that were supposed to be no bigger than spaniels. As I dwelled on everything we'd been through in order to accommodate them, a car slowed on the lane and then pulled into the drive. I recognised the sound of the motor immediately. Heading for the yard, I expected to see my wife back early from work. Instead, the gate opened to reveal what looked to me like a woman who had just climbed out of her own grave. Emma was alarmingly pale with dark rings under her eyes. Instead of the upright, confident individual I knew her to be, she looked quietly tortured.

'I think it's time I took myself to hospital,' she said.

'I'll drive you there myself,' I told her, taking the car keys from her hand. 'Just in case you change your mind on the way.'

The journey took far longer than expected. The falling snow had remained little more than a flurry throughout the day. Even so, according to the forecast on the car radio, a lot more was on the way. Judging by the heavy traffic, queuing at every junction, I could only think people were anxious to get where they needed to be before conditions worsened. As the roads had yet to be gritted, and with Emma looking in serious need of some medical attention, the drive proved to be quite a challenge.

It didn't help that I'd been forced to bring the children with me. Before we left, I'd considered leaving Lou in charge. As I found her in the front room, having a huge bust-up with the little ones about possession of the television remote, I felt it best to round everyone up and hurry them into the car. That took far longer than I would've liked, of course. First, Frank and Honey defaulted to finding their DS's, while May insisted that Hercules come with us.

'We could be ages,' she had pleaded. 'You never know with hospitals. In fact, we should probably take Sesi, too. Otherwise she'll be lonely.'

'This is ridiculous,' Lou had muttered. 'Why does everyone have to take something?'

In a way, Lou only had herself to blame when I sent her back to scoop up Justin and Beyoncé. On complaining that the twins were getting flour all over her lap, Emma placed them on the dashboard. It meant every time I turned a corner, the twins would slide one way and then the other. So it was for several reasons that I sighed in relief on pulling up in the hospital car park. Sesi had travelled in the boot the whole way there, while Hercules had gone from one lap to another in order to avoid a squabble among the kids about fairness. He looked happy enough, however, unlike Emma, who was clearly in a lot of pain. She didn't make a fuss. If anything, she expressed it in her stubborn refusal to accept any help.

'Shall I fetch you a wheelchair?' I asked.

'Absolutely not,' she said, wincing as she eased herself out of the car. 'I'll get going while you sort the parking ticket. The quicker I'm seen, the faster we can get home.'

With a sigh, I watched my wife hobble towards the main entrance.

'Please don't grow up thinking you're invincible,' I told the children. 'Sometimes, it's OK to accept help.'

Leaving May and Lou with the dogs, under strict instruction not to fight, I escorted the little ones across the car park. This involved halting for a passing ambulance at one point and reminding them that road safety began with not playing videogames on the move. Emma hadn't made much progress. We caught up with her in the corridor.

'Watch out, kids,' I said, as a porter breezed by pushing a patient in a wheelchair. I glanced at Emma; she had paused for a moment and was leaning against a radiator. 'Is that on?' I asked, concerned.

Emma's mouth tightened, as if regrouping her energies, before she headed for the crash doors ahead.

The burns unit was located at the far end of a side corridor. A sign on the door insisted that all users cleanse their hands with gel from the dispenser on the wall. It also sternly forbid the presence of children.

'I forgot about that,' muttered Emma. 'They have seriously strict hygiene standards in there.'

'We can't leave them on their own,' I said, as Frank and Honey resumed the game they were playing.

As if in response, a speaker over the door crackled into life.

'*You can bring your kids in with you, but they'll need sterilising first.*'

I stepped back, and realised we were being monitored by CCTV camera. At the same time, a nurse approached the door from the other side. She didn't open up, but just peered through the glass at us. When Emma introduced herself, and explained the reason for her return, the nurse looked warily at Frank and Honey.

'Have you all washed your hands?' she asked, and took a step back from the door. 'Let me see them use the pump,' she added, gesturing at the little ones.

Having supervised Frank and Honey, the nurse then motioned for me to do the same. She watched me closely as I rubbed the gel into my palms. She didn't respond when I showed her that I'd finished, which made me feel like I hadn't done it properly. Once Emma had cleaned her hands, I took another hit from the pump, which finally seemed to satisfy her.

'Listen up; this is the drill,' she said, addressing us through the glass. 'Children aren't allowed on a burns ward because of the infection risk, but you can keep them in the Family Room. Take them directly there, as quickly as you can, without allowing them to touch anything. Once inside, they must stay there until you're ready to leave. *Is that clear?*'

'Absolutely,' I said, aware that both Frank and Honey were locked onto their DS's once more. 'They're great at occupying themselves.'

The nurse released a lock. Warily, she cracked open the door.

'Hurry!' she said, and stabbed a finger at the first room on the right. 'Go as quick as you can!'

Baffled by the urgency, and feeling like the father of two carriers of the Ebola virus, I steered the little ones into the Family Room. It didn't take long to settle them. I just plonked them both on a sofa and left them to focus on their game. I'm not sure they heard me leave. I even wondered whether one of them would look up at some point and wonder how the hell they had got there.

Across in the reception area, I found Emma at the desk. Several nurses were talking to her. They seemed familiar with the new arrival. I guessed they had treated her the first time around. When one of them handed Emma a tissue from a box on the counter, I realised she was crying.

'This is my husband,' she said, and dabbed her eyes.

The nurses stared at me for a moment.

'Aha,' said one eventually, a fresh-faced young woman with a biro behind one ear. 'The brander.'

I was aware that other people were seated in the waiting area. Several looked up to see who she was talking about.

'Not on purpose.' I laughed nervously and placed a hand upon Emma's back to comfort her. 'I'm not into that sort of thing.'

The nurse who had accused me seemed to relish the moment. I wanted to clarify what I meant by it, but already their attention had returned to the patient.

'Take yourself into room two,' she told Emma, and pointed at the door in question. 'The consultant will be along in a moment.'

Dutifully, I took a step back to let Emma go first. Then I wondered whether I should be joining her at all. I didn't want to look like some kind of wife harming control freak if I followed. At the same time, hanging back might just make me seem like I didn't care about her suffering. So instead of making a decision, I just stood there feeling awkward.

'Are you coming in?' asked Emma from the door.

'He can take a seat in the waiting area,' the nurse replied. 'Just until you've been seen.'

So, feeling like a knucklehead who couldn't be trusted, I squeezed myself into a seat between a lady with a bandaged hand and what looked like a taxi driver awaiting a pick up.

'It was an accident,' I said quietly, as Emma closed the door behind her. 'With a hot-water bottle.'

The woman ignored me, while the cabbie checked his wrist-watch. I glanced at the only nurse to remain at the desk and found she was already looking at me. Turning my attention to my shoes, I made a note to ask Emma if she'd mind using a less emotive word to describe what had happened to her leg. With all this talk of branding, Lou and May had already made me feel terrible. Now I found myself waiting in a room with a bunch of people who quite possibly thought I'd finally agreed to let my wife out of the cellar so that she could seek some medical treatment.

Maybe I was just getting myself into a stew about the whole situation, because I began to worry that the consultant wouldn't be first to arrive but the police. As a result, it came as a relief when a harassed-looking man with a neat beard and white coat showed up. Following the nurse, he headed straight for the examination room. Not only did it help me to take a reality check, it meant that Emma was in good hands at last. I could just about hear them talking, along with more muffled sobbing, which wasn't great. I turned my attention to the skylight overhead, noting that it was almost covered in snow. A few minutes later, the door opened up from the inside and the nurse invited me to join them.

'Mr Whyman, you did the right thing bringing her back in.'

The consultant was washing his hands at the sink as he said this. Emma was on a gurney, lying on her front with her calf exposed. The doctor had removed the bandage. One glance at the wound was enough for me to understand why.

'That's not good,' I said, which was all I could think to say without totally alarming my wife.

For what I faced looked horrific, and far, far removed from the three little blisters where this had begun.

'It really hurts,' said Emma from the gurney. I moved around it so that she could see me.

'The site is acutely infected,' said the doctor, though I wouldn't have needed five years at medical school to reach this conclusion. 'We'll switch to a stronger course of antibiotics, and then keep things closely monitored.'

Outside, through the window behind him, I could see that the snowfall had picked up considerably. The flakes were no longer twirling to the ground but rushing diagonally past the glass. As the doctor prepared to dress the wound, I wondered how long it would take us to get home.

'So, when should we come back?' asked Emma, who was propped on her elbows now. 'A week?'

The doctor swapped a glance with the nurse.

'Oh, we can't let you go home,' he said. 'We'll need to keep you in until tomorrow, at least.'

Laser Eyes surprise!

So Long. So Wrong.

# part three

Busted in the wood.

The path home.

# 23

# Housebound

Overnight, the snow fell relentlessly. It should've been accompanied by a howling gale. Instead, I couldn't help thinking that the End Times had arrived in silence.

For once, I didn't wake to hungry, honking minipigs. When I opened my eyes, and pulled focus on the clock, it took a moment for me to locate the hour hand. I was so used to seeing it pointing any place before six that it came as quite a shock to find that I had made it through to the other side. I turned to report this to Emma, which is when events from the previous day returned to me.

'What a nightmare,' I croaked to myself.

If the drive to the hospital had taken some time, the return journey felt like it would never end. Many of the roads were clogged with stranded cars or impassable on account of the drifts. With four fractious children in the back, plus Sesi in the boot and a restless sausage dog puppy trading places every five minutes, I had to fight to keep my attention on the road. When we moved, it was at a crawl on account of the ice. Several hours after we had set off, the last leg proved the hardest. The car just would not get up the lane to our house. With the snow building, and ice underneath, I got about twenty metres up the incline before the wheels lost all purchase. All I could do was ease the car around and add another thirty minutes onto the slog by driving around the village so we could come in from the other end of the lane. By the time we finally pulled up in the drive, it was close to midnight. I had never seen snow like it, not in this part of the country, and hoped the thaw wasn't far away.

Standing at the bedroom window, looking out under a clear morning sun, it was quite evident that the snow was here to stay. Nothing looked familiar to me. A moment passed before I realised I couldn't actually see the minipigs enclosure. Struggling to take it all in, I realised that a small rescue mission was in order.

'I'm coming!' I called out, as I fought my way across the garden. The snow had settled evenly here. It's just it came up to my knees. There was still no sign of Butch and Roxi as I waded towards the gate. 'Come on out, guys. It isn't going to hurt you.'

I had brought both dogs with me. Sesi bounded into the snow, throwing up a spray as if she had just sunk into sea shallows. Hercules followed close behind, belly-flopped into the drift and all but disappeared from sight. I reached down for him, only for Emma's puppy to resurface a few feet ahead with a determined jump and a yelp of joy. Once again he vanished, but it didn't seem to stop him motoring onwards. For a moment, I watched the sausage dog popping up and down after Sesi, his ears bouncing out of time with his body, and figured he would be fine.

Returning my attention to the minipigs' enclosure, I looked in on their sleeping quarters to see them both peering out. Roxi snorted derisively. Butch just blinked in the sunshine.

Judging by the layer of pristine snow that covered their enclosure, they hadn't been out all night.

'Wow! Awesome snow!'

I turned to see Lou at the step to the garden. She had trailed out after me, wearing boots, pyjamas and a blanket around her shoulders.

'What is this? Refugee chic? Go inside and get dressed.'

Lou tightened her grip on the blanket. I was about to suggest that she should attend to her flour babies, before remembering we had left them in the car overnight.

'I might go back and get my phone,' she said, on spotting Hercules pop up through the drift. 'A clip of that could earn me a whole bunch of friend requests.'

'You'll catch a chill,' I warned her. 'And your mother will blame me.'

Ignoring me still, Lou's gaze drifted away from the snow-covered sausage dog.

'Where are the chickens?'

I looked around as she did. The snow was so thick it had entirely blanketed their hen house. I could hear them cooing inside, oblivious to the conditions. Roxi grunted just then. Head tipped, she was staring at the snow with one eye, as if hoping somehow that would make it disappear so that she could reach her food trough. I kept a shovel stored in the shed. Not that I had ever used it before. With a sigh, I asked Lou once again to dress herself, adding that she would have to oversee breakfast for the little ones. For before this day could begin, I had some real work to do.

By the time I had finished clearing the snow for the minipigs and the chickens, the small of my back was damp with sweat. Butch and Roxi could now shuttle freely between their sleeping quarters, food and water. My flock of four, meanwhile, had an exercise yard in which they could socialise. Having started out life as battery chickens, locked down in what was effectively a poultry prison, I figured they could put up with these conditions while it lasted. I wasn't going to be beaten by it either. As far as I was concerned, this day would be like any other. All I had to do was get the kids to school and then set off to collect Emma.

'School is cancelled,' said Lou, when I finally returned to the house. She was sitting at her mother's laptop, scanning a page intently. 'It says so on the website.'

I cursed under my breath.

'Excellent,' said May. 'We can go sledging.'

'Don't get too excited,' I said. 'You'll all have to come to the hospital with me.'

'Dad, you'll never get there.' Lou turned to the window. 'No cars have gone by since we got up. We're snowed in.'

'We'll make it,' I told her. 'Chances are it'll thaw out in an hour or so.'

From the boot room just then came the canine equivalent of a polite cough. On hearing Sesi, I turned to see her looking at me expectantly.

'I haven't forgotten your walk,' I told her, even though it had slipped my mind completely. 'It's just we're a little out of routine today.'

'Wait!' May sprang to her feet, almost tipping over her cereal bowl in the process. 'You do know what day it is, don't you?'

I glanced at May and the little ones, who looked back at me blankly.

'Well, it's a day off school,' I said. 'We've established that already.'

May bunched her lips to one side. Then her eyes narrowed in reproach.

'I can't believe you've forgotten! Mum wouldn't forget.'

'Forget what?'

'*Hercules!* It's safe for him to go for a walk as well today. It's been two weeks since his jabs against all the bad stuff. You can take him out into the woods and he won't die.'

What with the snow and Emma's surprise stay in hospital, I hadn't given the puppy much thought. In fact, I realised with a twang of guilt, his existence had completely slipped my mind when I came back in from the garden with Sesi.

'Excuse me a moment,' I said, and hurried for the boot room. As soon as I opened the back door, I found Hercules awaiting me expectantly. Immediately, he hopped over the threshold and shook himself down. I faced my children, who were watching from the kitchen, and prepared for the inevitable accusation of neglect. 'He's fine,' I said, and picked him up before he could jump at my dog. 'Does he look upset in any way?'

'I'm telling Mum.' Lou reached for her phone. 'He's bound to be feeling neglected.'

'Let's not trouble her unnecessarily,' I said, and plonked the puppy on the safe side of the child gate. 'Hercules just needs a good breakfast and he'll be fine. Then, once I've taken Sesi for a proper stretch, I'll pop out with the puppy. Clearly a little snow won't stop him.'

My dog enjoyed a long walk. There was no way that Hercules was ready for the kind of distance Sesi liked to roam. Nor was I in any hurry to take a sausage dog out in public. Even so, I knew that I couldn't just skip the walk altogether. The kids would never allow it. In a way, I was thankful that the snow had kept everyone inside. It meant that when I did step out with him, nobody would see me.

Leaving Lou in charge, and Hercules to bolt his breakfast, I headed for the woods with Sesi. The snow that covered the lane was completely unspoiled. Not a single tyre track cut through it. We made our way down the lane for a short distance before slipping between the bars of a gate. Here, a path led across a field to the woods beyond. Exposed to the open air, the snow was so deep in places that it almost came up to my waist. Sesi pushed on through it without a problem. Nuggets of ice began to catch and collect on her coat, but she didn't seem to mind. This was a whole new world to her, after all, as much as it was to me. We just didn't live in a part of the country that was prepared for this kind of weather. Generally, we freaked out at the first sign of frost.

I decided that our usual loop was a bit ambitious. Instead, I aimed to make it as far as an abandoned chicken farm. It was visible through the trees midway along the circuit, and a spooky place at the best of times. On this occasion we didn't get within eyeshot before I began to sense that things weren't right. Very soon after clearing the field, just inside the woods, I had the strangest feeling that I was lost. With no path visible, and everything familiar rendered different by the snow, I found I had no visual reference as to where we were. Even Sesi seemed a little hesitant. Where she would usually stride ahead, she hung back with me.

Within minutes, I decided it might be best if I retraced my footsteps. I didn't want to be the man who became confused and disorientated in woodland that was no more than half a mile square. It seemed ridiculous, but just then I was unable to work out which way we were heading. I even began to see myself being forced to make camp with my dog and then forage for berries in a bid for survival.

\*　\*　\*

'That was quick,' said May, after I had returned Sesi and a lot of snow to the boot room. 'Are you sure that's enough exercise for a dog of her size?'

'It is today,' I told her, and began to unzip my jacket.

'I wouldn't take your outdoor clothes off just yet,' she said, and drew my attention to the floor between us. There, watching me intently, sat the sausage dog. As soon as I met his eyes, he wagged his tail.

'May, it isn't suitable for him out there. The snow is really deep.'

'You can't keep him inside all day,' she said, gearing up to be unreasonable with me. 'That's like imprisonment.'

'It's common sense,' I told her. 'Maybe tomorrow, eh?'

May folded her arms. I could see the tension building behind her eyes.

'Look at him,' she said, while staring at me. 'If you don't take him out, depression will set in.'


I didn't buckle because of the dog. I could've lived with his disappointment. It was the fact that May was off school and on my case that persuaded me to leave the house once more. Had I refused, my daughter would've cast a shadow over my day. Reluctantly, with my boots back on, I attached Hercules to the retractable lead and prepared to set off. Fortunately, in the short time he had been with us, he'd grown enough not to be jerked off his paws when I released the lock button. Even so, conditions were totally unsuitable for a dog of his build. Once again, as we left the yard for the drive, Hercules just disappeared under the drift before temporarily popping up for air a couple of feet ahead. As I let the lead extend, as if to distance myself from him a little bit, I couldn't help thinking he moved like one of those dolphins that powers ahead of a boat prow.

After seven years of walking a dog that was waist-high to me, this all seemed quite wrong. I'd grown used to having Hercules around the house and in the garden. This was a new environment, however. For one thing, his hot pink collar seemed like the only note of colour amid the snow. All of a sudden, despite the fact that nobody was around, I felt completely self-conscious and stupid.

Without further thought, I pressed the brake button. Hercules had just launched from the snow when I did this. My action brought him flat down into the drift with his little legs splayed. He turned and looked at me indignantly.

'Sorry,' I said, and shook my head. 'I'm not ready for this yet.'

Ten minutes later, having loitered behind our woodpile for that time, Hercules and I returned to the house.

'How was it?' asked May, who was still picking through the magazine.

'Brilliant,' I told her, just as the puppy scurried off to find the little ones. My daughter watched him leave. 'That's just what dogs do when they're overtired. He's sure to conk out shortly.'

I noticed May had placed the house telephone beside the magazine.

'Mum hasn't called,' she said, having noted the focus of my attention. 'I thought she'd have rung by now.'

I glanced at my watch. It had only just gone nine o'clock. I'd been thinking about Emma while I waited until it was safe to come back inside. It had come as a shock when the doctor recommended an overnight stay. At the same time, I was relieved that she was in good care. Now she'd been admitted, there was nothing for her to do but let them get her back on her feet again. Even so, I was worried about her.

'She's probably waiting to be discharged,' I told May, and reached for the phone. 'Let me try her mobile anyway.'

Unusually for Emma, her phone rang a few times and then went to answer machine. Normally she would pick up straight away, only to tell me she couldn't talk because she was busy. Wondering why she had so clearly killed my call, but unwilling to alarm May, I left her a message and returned the phone to the table.

'Should we ring the hospital?' asked May, as Hercules tore back into the kitchen with the little ones close behind.

'Even better,' I suggested, 'why don't we go and see her? She'll probably be packed and ready to come home by the time we get there.' I glanced at the window. It had just begun snowing once again. 'The lane looks like it might be a bit of a challenge, but the main roads will be gritted by now.'

May tutted and pulled her feet under her chair. This was because Frank had dropped down on all fours and followed Hercules under the table.

'Do you think we'll even get the car out?' she asked, looking tense all of a sudden. 'What if we end up stranded?'

I chuckled and shook my head.

'You're such a worrier!' I said. 'Tell everyone to get ready and we'll set off in a couple of minutes.'

'What about Justin and Beyoncé?' she asked, in her unofficial role as the flour babies' foster mother.

'They're good to go,' I assured her.

With the dogs on board as well as the children and two packs of flour that had spent the night on the dashboard, I gunned the engine and prepared to reverse out of the drive. The snow was deep, but also powdery. I really didn't think it would present a problem. Sure enough, with a little play between the clutch and the accelerator, I eased the car out into the lane.

Returning the vehicle to the drive, having discovered that the wheels just span uselessly in first gear, took me the best part of an hour.

In that time, I conducted epic arguments with my children over issues that did little to help me get the car moving. Lou chose her moment to ask for a sleepover; May fretted that the dogs might suffocate unless every window was wide open, which only served to bring her into direct confrontation with Frank and Honey, who had left the house without coats on. At one point I asked the big girls to shut up and help me try to push the vehicle clear. On the count of three, I swore using words I would never usually deploy in front of an adult, let alone anyone under sixteen, before ordering the pair back in the car and making good use of the shovel for the second time that day. It was the digging that took so long. Not just clearing the snow in front of each wheel but breaking the ice underneath. I had held out hope that someone would come along with a tow rope, but the lane was free of all traffic for good reason. One desperate moment saw me seriously consider ripping open Justin and Beyoncé and sprinkling their innards on the ice in the hope that it might create some grip. Had May not been with me, I would've done just that. Instead, using the hearth rug I had ordered Lou to collect from her bedroom, which I wedged under the front wheels, I got the traction we so badly needed. The carpet was ruined, but by then I really didn't care. Had I been able to lay my hands on a petrol can and a box of matches, I'd have gladly set fire to our piece-of-crap people carrier and spent the rest of my life on foot.

Instead, off the lane at last, I killed the engine, sat back in my seat and closed my eyes.

'I did warn you,' said May, only to stop right there when I raised my hand to signal that it would be in her best interests.

'Just don't talk to me for a minute or so,' I said.

My wish was granted for a couple of seconds at most. Then my mobile rang.

'It's me,' said Emma, though it sounded like a spaced-out version of her. 'How are you?'

'We're all fine,' I told her, glaring in my rear-view mirror. 'But never mind about us. How are *you*?'

'OK,' she said, after a pause. 'I was with some surgeons when you called. I'm having an operation this afternoon.'

'*What?*' I stared through the windscreen, oblivious to the squabble that had broken out behind me about whose turn it was to have Hercules on their lap. 'Why?'

Again, Emma failed to respond straight away. Either she was being held hostage, and had to repeat whatever her captor was prompting her to say, or she'd been given an awful lot of medication.

'Something to do with cutting out this deep tissue infection,' she said eventually. 'I'm sure it's nothing.'

'I'm coming in to see you,' I said straight away.

'There's no need,' she said. 'I'll probably be asleep anyway.'

I was about to insist. I just couldn't ignore the fact that we'd just failed spectacularly in our bid to leave the house.

'OK, but if you need me at any time, just call.'

'Of course,' said Emma. 'Give the kids a hug from me, tell them not to worry, and don't forget to walk Hercules.'

'Already done,' I assured her.

# 24

# The Downhill Run

According to the radio, the entire country had been hit by the biggest snowfall in three thousand years. At least that's how long I thought they said. It was hard to hear that morning on account of all the children and animals that vied for my attention. To be fair to May and Lou, they could see that I was struggling, and elected to help out with the chores. Unfortunately, their enthusiasm didn't quite match their skill in finishing any job, from the washing up to the vacuuming, which created just more work for me. Even so, I was grateful for the effort they made. I just wished that I could make the pets aware that we were in the middle of an emergency situation.

In particular, Roxi the minipig was keen to make her presence known. This she did by standing outside the shed and mewling like a lost kitten. I only heard her by chance, having taken Hercules out for a plunge in the snow in the privacy of our garden. This strange noise meant only one thing. Our minipig was in season, and this was just the start of her day-long call for a mate. Being castrated, Butch was no good to her. He also knew what was ahead, which is why he'd buried himself behind a mound of straw in their sleeping quarters.

Every three weeks, in accordance with a female pig's fertility cycle, Roxi would start out making gentle feline noises and slowly build from there. She didn't honk. Instead, at her worst, she would draw so much air into her lungs that her sides went convex. The screeching, when it came, was positively pre-historic. It was also loud enough to be heard from the other side of the woods, as I knew from experience. There was nothing I could do about it. I could try to talk her down, rub her flanks or distract her with some food, but nothing served to shut her up. In a way, it was always a small mercy when her special lady time fell during the week, because at least then most of our neighbours were out at work.

That day, the snow didn't just keep people away from the office. Lying so thickly all around, and with not a breath of wind, it also served to amplify every sound. It didn't help that the lane was totally impassable by car. It just meant everyone got around on foot. In fact, by mid-morning we had a steady stream of people walking by our window. Every single one stopped to peer over the fence at Roxi, whose lovelorn calls caused crows to take flight from the treetops. Given that we had endured the din every three weeks, we were kind of oblivious to it. What caught the kids' attention, however, was the fact that many people who looked in on our garden were also dragging sledges with them. As soon as they saw what was going on, they begged me to let them go out and join in.

'I'm afraid we don't own a sledge,' I said. 'This is the first time it's snowed in years.'

'You've got a worktop in the shed,' Lou pointed out. 'Make one.'

'Out of what?'

My eldest looked at me like I really should know the answer. 'Wood is good.'

'Lou, I'm not a carpenter. You're mistaking me for Jesus. I can't just knock together a sledge like that.'

Now it was the little ones who appeared to be disappointed. I couldn't help notice that they had even left their games consoles on the sofa to look outside. For once, here was an opportunity for them to take up an activity that didn't involve looking dead-eyed at a screen while furiously smashing buttons.

'If Mum wasn't turning into a zombie, at least she'd have given it a go.' May was looking at the floor when she said this. I waited for her to flick her eyes at me, if only so I could sigh pointedly at her. I had broken the news of Emma's operation as gently as I could. The little ones had seemed alright, while Lou was deeply worried and distressed. Then a text had come through from her boyfriend which seemed to cheer her up far more than was appropriate. As for May, somehow she could not let go of the fear that all this talk of a hot-water bottle burn was a cover for an altogether more sinister affliction. 'Mum would never stop us from having fun,' she added, and dropped her gaze once more. 'Dead or alive.'

'If Mum was here,' said Lou, as another family trudged by the window pulling a fine, vintage-looking sledge, 'she'd tell you that if the shed worktop continues to gather dust then we should take it out and use the space to store a trampoline.'

'You're not having a trampoline,' I said. 'They're dangerous.'

It was then that May turned to Lou. She seemed to consult her without saying anything, before addressing me.

'I guess it's tough for you with Mum in hospital,' she said, and glanced once more at her sister. 'Lou and I will just have to make a sledge ourselves.'

I waited for May to look back at me, well aware that I could hardly just let them get on with it. In many ways, I saw myself reflected in her gaze. Somehow, with Emma in trouble and now all the snow, I had gone into a kind of lockdown. But I

couldn't just put everything on hold, I realised. It was important that I tried to keep things as normal as possible for the
sake of the family. Throughout this, quietly going about his
own business, Hercules was busy coupling with a soft toy
monkey he had taken a shine to lately. The monkey belonged
to Frank, who was watching with interest. It wasn't healthy
for us to be cooped up indoors any longer, I admitted to myself.

'Leave the sledge to me,' I said, and extracted Hercules from
the situation. 'Some of us could use the fresh air, after all.'

What I came up with wasn't rocket science. Nor was it made
from wood. One glance at the inside of the shed persuaded
me to abandon any hope of actually nailing something
together. First and foremost, I realised that I didn't own a
hammer. Nor did I have any timber at my disposal. Then there
was Roxi, whose screeching just got worse in my presence. I
could see her through the window of the shed, and she had
a clear view of me. Standing at the far end of her enclosure,
with her tail switching back and forth, she glared at me as if
I was fully responsible for not providing her with a mate who
could satisfy her needs. I was fairly sure Hercules had ruled
himself out, but that didn't stop him responding to her in a
way that took me by surprise.

For the first time in his short life, the Dachshund stopped
squeaking. Instead, with a force that commanded my attention,
he barked.

As I quickly learned, a sausage dog makes a noise like no
other. With lungs that occupied a broad chest, and a body that
served like the bellows of an accordion, Hercules effectively
punched through the peace. The noise he made was crisp, like
the clap of a drum machine – one wired to a pimped-up car's
sound system. The resulting pig/dog duet offered little by way

of melody. It didn't help that I added to the noise by yelling at Hercules to be quiet. Altogether, it explained why I didn't hear my neighbour joining in until his head and shoulders appeared over the fence.

'Mr Whyman, if you can't silence your pig then please control your little dog. That yapping is just too much.'

Roddie appeared to be dressed for a round of golf, which was wishful thinking given the weather conditions. I was surprised to see him, and also a little put out by the way he had described the noise made by Hercules. Yes, he was being a bit loud, but this dog wasn't like the little psychotic balls of fury that slammed against the gates when you passed them on the lane.

'He's a Dachshund,' I said, as if that might make things better. Roddie looked like a man who disliked terriers, I thought to myself, in the vague hope that we could bond. He didn't seem terribly appreciative, however. Hercules hardly helped. Instead of barking at Roxi, he focused on my neighbour instead. 'It's just his way of getting to know you,' I added over the din. 'But don't worry, we're about to head back inside.'

Roddie switched his attention from Hercules to the pig under his nose. She and Butch had been here for so long that he was familiar with the noise patterns, and aware that I did my level best to keep it to a minimum.

'Would Roxi care for some apples?' he asked. 'I have a few more windfalls left in my store, if that would help to keep the peace. They're quite brown now, but I know that's how they like them.'

'That's very kind of you,' I said, as Hercules continued to bark. 'Just toss them over, and take care of yourself in this weather. If there's anything you need, just shout.'

Roddie offered the dog a withering look.

'That's if I can make myself heard,' he said, before sinking out of sight.

I shook my head at Hercules, who chose that moment to curl away and plunge back into the snow. Roxi caught my eye, grunted and then shovelled a spray of snow in my direction. Aware that she was frustrated by my refusal to serve as her pig pimp, I ducked back into the shed. There, I picked out what I believed would make a good substitute for a sledge before heading back to the house.

'What's that for?' asked May, who found me in the kitchen. I was watching Hercules sniff around the pet carrier I had brought back with me. 'You can't take him away,' she said with concern. 'Just because he's frisky.'

'Observe.' I placed the cat basket in front of me, and then sat down upon it. Ignoring the sound of creaking plastic, I grasped the handle I had just fashioned from garden twine and attached it to the mesh at the front. 'Mark my words,' I added and lifted my feet to demonstrate how this would work. 'It'll go like a bullet.'

'But what if we ever have more pets?' asked May. 'Now you've turned it into a rubbish sledge, how will we get them here?'

'Hercules is the last,' I told her with some confidence. 'So, we might as well put it to good use.'

'I'm calling Mum.' Lou was standing at the kitchen door. As she never went anywhere without her mobile phone in hand, she was already scrolling for the number when I told her to think again.

'The last thing she needs is her daughter phoning to moan at her.' I climbed off the pet carrier and picked it up with one hand. 'Why don't we give it a go? Then maybe we can call her with some *good* news?'

Lou thought about this for a moment, before shaking her head and punching in more numbers.

'Dad, there are people out there who I know. People who will *talk*!'

'What if I said you could leave the twins behind? They still have a little bit of warming up to do after their night in the car.'

'Really?' Lou's expression brightened. She glanced at the pet carrier once more. 'I suppose it might work,' she said, and pocketed her phone.

Our village is located in the fold between two gently sloping hills. I had assumed that the fields amid the woodland would be ideal for sledges. By the time we stepped outside, it was clear the residents had settled on a more ambitious run.

'Wow,' said May, as the little ones spotted friends and raced ahead to join them. 'Isn't this a bit, y'know . . . *dangerous*?'

The crowd had gathered a little way down from our house, beside the gate into the field. From there, men, women and children were positioning their sledges in the middle of the lane and then launching themselves at full tilt. I watched one man, a lawyer who should've known better, setting off belly down like this was some kind of luge run. He passed several people on their way back up, who cheered him on as he continued to pick up speed. From here, the lane didn't level out for almost a quarter of a mile. By the time he came to a halt, adjacent to Tom's smallholding, the lawyer was little more than a speck – a triumphant one all the same, judging by the way he punched the air and whooped with delight.

It was highly irresponsible, totally unsafe, and everyone was at it. I had to give it a shot.

By now, I had pretty much forgotten the means by which

I planned to take part in the fun. As we joined the group at the top, I noticed several people glance at the pet carrier in my hand.

'Don't do it, Dad,' said May.

'I'm sure it isn't as lethal as it looks,' I assured her.

'I mean don't embarrass us,' she said, addressing me with her back turned purposely to the gathering.

I glanced over her shoulder. Certainly I had attracted some attention.

'If I back down now,' I told her, 'it'll look like I lost my nerve.'

As I said this, a little girl in mittens set off down the lane on a plastic tray sledge. I drew May's attention to her. The girl was no older than Honey. If she could do it, I had no reason to bail. May looked stricken.

'This could be the worst day of my life,' she said.

Lou appeared behind just then. She had a friend from school in tow, who was carrying a pack of plain flour in the crook of her elbow.

'Can we fetch Hercules?' she asked me. 'Everyone wants to meet him.'

While I felt no sense of embarrassment about attempting to travel the lane by pet carrier, the prospect of trotting out a sausage dog filled me with dread. It was irrational and unreasonable, but I just wasn't in the right frame of mind. I had already bailed out of walking him, and the lane was entirely deserted back then. Now several villagers were out with their toboggans. If I was going to keep my head up high in public, with a sausage dog at my side, then my wife would need to be holding the lead. Just then, I missed Emma more than ever.

'The temperature has dropped since this morning,' I said,

after a moment to think of a good excuse. 'He's too young to be out in these conditions.'

Lou didn't seem at all happy with my reason, but there was little she could do about it. Anxious to move on and create some distance from the issue, I set down the pet carrier. Looking towards the foot of the lane, it was clear that so many runs had been made by the sledges that the surface was basically polished ice. All of a sudden, I didn't feel quite so confident. Nevertheless, I positioned myself on the roof of my chosen means of transport, grasped the handles and focused on the slope. As I did so, I noticed a small boy making his way up the side. I didn't recognise him. Nor could I be sure of the breed of his little toy dog that was scrabbling for purchase on the ice. The Pekingese, if that's what it was, appeared to be made entirely from long lengths of string, much like the head of a floor mop, and was wearing a tailor-made duffel coat with a hood.

'That's what we need for Hercules!' declared Lou, and pointed at the dog. 'Fashion accessories!'

'We'll see about a canine coat once we can get to the shops,' I told Lou, with no intention of following it up. 'Now watch the little ones for me and stand well back,' I added, lifting my heels from the ice. 'It's time I headed downhill!'

I appreciate it looked unconventional, and probably wouldn't catch on, but the pet carrier was by no means nailed to the floor. The plastic base slid nicely over the ice, and quickly gathered momentum with me on board. I glided past the boy, who stopped to watch in what looked like admiration. I didn't have a chance to check out his toy dog in closer detail. By then I had picked up the pace and needed to concentrate.

Midway down, it occurred to me that if Emma was here

she would've stopped me from doing something so foolish. This I realised on exceeding a speed where I felt it would be safe to bail. Emma might've been impulsive when it came to taking on pets, but not with matters of personal safety. Without me, our household would probably be host not just to a sausage dog and two minipigs but chimps and a trained gazelle. In Emma's absence, I wasn't sure I would survive the day without an accident of my own making.

Astride the pet carrier, my eyes were smarting and I felt every bump and ridge through my spine. My knuckles had turned white where I clung onto the handle – but only until the twine gave way. Then all I could do was clutch the lip of the roof and pray this wasn't going to end in a hospital visit of my own. Just then, I rocketed past the lawyer, who was making his way back up the hill. His sledge looked sleek and very expensive.

'Dude, you're shredding it!' he shouted, and gave me the sign of the horns with his index and little finger.

*What are you, twelve years old?* I thought to myself, in no position to let go and return the gesture.

'Thanks!' I called back instead, and then took a breath because the carrier started to rotate.

I was dimly aware, as I found myself facing backwards, that the lane was still open to traffic. No vehicle had passed all day, but there was always a possibility that I was about to find myself hurtling towards an incoming gritting lorry. In a way, it was fortunate that the plastic housing gave way under my weight at that moment. With a splintering crack, my bottom dropped through the roof. It was a shock, but strangely gave me more stability. It meant I could push my heels into the ice in a bid to stop the pet carrier. This I managed where the lane levelled out, with not a great deal of grace and just one witness to the event. As I skated to a halt in front of Tom, my smallholding friend, all I could do was smile sheepishly.

'Well, that's one more tick on the list of things to do before you die,' he said, eyeing the remains of the carrier. 'Congratulations.'

Breathless and a little winded, I gladly accepted his hand so that he could haul me from the wreckage. Tom was a man at one with the outside world. Unlike everyone else, he wasn't wrapped up in a winter coat. His only visible measure against the cold was a short, thin scarf. Everything else, from his patched-up jumper, boots and jeans, he wore whatever the weather. He was also dragging what at first looked to me like an assault craft that the army might use to land soldiers on beaches. As a sledge, it was formidable. The hull, if that's what it was called, sported a solid top and a prow that would probably win out in a collision with a gritter. I realised this was no longer a risk, however, when I saw that Tom had left his Land Rover at a right angle further down the lane.

'Nice parking,' I said, on brushing off all the ice I had collected on my way down.

'Safety first.' Tom watched the next person make their descent. 'It's not like anyone is going places today, is it?'

I couldn't disagree. As a village, we were completely snowed in. And as a community we had gathered here to make the most of what were frankly freak conditions.

'So,' I said next as we set off on the climb up the hill, 'how long did it take you to make this?'

I drew his attention to the sledge. This didn't boast a handle made from crappy garden twine. Tom was hauling his creation using a rope slung over his shoulder.

'An hour,' he said without looking round. 'Maybe less.'

'What's it like on the slope?'

'I'm about to find out. This is the maiden journey. You and the kids are welcome to climb on first if you like. There's plenty of room.'

I was still trailing the shattered remains of the pet carrier. Bits of plastic were breaking off as I dragged it along by the ditch.

'I think perhaps you should be the test pilot,' I told him. 'Or maybe just fit some safety belts.'

We trudged on together, pausing only to watch several more villagers whizz down.

'I haven't seen you around very much lately,' said Tom. 'How are things at home?'

I told him about the accident that had earned Emma a stay in hospital. When I added that she was in theatre that afternoon, he stopped and waited for me to face him.

'You should be with her.'

'I tried,' I said. 'That was when I discovered we're currently living on a piste. Besides, she was adamant that I stay at home to take care of the kids and the animals.'

We continued up the hill in silence for a moment. Not that it was soundless all around. We were close enough to the gathering at the top to hear them laugh and chatter, but beyond that Roxi was making her presence known.

'Sounds like your minipig is in season,' said Tom.

I sighed on hearing her screech. 'Sometimes, I think it sounds more like Godzilla has come to the countryside.'

Tom smiled to himself. 'When my girls make that noise,' he said, 'I know it's time to bring in the boar. That keeps them nice and quiet.'

'I'm not breeding Roxi,' I told him. 'It wouldn't be right.'

'But there's money in minipigs, so I heard. You could make a lot from a litter.'

'Have you seen her lately?' I asked. 'She's *massive*, and Butch isn't far behind.' Despite the weight of his sledge, Tom was striding up the lane. I had to hurry to keep up.

'Do they hang out in the living room any more?'

I laughed out loud at this.

'Roxi wouldn't fit through the door,' I told him.

We were close to the summit now. Near enough to see that Frank and Honey had fallen out over who got to sit at the front of one of the many fertiliser bags some bright spark had brought with them. Those kids who were using them appeared to be travelling at a much safer speed than I'd experienced. The boy with the toy dog had just sat down on one. He stationed his pooch between his legs, before easing back the hood of its canine duffel coat. Not that the dog could see much behind such long white hair. Then, with a huge grin, the boy set sail down the slope.

'Hold on tight!' Tom called across, and stopped to watch them pass. 'Isn't that great? Those two look like they're having the time of their lives!'

I studied Tom as he followed their course down the lane. His reaction surprised me. I just assumed he'd be like me, and dismiss the toy dog as a joke. Then I thought about what he'd just said, and realised he was right. Back when I was that boy's age, if my dad had relented and presented us with a puppy I really wouldn't have cared what breed it was. Even if he'd lost his mind and gone for a sausage dog, I'd have devoted myself to it. I'd done just that with an orphan bird, and it brought out the best in me. When Tom turned back to finish climbing the hill, I had already decided that I needed to come out about Emma's latest pet acquisition. Hercules was nothing to be ashamed about, after all. At least that's what I needed to work towards convincing myself.

'I might as well tell you that we have a new dog in our household,' I said. 'It seems a shame to leave him out of all the fun.'

Tom was about to respond, only to be silenced momentarily by yet another plaintive shriek from our back garden. For all the wrong reasons, the minipigs never left me. Even out here, away from the house, I was still reminded of their demanding presence in my life. Abandoning my attempt to tell Tom about the Dachshund, I closed my eyes for a second and sighed.

'Can I make a suggestion?' he said, as the minipig fell quiet and people started talking once more. 'Why don't you arrange for Butch and Roxi to go on a little holiday?'

'Eh?'

'If it helps, they could come and stay on my smallholding for a while. It'll give you a break, let the pigpen rest, and they'll get to root around somewhere new. You never know,' Tom said to finish, and nudged me on the shoulder, 'my wife could even fall in love with them. You might never get them back!'

'Really?' I faced him directly, wondering if there was a catch. The subject of Butch and Roxi's future was a sensitive one between Emma and me. We both recognised our responsibilities for their welfare, even if their presence in our back garden meant no back garden. There had never been any question of rehoming them because, frankly, I couldn't think who in their right mind would want to take on two oversized pigs as pets. Nor did I think Emma would even consider it as an option. But this was a bit different. It wasn't permanent. Not on paper, at any rate. What's more, Tom's smallholding was only a short walk down the lane, and provided everything that a pig could need. Without question, Butch and Roxi would be extremely well cared for. All of a sudden, I wondered what it might be like to wake up naturally one morning, without any squealing to flood my body with adrenalin. 'If you're serious,' I said, 'that would make our lives so much easier.'

'Not a problem,' said Tom, as our hormonal minipig screeched once more.

'One thing,' I added. 'Promise you won't bring the boar to her. There's only room for one Roxi in this world.'

'Of course not. She can make as much noise as she likes down there.'

'And swear to me you won't eat them.'

Tom looked hurt at this, but then his grin returned and I knew he was just playing with me. At least I hoped he was, because this was one proposal I couldn't refuse.

'So that's settled,' he said, and began the process of lining up what was basically the mother of all sledges. 'Let's make the most of this snow while it lasts. Once it thaws, Butch and Roxi can pack their suitcases and leave you to learn how to relax.'

'Even without the minipigs, I can't see that happening,' I said. 'Not with my family.'

'How so?'

Tom looked at me quizzically. Now was the time to tell him.

'Emma's got a Dachshund,' I confessed. 'A miniature one. He's called Hercules. It's supposed to be her dog, but with things as they are he spends all his time with me.'

I was braced for a burst of laughter, but he didn't even blink.

'Then let's hope she gets well soon,' was all he had to say on the matter, before climbing aboard his sledge. Digging his heels in as an anchor, he gathered the rope in both hands and then looked around to see if anyone wanted to join him. In response, everybody stood well back.

'God speed,' I said to him. 'Though let's hope that's not too fast.'

'We'll soon find out . . . wait a minute!'

Midway down the slope, on the way back up from a successful ride, a toy dog in a hooded coat had broken free from his young master. It was desperately trying to scamper to the top, but the ice and steep angle prevented him from making any headway whatsoever. The harder the dog tried to run, the further back he slipped. The boy wasn't far behind. He seemed to think it was hilarious, and went so far as to mimic the dog's running action. On grabbing the trailing leash, he even earned a cheer from the group by the gate. With his four-legged friend safely in his arms, the boy then stepped aside so that Tom was free to make his first run.

'This new dog of yours,' said Tom, lifting his feet onto the great sledge, 'I'm sure in time he'll find his feet.'

'Hercules won't have to look far,' I replied as he took to the slope. 'But let's hope you're right.'

# 25

## Unexpected Guest

With Emma in theatre, I tried to keep busy all afternoon. It wasn't difficult, being snowed in with such a high-maintenance family.

The hens, in particular, needed my attention, after I discovered that several had attempted a kind of jailbreak from the snow walls of their confines. Somehow, by a process of mad flapping and brute force, they had made their way across the drifts and taken refuge in the flower-bed. I considered returning them all to the pigpen, where much of the snow had been trampled down by Roxi. In a way, I thought they'd serve to distract her from her calls for a boar capable of meeting her needs. Then I decided that in her frustration she might turn to comfort eating and scoff my flock.

It was yet one more dilemma associated with the minipigs – but hopefully that wasn't going to last much longer. As soon as Tom had invited them for a holiday, I saw a chance to get our lives back in order. All I had to do was sell the proposal to Emma, and I could look forward to the return of my lawn. It was just a question of pitching it at the right time and place. With Emma in hospital, that wasn't here or now. I was just debating whether I should call the burns unit for an update when Sesi leapt from her bed and delivered a masterclass in forceful barking. With Hercules adding some top notes, it told me just one thing.

Somebody was about to ring the doorbell.

'Hi. Is she in?'

I had opened the door to find myself faced with an undernourished youth of indeterminate gender. S/he was wearing a beanie hat pulled down to the brow, with highlighted hair splayed to the shoulder and a face not unlike a sparrow.

'Who would she be?' I asked.

'*Alfie!*' cried a voice from the staircase behind me. I turned around to face Lou, who looked overjoyed. 'You made it!'

Returning my attention to the visitor, I saw his gaze drop to the object cradled in my arm. 'Cool dog,' he said, and tickled Hercules behind the ears.

'It belongs to Lou's mum,' I said quickly.

'Legend.' Alfie nodded, seemingly lost in thought as he continued to focus on the dog. 'She's bang tidy, your wife.'

I took so long to realise that Alfie was trying to be complimentary, rather than breathtakingly out of order, that Lou had bundled into the boy's arms before I could reply.

'I didn't believe it when you said you'd walk all this way for me!' she purred from his shoulder.

'I wasn't going to miss our anniversary,' he said, with his arm wrapped around her in a display of staggering self-confidence.

'Anniversary?' I didn't quite know where to look as he said this. I had only ever seen my eldest embrace one other male, and that was me. 'How long have you been going out with each other?'

Alfie looked at his watch. Then he pulled back from the hug and beamed at Lou.

'Five days, two hours and ten minutes.'

'Right,' I said, thinking this relationship wasn't going to end well. 'So, you came here on foot? That's quite a commitment in these conditions.'

'It was nothing,' he said with a shrug. 'Not for my girl.'

I wasn't sure I liked the sound of any of this. At the same time, I was wise enough to know that Lou would consider any further conversation with the young man to be some form of interrogation.

'Come in,' I said instead. 'You must be freezing.'

As well as the beanie hat, Alfie was dressed in skin-tight jeans and baseball boots, some rock-band T-shirt featuring boys who looked like clones of him, all finished off with the kind of long cardigan Emma would wear.

'We'll be upstairs if you need us,' said Lou. 'Just chilling in my room.'

'Hang on,' I said, only to falter as the pair looked back at me from the stairs.

'May is with us,' said Lou, and shot me a glare as if to beg me not to embarrass her.

Before we moved here, the wall between two of the children's bedrooms had been knocked down to create one shared space. We decided to keep it like that as May and Lou were so close. Now, with the girls so much older, we'd been thinking about blocking it up again to give them both some privacy. Watching Lou lead her new boyfriend upstairs, however, I decided that such a plan really ought to be postponed indefinitely. Setting Hercules on the floor, I returned to the kitchen and fretted. We had no ground rules for this kind of visit, after all. On paper, as an advice columnist, I regularly stressed the importance of having that conversation long before any love interest showed up, just so that everyone was clear about the boundaries. Had I actually found a way to talk it over with

Lou, of course, that boundary would've stopped at the foot of the stairs. Alfie was welcome to visit. It's just I would've liked him within a two-metre radius of me at all times. As it was, my eldest daughter had brought her first ever boyfriend back to the house, and within seconds they were in the bedroom.

'Well done,' I said to myself bitterly. 'That went so well.'

Over the course of the next twenty minutes, if I stayed very still and held my breath, I could just about hear them talking upstairs. It was the pauses in between sentences that troubled me, however. When one such break surpassed the ten-second mark, I had to stop myself from marching upstairs and closing down the whole sleazy operation. Such was my focus on proceedings above the ceiling that I jumped when my mobile started ringing. On seeing who was calling, I almost fumbled it to the floor in my hurry to pick up.

'Emma! How are you?'

At first I thought it was a bad connection. When she finally answered me, I barely recognised her voice.

'Sleepy,' she said in a hoarse and detached-sounding whisper. 'My throat is also sore from the tubes.'

'What? For an operation on your leg?'

'It was complicated,' she said. 'The burn went much deeper than they thought.'

My instinct was to close the call and jump in the car. I needed to see my wife, and find out what had happened to her, but conditions outside were much the same. Realistically, I was going nowhere.

'Are you comfortable?'

'On the drugs they've given me? I wish I could feel this way forever. All I want to do is sleep.'

I explained that we were still snowbound, but that I would

move heaven and earth to be with her the next day. I wasn't quite sure what that would involve. If Alfie could walk a few miles in the name of teenage love, I would just have to set out across the county and strive to make it to the hospital by nightfall. As it was, I just hoped that a thaw would kick in. At that moment, much to Hercules's delight, the little ones trotted into the kitchen. Still listening to Emma, I retreated to the window and let them pass, along with May as she ushered them into the boot room.

'We're going sledging again,' she said, but I just scowled at her and pointed at the phone. I didn't cope well with people talking at me while I was taking a call. It was just one of those multitasking challenges I had never overcome, like picking up the dirty laundry basket before I came downstairs. I was already focusing on two things, I would argue: walking and breathing. Besides, at that moment I had to really focus on what Emma was saying because her voice was just so faint.

'When do you think they'll discharge you?' I asked.

'I can't think that far ahead,' she replied. 'I'm too woozy.'

I promised her I would press the doctors for details just as soon as I made it in. Emma told me not to hurry, because they didn't do their rounds until at least mid-morning.

'I miss you,' I said, aware that she was about to wind up the call. At my feet, a little lost now that Frank and Honey had forsaken him for the village slope, Hercules looked at me in hope of some attention. 'Someone else misses you, too.'

I didn't have to tell Emma who I was talking about.

'Aw, that puppy has really helped me through this. I've been thinking about him loads.'

'What would we do without him?' I asked, thinking how much easier life would be at this difficult time if he hadn't been here at all. 'He's certainly one of a kind.'

I considered going on to tell her about Tom's offer to take the minipigs for a never-ending holiday. Like any pitch, however, I reminded myself it was best done face to face. When Emma finally spoke, to ask me to send her love to the children, it sounded like I would never hear from her again. I felt really odd about saying goodbye. When fit and healthy, my wife wasn't someone I had to worry about. It was the rest of the family that would fall apart at the seams without an adult present. Now Emma was away from home – and in trouble, it seemed. She'd been vague about exactly what the operation had involved, presumably because she didn't know herself. Being stuck here at home hardly helped my sense of helplessness. I wanted to be at Emma's bedside, doing everything I could do support her. Tomorrow, I decided, it was time to take control of the situation.

A second later, I realised that May's decision to take the little ones sledging had left me with a more immediate issue to deal with. It was an instant reminder as to why I was needed here. Holding my breath once more, I looked up and focused on the ceiling.

In the bedroom above, where Lou and Alfie were now alone, all the chatter had ceased.

As an agony uncle, when presented with a situation like this, I could've sat down and written a clear, balanced and non-judgmental approach to resolving things constructively. As a father with no prior experience of dealing with a boy in my teenage daughter's bedroom, I froze. I couldn't just steam upstairs and put a halt to whatever was going on. That would be heavy-handed and counterproductive. Nor could I turn a blind eye and hope for the best. That would be cowardly and irresponsible. All of a sudden, this rake of a kid had transformed in my mind into some morally-bankrupt

Lothario. What designs did he have on my daughter? Why wasn't he outdoors engaging in less upsetting activities, as I did at his age, such as learning to smoke roll-ups in back alleys?

Aware that I had to do something, I went for the compromise move. Firstly, this involved creeping to the foot of the stairs. Since there was no sound from upstairs, I proceeded to stage two.

'Guys? Would you like a cup of tea or anything?'

Holding still, I strained to make out just what was going on up there.

'No thanks, Dad.'

'Right. OK.' I retreated to the kitchen, hating myself. I was also well aware that Lou hadn't replied for several seconds. Fearing the worst, I retraced my steps. 'How about a cup of tea and a slice of cake to go with it?'

From the bedroom, I heard one of them tutting.

'Dad, we're fine. Thanks all the same.'

Each time I shuttled between the stairs and the kitchen, Hercules had followed dutifully. Just then, he was at my feet, looking up at me with interest. I peered down at him, and realised he might just be able to help me out here. Quietly, I opened up the child gate. Climbing the stairs hadn't been a problem for him, and I would be here to help him back down once he'd undertaken the task I had in mind for him. I gestured for Hercules to seize the opportunity, which he did tentatively at first, before taking the last few steps at a bound. If I was an army man, this would be the equivalent of sending in the remote-controlled surveillance robot to scope out the enemy.

I figured Hercules would make a beeline for the first sound of activity and quickly make his presence known. I would then have every excuse to hurry after him, apologising profusely for the canine interruption while simultaneously putting a stop to any funny business.

Watching the dog's hind quarters negotiate the last step, I imagine he'd already made it into Lou's bedroom. I waited several seconds, expecting to hear Lou acknowledge him at least. When that failed to happen, I began to fear she was too distracted to notice.

That's when I heard a sound that caused my heart to miss a beat. A steady, rhythmic creaking that could only mean one thing.

'OK, that's quite enough!' I covered several steps at a time in my hurry to reach the landing. 'Stop what you're doing right away. Have some decency for crying out loud!'

The door to Lou's bedroom was ajar. I didn't stop to knock, and so it came as no surprise that my sudden arrival startled them.

'Dad! What are you doing?'

Lou was at her laptop, with Alfie at her side. He had an exercise book in his lap and a calculator in one hand. Both looked deeply alarmed by my appearance. I glanced at the screen, which showed a spreadsheet.

'What is that?' I asked, panting a little bit.

'Maths,' said Lou, whose confusion at my sudden appearance looked set to turn to anger. 'Alfie is helping me with my homework.'

I drew breath to explain myself, and thought better of it. At the same time, the creaking sound that had prompted me to take emergency action returned to my attention. Only it wasn't coming from Lou's bedroom.

'What is *that*?' asked Alfie, turning my question on me as we faced the open door. Frank and Honey's bedroom was directly across the landing from here. The door was wide open, and the source of the noise clear for all to see.

'Eeew!' Unusually for Lou, she didn't reach for her camera phone to capture the moment. More likely, she'd seen enough already. Without a doubt, Hercules had just pushed things too far. For what he had found here wasn't just one stray soft toy. Frank liked to trail the odd one downstairs in the morning, where it would be vigorously defiled by the sausage dog until someone retrieved it. Instead, Hercules had discovered my son's entire collection. He kept them at the foot of his bed, from dolphins to dragons, lions, bears and a turtle, only now they were strewn across the floor and helpless to the little Dachshund's advances. Frankly, the dog didn't know where to put himself.

'Awesome,' said Alfie, straining to look around me for a better view. 'Didn't the Romans enjoy this sort of thing?'

After tea, later that afternoon, I felt bad about sending Alfie home. The sun was beginning to set, after all, and the temperature could only drop further. Then again, with no means of driving him, my only other option was to offer him a bed for the night. Having given that about a second's thought, I decided he'd be better off taking his chances with the elements. Fortunately, in a bid to impress my eldest, Alfie himself had insisted on making the return journey on foot.

'My Dad said if I walked here then I'd have to walk back. He's hard-core like that.'

I doubted my children would ever describe me in the same way. Then again, I'd never have let them walk several miles in these conditions. For a moment, I thought perhaps I really should extend the offer of an overnight stay, but Alfie didn't look at all fazed by the prospect of the trudge ahead of him.

'Can I lend you something?' I asked, and gestured at what

was hanging on the hooks. Alfie regarded my collection of coats like I'd just confessed to being a flasher.

'I'm good,' he insisted, and glanced at Lou.

All of a sudden, I realised they were looking for a private moment in which to say goodbye. I figured it was only fair that I gave them the chance, so I headed into the kitchen, turned on my heels and headed straight back to join them.

'Bye, then,' I said, holding the door open, and offered him my hand.

'Safe.' Alfie clasped it in a slightly odd way, I thought, as if preparing for an arm wrestle, and then stepped out into the snow.

I watched the boy trudge down the lane, buttoning his cardigan to the top. Lou began texting him before I'd even shut the front door, and he duly replied moments later. I figured if he ran into problems we would soon know, so it didn't feel like I was totally abandoning him. Besides, I had more than enough to manage without a young man milling about the house. The minipigs needed extra straw to keep warm throughout the night, which was only something I was able to get on with once I'd convinced May that we couldn't accommodate them indoors. Those days were long gone, I told her, and there was no way that I would think about fixing them a hot-water bottle. Fortunately, a day spent sledging meant the little ones didn't complain too much when story time beckoned. Once they were tucked up, I was free to fret about Emma and the discovery that we were running low on vital supplies.

* * *

'What are you looking for?' asked Lou, who had just found me on my hands and knees, rummaging through one of the cupboards under the kitchen worktop.

'We're out of wine.'

I emerged grasping a dusty, squat, purple bottle. Sesi watched me from behind the child gate bars. Hercules was with me, and stretched forward to sniff the bottle cautiously. Lou just looked at me disapprovingly.

'Can't you manage without?'

'Of course!' I said, and unscrewed the cap from the peach schnapps in my hand. 'It's just this really does need drinking. We've had it since Christmas 1997.'

As Lou turned her attention to what snack she could fix for herself, I took the bottle and a glass into the front room. I had lit the log burner early. All I needed to do was turn down the air flow so the blaze behind the glass stopped resembling something like the space shuttle's afterburner. With the flames flickering, I settled down on the sofa and watched with amusement once again at Hercules stretched out on the hearth. It should've felt cosy and relaxing. Instead, I sat there with a strong sense that someone was missing.

My thoughts were interrupted by my dog whining from the boot room. She wasn't who I had in mind, of course, but it seemed unfair to keep her out in the cold.

'Sesi, it's been a long day,' I said, addressing her from the other side of the child gate. 'Please don't make it any longer by menacing Hercules. He's been here long enough for you to know that he's no threat.'

Sesi looked at me as if she understood every word. She didn't, of course. I could've read her the TV listings and she wouldn't once have broken from my gaze. My dog just knew how to appear in order to earn what was coming: time out for good behaviour. I lifted the gate to swing it open, but she did that last bit for me. Such was her eager-ness to get through that she pushed me to one side and then tore across the tiles in the direction of the front room.

'Don't hurt him!' I yelled, and sprinted after her. All of a sudden, it seemed to me that Sesi had been biding her time, just waiting for this moment to arise before seeking retribution for being so sidelined. I crashed into the front room, fearing the worst. There was my Canadian Shepherd, standing stock-still over Hercules with her head low on muscular haunches. At first I feared she was busy tugging out the sausage dog's guts. Hercules was on his back, though all I could see of him behind my massive hound was his front paws on one side of her and rear legs on the other. I circled cautiously, until a clearer picture emerged. Sesi hadn't eviscerated Emma's latest pet. Hercules was simply sound asleep in front of the wood burner with his head crooked sharply and his ears flat on the hearth. With his rear legs splayed, Sesi was doing what comes naturally to a dog and just sniffing at his privates. 'I don't suppose there's much to explore there,' I said, feeling only relief when she then settled down as well.

I returned to my spot on the sofa. There, over the course of the next half an hour, I grimaced my way through a small glass of peach schnapps. In that time, encouraged by the warmth from the burning logs, Sesi stretched out and then flipped over, legs splayed, at a right angle to the sausage dog. Together, they looked ridiculous. More importantly, both appeared to be oblivious to the presence of the other. Hercules wasn't tormenting Sesi, while she appeared to have accepted that there was no competition for my affections from a dog that God must have placed on this earth just to mix up what it meant to be a canine. For the first time since Hercules arrived, I felt comfortable with him in the house. He was alright, for such a strangely shaped dog. In a way, I quite admired the fact that he wasn't intimidated by Sesi in any way whatsoever. Awake, he might've annoyed her by constantly bouncing at her head, but he wasn't aggressive like all the psychopathic little dogs down the lane. Watching them at rest proved quite soporific, as did the second glass of peach schnapps I managed to struggle down. It was one of those moments where I had no idea what point I fell asleep, but when I awoke it was with a deep sense of alarm.

'Dad? *Dad!*'

I opened my eyes to find Lou standing over me. She had shaken my shoulder to stir me. As I found focus, her expression switched from fear to relief to some annoyance.

'What's up?' I asked.

'Panic over.' She turned to May, who was at the door, stricken by anxiety and with her eyes locked on the two sleeping dogs. 'They haven't been gassed.'

'Eh?' I sat up straight, feeling groggy from the schnapps.

'May came downstairs to say goodnight, took one look at the three of you and assumed you'd succumbed to carbon monoxide poisoning.'

To be fair, both Sesi and Hercules looked like corpse dogs. With their crooked legs in the air, I could see why she has assumed the worst. I turned to May, and realised she had been on the brink of tears.

'They're just conked out after another busy day,' I told her.

'I thought we'd lost you, too,' she said quietly, and stopped there as her voice was quivering. Even so, I knew what was troubling her.

I rose from the sofa and clasped May by the shoulders.

'This is about Mum, isn't it?' I said. 'She's coming back, I promise.'

May drew breath to reply. At the same time, her tears began to spill. 'What's happening to her?'

'Your mother's not a zombie, OK? It's just a burn. A bad one. But she'll get better, I promise.'

May smiled, and used the heel of her hand to wipe her cheeks.

'I just want her home.'

'I know that,' I said, and hugged her. 'We all do.'

# 26

# A Bad Way

The gritting truck came in the night. From my bed, unable to sleep, I heard it powering up the hill. It should've left me feeling liberated. Instead, with Emma weighing heavy on my mind, the sense of suffocation left me staring at the ceiling. As the vehicle passed the house, both dogs stirred and let loose very different brands of barking.

At first light, I was ready for the minipigs before they had opened their eyes. Roxi was asleep in her usual position, with her head lolling at the entrance to their sleeping quarters and Butch tucked up against her formidable butt. All it took was the sound of the gate latch lifting to wake them. Before I did that, however, I considered taking a big breath and squealing. I just didn't think a taste of their own medicine would get them off to a good start.

'Rise and shine,' I said as the pair bundled out into the crisp, still dawn. 'And watch where you put those trotters. It's icy, and one casualty is quite enough in this household.'

Emma was the reason I had seized the day. I wanted all the chores out of the way before the hospital opened its doors to visitors. I was half hoping she would be ready for collection as well. We'd only passed a couple of days without her, but having been snowed in it felt like an age.

With Butch and Roxi guzzling, I turned my attention to the

dogs. Sesi was stretched out on her bed. She was clearly in no hurry to head out into the cold, and I didn't blame her. Hercules, however, was sitting up in his crate with his tail switching one way and the other.

'OK,' I said, mostly to myself. 'Let's do this.'

The day before, I had made it no further than the drive. Today, for the sake of the sausage dog, I refused to be overwhelmed by embarrassment. I reminded myself that I had got things all out of proportion, much like Hercules himself. There was no shame in walking him. I might've been dying on the inside, but so long as I didn't *look* uncomfortable, nobody would pay me any attention whatsoever. Having knocked on Lou's door to tell her she was in charge for a couple of minutes should any of her siblings wake, I prepared for the Dachshund's maiden voyage.

'Are you ready?' I asked the dog, on opening up the yard gate onto the drive. 'There's no backing out now.'

Hercules responded by plunging into the snow, as he had the day before, surging forward and then surfacing with some expertise. I focused on the fact that the lane was basically just covered in slush now. Once we had cleared the drive, he would have no choice but to walk normally. It still felt weird being out with something so slight in comparison to Sesi. It was like swapping cars after years spent driving just one vehicle. The set-up was basically the same and yet *everything* felt different. Nevertheless, I could sense myself getting into something close to a stride. Hercules did likewise just as soon as he hit the lane. In the interest of safety, I reeled him in a little bit, but not so close as to cause me to skip. It wasn't easy, however. With the environment being so new to him, he stopped dead in his tracks several times to sniff the tarmac. On the third occasion when he came to a sudden halt right in front of me, I sort of goose-stepped my way over him.

'For crying out loud!' I turned to face the sausage dog, who looked up at me like this might be the start of a fun new game. 'Focus, Hercules. *Please!* It's important that we both make an effort here.'

I spun back around on my boot heels, bringing the leash in a little tighter so that the dog was at my side. Then, with a gentle tug, we set off again. This time, Hercules fell into line. I found that if I held the leash outwards a little bit, so it led vertically to the dog, I had far more control over him. It was only when I heard a vehicle powering up the lane, however, that I realised it basically made me look like I was mincing.

Maybe that was all it took to prick my fragile confidence. For as a four-by-four splashed into view at the foot of the lane, I panicked. In no way was I ready for this. I'd simply been fooling myself. Aware that I was too far from the house to get back in time, I seized the only course of action available to me.

Scooping the sausage dog off the lane, I sprinted for the farmer's gate. Holding him in the crook of my arm, I dipped through the bars and took refuge behind the hedge. The sound of the vehicle grew louder, powering through the slush. I waited for it to pass, and grimaced as it began to slow instead. Now I just felt foolish. I quickly set Hercules on the ground. In a bid to pretend I hadn't just run for cover, I set off towards the woods. The trouble was the snowdrift still lay thick on the ground. For Hercules, it proved impassable. He attempted his technique of plunging into the snow and then surfacing, but it was just too deep. Aware that he could possibly perish, I tugged him free and then crouched to brush away what was basically a coat of ice crystals.

'Look at you with your new special friend.'

Recognising the voice, and resigned to the fact that I had been spotted, I turned to face the farmer's fence. Behind it, Tom had pulled up in his Land Rover and wound down the passenger window. I wasn't sure whether I should be relieved it was my friend, or all the more uncomfortable.

Rising to my feet, I gestured casually at the sausage dog. 'I'm just exercising him for Emma. You know? Until she's home and well enough to do it herself.'

'Where's Sesi?' asked Tom, and looked around. 'Don't tell me *she's* got hang-ups about being seen out with a dog that long?'

I tried not to smile, and failed. Tom knew I had issues with Hercules. Clearly this was his way of telling me not to take life so seriously.

'Sesi will get used to him,' I said. 'Give it time.'

Hercules shook off the last of the ice just then. It was a process that began at his head and then passed down the length of his body all the way to the tip of his tail.

'It's sweet how he does that,' said Tom. 'Emma must be thrilled.'

'She was until the accident,' I told him. 'I'm going to see her later this morning.'

Tom nodded, and glanced up the lane.

'Can I do anything to help?' he asked. 'Who's going to look after Hercules?'

'Lou will have to hold the fort,' I said. 'I imagine school will be closed until the last flake of snow has thawed.'

Tom shook his head like I'd given him an incorrect answer.

'Drop him off with the kids at my smallholding,' he said. 'I'll be there with the missus all morning. We can start setting up Butch and Roxi's holiday home.'

'That's kind,' I said, feeling buoyed all of a sudden by the reminder of his proposal. 'Are you sure?'

'It'll be our pleasure.' Tom gestured at the dog on my boot. 'Then you're free to collect his rightful owner.'

It was no surprise to learn that school had been cancelled. Not just for a second day, according to the website, but for the rest of the week. All four kids cheered the news, and then complained when I told them where they would be spending the morning.

'Do we have to go?' asked Lou. 'You can't get a phone signal at the bottom of the lane.'

'You'll survive,' I told her.

'But what if Alfie wants to speak to me?'

'Alfie can wait,' I said, in no mood for delays. 'In my day, we didn't have mobile phones to keep in touch with dates.'

'It's different now,' said Lou. 'You *can't* be uncontactable.'

'Just get in the car,' I told them all. 'The good news is that Hercules can go with you.'

This was enough to persuade Lou and the little ones to head for the back door. Only May seemed hesitant.

'Won't Sesi be lonely?' she asked.

'Sesi is a guard dog,' I reminded her. 'It's what she does.'

'What about Lou's flour babies? We can't leave the twins home alone. Social services would take them away if they found out.'

'Good,' Lou muttered, and turned back to glare at her sister. 'Why don't you let me worry about them?'

'Because you're not worried,' May said flatly. 'If it wasn't for me they'd be starving hungry.'

I caught Lou's eye. She looked as bemused as I did by this, and equally unwilling to press May for an explanation.

Nevertheless, I knew that leaving Justin and Beyoncé behind would cause me yet more grief.

'OK, go fetch the twins,' I told May. 'Just don't feed them any more.'

The drive to hospital was a challenge. The roads had been gritted, but were still treacherous. I was relieved not to have the children with me. Their safety was paramount, while I was free to fishtail on the ice every now and then without hysterical shrieking from the back seat. The journey took a long time. From start to finish, however, my thoughts were with Emma. All I wanted to do was bring her home.

Outside the burns unit, as I cleaned my hands at the antibacterial pump dispenser, I faced the same interrogation by intercom. This time, I confirmed that I was alone. The nurse on the other end sounded relieved, and buzzed me through. Once again, I made my way through to the reception area. The nurse was behind the desk, waiting for me. I recognised her from my previous visit. This time, she didn't have a biro behind one ear. Instead, she'd used it to pin her bun in place.

'So, the brander is back,' she said, straightening her papers as I approached the desk. 'Do I need to frisk you for hot-water bottles?'

'How is she?' I asked, doing my level best to rise above the teasing.

The nurse nodded, which was hard for me to read, and set her papers on the desk.

'You can see her now,' she said, and invited me to follow her through to the ward. 'She's been looking forward to seeing you.'

Beyond the reception doors, I felt as if I had walked into a different world. Staff pushed steel trolleys across a spotless white corridor. The smell of antiseptic quickly worked inside my nostrils. This wasn't a general ward, however, with beds in facing rows. I was well aware that in every room we passed lay someone who had been through an unthinkable trauma, and whose burns left them vulnerable in every way imaginable. As we passed each open door I just looked straight ahead. Somehow just being here felt like an invasion of their privacy.

Finally, the nurse stopped outside one door and invited me to go through. I dared to turn my eyes, and saw Emma. A drip stand was stationed at her bedside, with a vast clock on the wall behind her. With her hands clasped together, she seemed to be focused on just staring at the ceiling. As I entered the room, Emma turned her head and smiled. I smiled back. At least I think that I did. I was so shocked by how she appeared to me that I struggled not to take a step backwards.

\* \* \*

Some time after lunch, when I pulled up at the entrance to Tom's smallholding, I believed I had finally got a grip on my composure. I needed to be calm and cool for the sake of the kids. I couldn't let them see how worried I was about their mother. Checking my reflection in the rear-view mirror, I took a deep breath and climbed out of the car. It was freezing cold. The roads were clear, but snow still smothered the fields and woodland. Nothing matched the steep slope of our lane for sledging, but judging by the distant shrieks of delight it seemed that people had found other, safer places. I climbed the gate into the smallholding and looked around. Tom's pigs were slumbering in their arks. His horses were in the stable. My children were nowhere to be seen.

'Hello?' I called out. 'Anyone here?'

Tom's workshop was tucked away behind the stable. When I heard the sound of laughter, I knew where I would find them.

'Dad! You're back. Please don't say it's time to go home yet.'

I didn't quite register what Lou had just said. This was because she addressed me with a nail gun in hand. She was wearing protective goggles, but it didn't do much to ease my concern. Behind her, at his workbench, Tom was overseeing some project that Frank and Honey had undertaken. It involved two lengths of metal and a small blowtorch. May was working at the far end of the bench, hammering madly.

'One moment,' said Tom, without taking his eyes off the little ones' work. 'We're just finishing the runners for their sledge. You can't *not* have one. What kind of childhood are you hoping to give these kids?'

On the floor in front of him, I realised, stood the fruits of their labours. It looked like a proper sledge. The kind I would buy from the shops – that is, if I was ever inclined to spend money on something they'd get to use once in a blue moon.

'I'm impressed,' I said, and looked around. 'Where is the dog?'

'Out with the missus,' Tom told me. 'She *loves* Hercules.'

I didn't reply. This was because Honey had just waved the blowtorch a little too close to Frank's hands for comfort. I noticed that Justin and Beyoncé had been placed at the back of the worktop. Judging by the strip of gaffer tape across Justin's midriff, I could only think he had taken a nail from Lou's gun, accidentally on purpose, no doubt.

'Where's Mum?' asked May, pausing in her work for a moment.

'Back soon,' I said, as brightly as I could.

Tom switched off the blowtorch, much to the little ones' disappointment, and levelled his gaze at me.

'Guys,' he said, addressing the children, 'I think the sledge is ready for assembly. Why don't you lay out the parts we've built and start screwing it together like I showed you? The power tools are on the rack.'

'Is that wise?' I whispered as he crossed the workshop and motioned for me to leave ahead of him.

'All part of the learning process,' he said. 'Now, how's the patient?'

I waited until we were out of earshot, around the corner of the stable. Even then, I couldn't find any words to tell him. Ever since the snow came down, just as Emma was admitted to hospital, it felt like reality had been put on hold. I still couldn't believe a minor accident with a hot-water bottle had turned into something quite so grave. All the way back I had dwelled on the way I'd found her. The room didn't help. It was huge, designed for teams of surgical staff to work at the same time, and largely unfurnished, which made it feel sterile in all kind of ways. Emma was wearing a white hospital gown, propped up on pillows on top of the bed. One leg was crooked, I had noticed, which was when I saw what looked like a shark bite taken out of it. This went way beyond the scope of the burn when she'd been admitted. I struggled to understand why it hadn't been dressed. Emma was on a drip and a string of drugs. Her explanation made little sense, and so I had asked a nurse. Apparently, the surgeons had found the infection went so deep they'd been forced to cut away the tissue behind it to create a kind of firebreak. The resulting wound was now close to the bone, which they'd chosen to leave open so they could monitor things. What troubled me more than anything was that Emma barely seemed to register it. She was so medicated it felt as if I was talking to someone who was in the middle of a dream.

She engaged with me for short bursts, and then drifted off again.

Above all, I was frightened that Emma might lose her leg.

I really didn't want to ask, as it just seemed so crass. Without an answer, however, I couldn't shake the thought from my head. Now, facing Tom, I found I didn't dare put it into words for fear of my composure crumbling. As I fell in and out of an explanation, he stopped me with a nod like he understood just what I was going through.

'Sorry,' I said. 'It's all come as such a shock.'

'Well, you're doing a fine job keeping the family afloat while she's away.'

Just then, Tom's wife appeared at the gate. She called across to us, drawing our attention to the fact that Hercules could pass clean underneath the lowest bar.

'I'm not so sure,' I said. 'I can't even bring myself to walk her damned dog.'

Seeing me, Hercules launched into a sprint –, only to do so on the spot on account of the fact that he was on a leash. Tom laughed. Seeing the stationary dog's ears flapping up and down was enough to draw a smile from me, too. It was one that quickly led to a chuckle. A first in some time. Just then, I looked at the dog as a source of fun instead of stress. In view of what Emma was going through, I owed it to her to get over any doubts I had about him. By the time my wife was well again, I decided, I would be at one with her dog.

# 27

## Walking with Sausage Dogs

I returned home with a renewed sense of purpose. We might've been in crisis as a family, but I refused to be defeated by a Dachshund. As a result, the next few days brought out the very best in me. And also the worst.

In that time, my greatest achievement was in finding a way to take Hercules out in public. The solution, I discovered, was Sesi. The morning after I had visited Emma, I was in such a scramble to return to hospital that I decided to walk both dogs together. Once again, the lane was empty as we left the house. I had expected Hercules to menace my Shepherd. Instead, the joy of being outside served to focus his attention on scampering forward as fast as possible. Sesi liked to walk on my left, close by me, and so I allowed Hercules a little slack on his lead so he wouldn't get in the way. It wasn't quite Husky formation, but I certainly felt the pull from them both. Further down the lane, a young man was pushing his bike towards us. At once, I entertained the thought of hurrying to the farmer's fence. It wasn't far away, after all. Then I considered Sesi. Hercules might've been wearing a hot pink collar, but nobody was going to laugh when I had a white wolf at my side. As we walked on, Hercules picked up on the man's closing presence. I felt him straining harder on his lead. Then he began to growl and bark. Naturally, the target of his aggression looked less than intimidated. He smiled at Hercules and then at me.

'I guess he can play the big man with that kind of backup,' he said, and nodded at Sesi.

I drew breath to stress that the sausage dog belonged to my wife, but thought better of it. What mattered was that I looked in control and comfortable with it.

'They work well together,' I replied instead, which was a total lie but sounded like the right thing to say.

'Looks like you all do.'

The young man made this observation just as we passed one another. I stopped in my tracks and turned to face him, but he just pushed on with his bicycle.

It was only a brief exchange, but his compliment felt like a milestone to me. At last, I was beginning to master the art of walking with sausage dogs. And it really was an art. One that involved an inner confidence, a sense of total relaxation and, crucially, an ability to deftly sidestep the damn thing whenever he stopped without warning. Ultimately, once I'd worked out that this was a far more acceptable avoidance tactic than skipping over him, I started to think that we might go far. In fact, I kept my head high on seeing a builder's van climb the lane. It was clear that the three men in the front had clocked Sesi from some distance. When the driver started sneering, I figured Hercules had also come to their attention. The van even slowed on passing. I just nodded at them cheerily and continued on my way.

I still wasn't sure I could walk Hercules without Sesi, as I told Emma at her bedside later that morning, but it was a start.

'I can't wait to see him,' she said. 'Has he grown much?'

'Only in length and libido,' I told her. 'Frank has taken to calling one of his soft toys Humpy Monkey because of what Hercules keeps doing to it. I can't decide if it's an educational experience or an episode that's going to mess him up as an adult.'

'He'll grow out of it,' said Emma, who had just received a visit from the nurse to change her drip. I could barely bring myself to look at her leg, which was still without a dressing. According to the consultant, who had also dropped in to see her, the surgeons planned to operate again towards the end of the week. By then, so he said, he hoped that everything would be back under control. Emma barely blinked when she learned this. In fact, she only seemed to switch on after he had left, when I came to the subject of her puppy. 'I've been thinking,' she said. 'Once he's matured we could hire him out as a stud dog.'

'Hercules?' I laughed before I could stop myself. 'I'm not sure he's sexually attracted to anything that isn't plush. It's a fetish, I think.'

It was the first moment of light relief for me since I had arrived. The consultant had done his level best to sound reassuring, but I heard no certainties from him. He had talked about scarring as if that was the best possible outcome. I didn't care about anything like that. I just wanted Emma to come home, back where she belonged. Until then, I stuck to the subject of the sausage dog, because that's what brightened her expression, and hoped she couldn't see that I was worried sick.

'There's money in putting him out to stud,' she said next. 'Saves on the cost of castration, too.'

I thought about this for a moment.

'But that means he'll stay frisky,' I pointed out. 'I'm not sure how much more Frank's soft toys will take.'

Emma smiled, and closed her eyes. After half a minute or so, I wondered whether she would open them again. Once more, she'd managed a short burst of conversation before withdrawing into herself again. It was just so difficult for me to process. Here was someone who spent her working day being in charge of stuff, not lying in hospital looking like a ghost of her former self.

'I'm so tired,' she muttered finally, in a voice so quiet I barely heard her. 'My head feels like cotton wool.'

I thought she might open her eyes, but it didn't happen. I leaned forward, close enough to detect her breathing. It was comforting to hear, though I hated seeing her this sedated. I was also determined not to go home without a proper goodbye. It was for this reason that I decided now would be a good time to mention the minipig proposal. If anything was going to bring her back to me, I thought, this would be it.

'Tom's offered to take Butch and Roxi for a holiday on his smallholding,' I explained. 'If his wife takes to them, it might even turn into a permanent arrangement. Strictly speaking they'd still be ours. It's just we wouldn't have to lose sleep for the privilege. What do you say?'

Just then, I wouldn't have minded had Emma snapped open her eyes and told me to forget it. That would've been fine. At least I'd have regained that connection. Instead, when she failed to respond either way, I wondered whether she had heard me at all. Judging by the rhythm of her breathing, it seemed I might have missed my moment.

Reflecting on things as I drove home, my view began to change. I decided that Emma *must've* taken the proposal on board. It was often said that people in comas were well aware of their surroundings, and mercifully my wife wasn't that far gone. In a way, her silence suggested to me that she had no objections. Given that she was unlikely to be discharged for some time, I even wondered whether I could get it sorted before she was back in my care. The more I reasoned with myself, the clearer it became that this would be my way of making up for hospitalising her in the first place.

And so, on collecting Hercules and the kids from Tom and his wife, I confirmed that Emma would be delighted for the minipigs to take a break.

'It sounds like she's going to need as much rest as she can get,' said Tom, who then looked around at his land. 'Once the thaw comes, I can pick them up in the stock box if you like?'

I had to remind myself not to look too delighted by the way this arrangement was shaping up. Of course I cared about Butch and Roxi, but we just couldn't cope with them in our back garden any more. They had enough space. It's just by rights that space deserved to be a nice flower-bed.

Even though Emma hadn't raised any objections to the plan, I knew that I would face some from the children. That's why I decided not to tell them straight away. Instead, at tea time, I pitched it as a hypothetical question.

'But I'd miss them,' said Lou, when I asked how they'd feel if Butch and Roxi ever went away. 'We won't be the cool family with minipigs any more.'

'I don't think keeping minipigs can be considered cool,' I said. 'Gullible and foolhardy, perhaps, but hardly hip and trendy. Besides, you'll find other things to fill your Facebook page. How about Hercules?'

'Where is he?' asked May. 'Whenever he goes quiet, it usually means he's being gross with Frank's teddies.'

Over the sound of the little ones sucking spaghetti into their mouths, we listened out for the telltale squeaks of a soft toy being molested. I called the dog's name a couple of times, and was just about to look for him when he appeared at the kitchen door.

I wasn't the first to notice that something wasn't quite right about Hercules. It was Lou who drew my attention to the odd and ponderous way he moved.

'Is he in pain?' asked May, as Hercules looked up at me with worry in his eyes. 'Has he hurt his back?'

Certainly his spine seemed somewhat arched. Then I spotted what was stopping him from walking normally. For a moment, I thought he'd impaled himself on something that looked like a pork fillet. A feeling of sickness and disbelief rose up in me, until I realised that it was in fact very much a part of the dog.

'Good grief!' I declared, as Lou was next to realise what it was. With a shriek, she climbed up on her chair, which only startled everyone else to do the same thing, including me. 'Give me your phone,' I demanded of my eldest, just as she took a picture. 'I need to look something up.'

Opening her mobile's web browser, I ran a Google search on 'Dachshund' and 'Penis'. Very quickly, I confirmed that it was indeed what we had just been presented with, and in a state of some engorgement.

'That's revolting!' said May. 'And *huge!*'

Poor Hercules appeared to be as freaked out as us. He slumped sideways on his rear quarters, evidently unable to get comfortable. With his manhood lolling crossways onto the tiles, he looked up at us as if hoping we could put him out of his torment.

'It looks like it could bite,' said Lou. 'Do something, Dad. Make it go away!'

Frank and Honey looked equally startled, but also somewhat curious.

'Everyone stay calm,' I said. 'It's an adolescent thing, and clearly come as a shock to him.'

'Just make it stop!' wailed May.

I faced her for a moment.

'I should imagine this is the first time it's actually happened. All that soft toy humping has finally aroused him for real.'

'You need to comfort him, Dad.' Lou held out her hand for my phone. 'He looks scared.'

She had a point. I just felt a bit disgusted at the idea of going anywhere near a foot-long sausage dog with a penis that pretty much matched. Aware that I needed to control this situation for the sake of the children, however, I climbed off the chair to crouch beside the dog.

'It's OK,' I said, and hesitantly patted his head. At any moment, Hercules could've rolled over in my direction and flopped his swollen appendage on my foot. Instead, he remained in the same position, and allowed me to talk him into a sense of calm. In a way, I felt that I had let him down. The poor thing had clearly come looking for help, and my first response had been to behave like the maid from *Tom and Jerry*. Finally, with his retracting member looking more like the head of a lipstick, I rose to my feet and assured my children that it was safe to come down from the chairs.

'It won't happen for much longer,' I told them. 'Your mother had plans to raise him as a stud dog, but I'm ruling that out right here and now. As soon as he's old enough, Hercules will be paying a visit to the vet.'

There was one upside to the trauma this episode caused to the sausage dog. Normally, when reading with Frank at bed time, Hercules would set about making passionate love to the soft toys on his bedroom floor. Humpy Monkey was his preferred partner. If that was in the wash on account of his affections, he would often drag out a patchwork turtle from under the bed before ravaging it at our feet. That night, however, as Frank found his way through the words on the page, Emma's dog was nowhere to be seen. I wasn't surprised, given what he'd been through. It was only after I had said goodnight to the little ones that I discovered he had opted to take out his testosterone on a pastime with less upsetting consequences. For Hercules, at any rate.

'Oh . . . my . . . *God!*'

It took a moment before I registered what he'd been doing while I was upstairs. I had walked into the front room, thinking I should close the curtains, only to find there wasn't much of one left. Hercules was sitting at the French windows, looking thoroughly busted, behind what were basically ribbons of fabric. For such a low-slung dog, he had clearly gone to great lengths to shred the curtain as high as he had.

'You should've been watching him.' This was May, who had come downstairs shortly after me. 'This is what young dogs do when they're bored.'

I turned to face her, only for my attention to catch on the sofa cushions – which Hercules had disembowelled.

'It's what vandals do sometimes too,' I said, shaking my head. 'Sesi was never this destructive.'

'That's because you like Sesi,' said May, who crossed the room to collect Hercules in her arms. 'If you liked Hercules then he wouldn't do it,' she said, and planted a kiss on his head.

I looked around once more, shaking my head at the same time.

'Well, this is a low,' I muttered. 'That dog might have to go.'

May reacted like I'd just suggested a cull of the children in the house.

'No way!' she declared, clutching Hercules tightly. 'What kind of monster are you?'

'May, be reasonable.'

I didn't want to stress that his appetite for soft-toy sex and destruction went beyond what any pet owner could be expected to put up with. I felt the damage that surrounded me spoke volumes. My daughter continued to glare at me. It was unnerving, as if at any moment I would be forced to clasp my hands over my ears in response to some agonisingly intense sound frequency heard only by me. Maybe Hercules picked up on it as well, because he started wriggling in her arms just then. With her eyes still fixed upon me, May crouched and released the dog.

'Wait until I tell Lou what you said.'

As she headed for the stairs once more, Hercules saw his opportunity to avoid any consequences of his actions by hurrying after her. It left me alone to appraise the damage. I decided that the upper half of the curtain might be worth salvaging. I knew that if Emma had been here she would've written off the whole thing. In her absence, my standards weren't so high. I was midway through cutting off the shredded half of the curtain with a pair of nail scissors when May reappeared. This time, she didn't look so gleeful.

'I think you need to see Lou,' she said. 'It's serious.'

'What's the matter?'

'Alfie has dumped her.'

Having only just dealt with the fact that my eldest daughter was dating, I now found myself faced with the aftermath. Her bedroom door was ajar, but I knocked first on account of all the sobbing. When she didn't answer me, I let myself in anyway. Lou was slumped against the side of her bed with her knees drawn tight and her head buried in her hands. Her laptop was on the carpet beside her. So too was Hercules. Surprisingly, he showed no interest in Lou's much-loved but threadbare teddy. Its head and one arm were dangling provocatively from under her pillow, but the dog's attention was locked on Lou. With his head cocked, a whine formed in his throat. From where I was standing, it sounded like concern. Hearing this, Lou reached out with one hand and drew him closer. Hercules submitted, and rested his chin on her leg. Just then, despite all the upheaval he had caused, that dog seemed to me to be in just the right place. I saw him turn his eyes up at me, looking as if he felt her pain completely. Noting that Lou's laptop browser was open on Facebook, I wondered whether this had been a public kind of break-up.

'What happened?' I asked.

Lou looked up, saw me at the door and wailed.

'He . . . he changed his profile back to single,' she said, in a voice that failed to quite make it through the sentence. 'All because he couldn't reach me this morning.'

'But you couldn't get a phone signal at the smallholding,' I reminded her. 'That's understandable.'

Lou wiped her face, transferring her tears onto Hercules.

'There's more,' she told me. 'Guess what happened when I tried to send him a message just now to explain myself?'

'I hope he wasn't rude to you.'

Lou shook her head before blowing her nose. 'It's worse,' she croaked. 'He's *blocked* me!'

Before I could double-check if that really was a big deal in her world, Lou's composure broke once more. I'd seen enough. Collecting her from the floor, I offered my daughter a hug. She clung to me as if an abyss had opened up behind her. After all my failed efforts to communicate with her about sex and relationships, it did at least leave me feeling like she looked to me for something. As for the sausage dog, having served a useful purpose himself, he promptly turned his attention to the teddy. Fortunately, Lou spotted him dragging it from under the pillow. She broke off to deal with the situation, leaving me to find May at the door.

'Look after your sister,' I told her, on leaving the room. 'And stay away from boys, alright?'

'Who needs boys?' she asked, and gestured at the dog. He was looking up expectantly at Lou, as if hoping she would stop hugging the bear and toss it to him. 'We have Hercules.'

# 28

## Like Lassie, But Longer

What Emma's Dachshund had done for Lou wasn't much, but it made an impact on me. Just being there in her time of need meant Hercules went some way towards redeeming himself in my eyes. I only had to walk into the front room to reconsider my opinion, of course. Then something else happened that changed my view of him completely.

I was out in the snow, shooting a clip of the minipigs on Lou's camera phone. My aim was to create a little back-up material for my next hospital visit in case Emma had any doubts about moving Butch and Roxi to Tom's smallholding. I figured footage of them lumbering over the frost-capped mudsuck that was their pen should be sufficient. I had no intention of staying out for long. Hercules had followed me into the garden, unlike Sesi who didn't much care for such bitterly cold conditions.

By now, the sausage dog had perfected his tunnel-and-jump manoeuvre that allowed him to move through the snowdrifts. As I trained my camera on Butch in the pen, Hercules happily motored around the perimeter of the garden in this weird way of his. I paid him no attention, until he stopped mid-circuit and barked. Being so close to me, it came as quite a shock, as the jolt in the video clip would testify.

'Keep it down,' I muttered, before returning my attention to the viewfinder.

What had made his bark worse was the fact that the snow covering still made everything so still and quiet. Butch and Roxi grunted every now and then, but that really was about the only sound that I could hear.

Until, that is, a voice called out from the distance, which triggered another response from Hercules.

To my ear, it sounded like kids playing, and so I kept on filming. I only wanted thirty seconds of footage. When Hercules kicked off for a third time, I decided that I'd had enough. Pocketing the camera phone, I headed back inside. It was only at the door that I realised the dog hadn't followed. I had to call his name a couple of times before he appeared, but even then he paused at the door to sound off once more.

'That's *enough* now,' I said, and plucked him off the ground. 'You're not a terrier, OK? No more noise.'

With yet another day off school, the children had begun to turn feral. May and Lou were unlikely to surface before lunch, while the little ones were guaranteed to remain in their pyjamas until bed time. I found Frank and Honey at the kitchen table. Both were engaged in a furious bout of DS button-smashing. I asked what game they were playing. With no response from either of them, I decided that meant there would at least be no demands for juice and biscuits while I reviewed my footage of the minipigs. I was pleased that I had lingered on one upsettingly ambitious excavation Roxi had made. It was close to the back fence, which had come down once in the past due to her persistent digging. If Emma had any misgivings about sending them on holiday, this would surely seal the deal. I smiled to myself as the clip drew towards a close with a shot of Butch sidling back to his sleeping quarters.

And there, just as the minipig squeezed inside, that voice

could be heard in the distance. The footage stopped just as Hercules barked back, but this time I was able to replay it. With the phone to my ear, and the dog at my feet, I listened intently.

This time, focusing on nothing else, I heard it quite clearly. Not a child but an adult. A man, I realised. Nor was he far away, as I had thought. It was just very faint in volume as he called out for help.

Racing into the lane, having left Lou to hold the fort, I stopped a couple with a toboggan who were heading to the slopes. In such still conditions, it only took a moment to pinpoint the direction from where the pleas were coming. Together, we rushed towards my next-door neighbour's house.

I found Roddie face down in the snow. He had dragged himself some way through the drift from where he had slipped and broken his hip. Judging by the trail, and the basket beside the woodpile, it looked like the accident had happened as he was loading up with logs. He was dressed in slacks, deck shoes, a golfing jumper and a pair of marigolds. As he'd stopped responding to us some minutes before I'd spotted him, it was no time to ask him what was wrong with proper gloves. Instead, I made a hurried call to the emergency services, and stayed at his side while the others fetched blankets from his house. I had never seen anyone quite so blue before. It was evident that Roddie had been exposed to the cold for a long time. He was conscious, just about, but making little sense. I found myself talking to him as I would to a child, and held his hand until the ambulance arrived.

\* \* \*

Visiting hours were over by the time I arrived at the burns unit. Once I explained my reasons, however, the nurse with the pen in her hair let me into the ward. She also informed me that Emma had undergone her second operation. My wife had come round some time ago, so she said, but might still be dozy from the anaesthetic. As I made my way towards her room, I didn't think she could be any more zoned out than she had been the last time I visited. Even if she was a little spaced, I told myself, the story I had to share would surely bring her to her senses.

'I even called Lou at home and asked her to make a hot-water bottle for him,' I confessed to Emma, on finishing the account. 'It was only lukewarm, mind you. With hypothermia, it's important not to bring someone back to temperature too quickly.'

'Or burn them,' she added.

Normally, my daily news would detail Hercules's latest misdemeanour. This was different. According to one of the medics, I had probably saved a life. Naturally, I wanted to take all the credit. I just knew my conscience wouldn't permit it. The couple I encountered in the lane had been brilliant. Above all, however, had it not been for one miniature Dachshund then a confused old boy in washing-up gloves would've perished in the cold.

'Hercules is a hero,' I said. 'Like Lassie, but longer.'

Emma smiled.

'Well, it sounds like you did your bit.'

She looked as pale as ever, but her leg had at least been closed and dressed. Looking at her no longer made me feel so sick to the core about what had happened. I even felt that Emma's senses were a little sharper this time.

'Can you imagine how bad I would've felt if I hadn't played

back that film when I did?' I asked her. 'Imagine if Roddie had died, and I'd unwittingly caught him on camera crying out for help?'

'I don't think hitting the delete button would've erased that from your memory,' she said. 'He's a lucky man.'

'Well, it was all down to your dog.'

From her pillow, Emma seemed to read my gaze for a moment.

'You sound much brighter about Hercules,' she said finally. 'I'm pleased.'

I hadn't forgotten what he'd done to the curtains and the cushions, and Frank's soft toys were all but written off. Nevertheless, Hercules had proven himself to be a kind-hearted dog. He looked out for others, which was no bad thing in my book. Whether or not the sound of Roddie's voice just served to wind him up, I'll never know. I had planned on bringing the clip with me to show Emma. The problem was I had recorded it on Lou's phone. When I asked if I could take it, a distance of more than thirty miles from where she would be at home, she practically broke out in a stress rash before my eyes.

'The good news is that Roddie's going to be OK,' I said. 'And so are you, according to the nurse.'

Emma didn't seem so positive.

'I'm going to be fitted with a silicone implant,' she said.

'Really?' I looked at her in surprise. Before I could make a complete idiot of myself, she drew her leg from the bed sheet to illustrate where.

'It's a plug I have to wear for the next two years,' she said, and gestured at an area under the bandages. 'A kind of filler for the hole in my calf while it heals.'

Again, I felt the weight of responsibility on my shoulders.

'I'm sorry.' I clasped her hand and squeezed it. 'I feel I need to make it up to you.'

'I'm not looking for retribution,' she said in a way that made me think she had entertained the idea. 'There are people in this unit with injuries that make mine look like a scratch. It's been a humbling experience. Now I just want to come home and be with my family. If all goes well, I'll be discharged within the week.'

'We're already making plans for your return,' I told her, and decided there and then that the details of Butch and Roxi's holiday would make a nice surprise.

On the way back from hospital, I stopped off at Tom's small-holding to check his offer still stood.

'They're welcome any time,' he told me, when I found him in his workshop. He was cleaning down what looked to me like a shoulder-mounted rocket launcher. As I'd seen him use it, however, I knew the device was something that helped him drive fence posts into the ground. 'My wife's really looking forward to having them here,' he went on. 'She's been telling friends we're about to have two minipigs come to stay.'

'She hasn't been looking at pictures on the internet, has she?'

Tom grinned.

'Don't worry. I've prepared her. She just loves pigs of all shapes and sizes.'

'I'm sure Butch and Roxi will love her too,' I said. 'And not just because she'll be feeding them.'

I watched Tom finish wiping down the Fencimator, or what-ever it was called. Then he propped it against the workbench and said: 'Would you like to see where they'll be staying?'

'Sure thing. At least then I can say that I carried out due diligence.'

Outside I followed Tom across a series of gangplanks. The ground was frozen, but at long last the snow was beginning to thaw. It wouldn't be long before the mud returned, but I wouldn't miss that one bit. Tom's pigs occupied several enclosures, and frankly didn't look much bigger than Roxi. What's more, everything here was tidy. Unlike my garden, I had a real sense that nothing was out of control or bodged together as a reaction to some unforeseen problem. I was also thrilled by the fact that very soon the pigs wouldn't be my concern.

'Here we are,' said Tom, and stopped at an empty enclosure that bordered the woods. 'Hotel Minipig!'

I clasped the gate and looked around. It was about three times the size of the pigpen in our garden. What's more, it featured a proper water trough and one of Tom's hand-built arks. He'd even lined it with straw in readiness for Butch and Roxi's arrival.

'They'll love this,' I said. 'As far as holidays go, all that's missing is a wet bar and infinity pool.'

Tom drew my attention to the ground. Unlike the churned terrain I was used to looking out upon from our bedroom window, here it was quite level.

'After the last pigs we had in here, I went over it with the roller a couple of times,' he told me. 'It'll give them something to root up over time.'

I faced my friend and invited him to shake my hand.

'After recent events this is one thing that makes me really happy,' I said. 'I can't tell you what a difference it's going to make to our lives.'

'Not a problem.'

I took a sharp intake of breath when his hand clasped mind and squeezed hard. Tom didn't seem to know his own strength sometimes. Nor the size of his heart.

I drove up the hill with a plan of action. As agreed with Tom, come the weekend he would show up with his stock box, and I would wave off Butch and Roxi on what I hoped to be an everlasting vacation in pastures new. Beforehand, of course, I needed to be sure the kids were fully prepared. I couldn't just pretend it was a hypothetical question any more. It was going to happen imminently. In particular, I knew that May would find every reason to worry. I had left them all in Lou's care, and figured that before I could speak I'd have to do a little clearing up. I didn't mind at all. At this difficult time, she did a good job in keeping her siblings safe and sound. Washing a few breakfast bowls was nothing compared to the hassle of finding childcare, after all. I figured once Emma was back this new-found freedom could proving to be quite a liberation for us. Then I stepped inside and discovered one of the pets had already made the most of the free time and space.

'What is that?' I said to myself, having been greeted by Sesi in the boot room. I was looking into the kitchen. The floor tiles were covered in a white powder. Then Hercules padded into view, drawn by my voice, and dragging the remains of Beyoncé in his jaws. 'Oh.'

I couldn't be sure quite where he had found the flour baby. I just knew that I had arrived too late to save her. It was a fight to make Hercules let go of the shredded pack. When he finally released her remains, she was good for nothing but the bin. I could hear two sources of activity in the house: the familiar bleeps of a Mario game from the front room, and girly chatter upstairs. I told myself that at least the non-edible children in the house hadn't come to any harm, and called out for Lou to come downstairs.

'How's Mum?' she asked breezily, on swinging into the hallway. There my daughter reacted as if she'd just stumbled upon a scene of wholesale family slaughter.

'My *baby!*' she shrieked, and threw her hands to the side of her head. 'Oh my God! I'm going to be so marked down for this!'

'Justin is unharmed,' I said, as if that might help, and gestured at the pack of flour on the worktop.

'I only left her for five minutes. I'd placed her on a stool to take a photo so I could show how she was developing.' Lou paused there, her voice cracking. 'And now she's gone!'

I contemplated the mess. Hercules did likewise from my foot. Given Lou's hysterical response, it served as his safe place. I realised there was a conversation to be had about being a responsible mother at all times, but figured that should probably wait.

'We can always replace her,' I offered instead. 'The supermarket has a whole shelf of Beyoncés.'

'It won't be the same,' she said, sounding both frustrated now and a little angry. 'Why do we have such nightmare pets?'

I glanced at the dog at my feet, who was entirely to blame here, and then at Sesi behind the child gate.

'To be fair,' I said in her defence, 'it's mostly Mum's pets that are the problem. The good news is I have a solution that I think everyone is going to like.'

By now, May had been drawn downstairs. She floated up behind her sister with her eyes locked upon me.

'You can't get rid of Hercules,' she said again. 'You'd have to get rid of me first.'

'We're not getting rid of anyone.' I held out my hands,

appealing for calm. 'You know the other day I asked how you'd feel if Butch and Roxi ever went away?'

'Sad,' said May, nodding all the same.

'Well,' I pressed on. 'I've lined them up with a little winter break.'

Both Lou and May stared at me as if waiting for the catch.

'Do you mean, like, skiing?' asked May, blinking first.

Patiently, I explained what I had arranged with Tom.

'It's perfect,' I said. 'They'll only be down the lane, in a proper smallholding, and we can visit them any time.'

'How long will they be away for?' asked Lou.

I didn't want to push my luck here. That Tom had suggested it could become a permanent arrangement was just too good to be true. Right now, I knew the children wouldn't stand for it. Give them a couple of weeks without being awoken by the livestock equivalent of the Kraken, however, and I felt sure they'd be in no hurry to bring them back.

'Just long enough to let the grass regrow,' I told them, while at the same time thinking some rhododendron bushes would thrive in soil so rich in manure.

# 29

## March of the Minipigs

Since their arrival, three years earlier, Butch and Roxi had pretty much never left home. There was one occasion where I'd been obliged to race into the village and rescue Roxi from a teenage sleepover party, but Lou had learned her lesson a long time ago. To transport livestock of any shape or size, you need a movement licence.

When I came to filling in the form, I realised with a great sense of pleasure that once transported they would require a twenty day 'stand still'. In order to prevent the spread of any disease, Butch and Roxi would not be allowed to relocate anywhere else throughout this time. Surely, I thought to myself, three weeks was long enough for Tom's wife to fall in love with a pair of minipigs? With the paperwork complete, it seemed I even had the law on my side when it came to my rehousing project.

Towards the end of that week, the snow had all but gone. What raised my spirits more than anything, however, was the news from the hospital. As the consultant had hoped, Emma's recovery was progressing nicely. All going well, I could expect to collect her within a day or so. And what a homecoming we had in store for her, as I kept reminding myself.

\* \* \*

Come Saturday, I was ready to put the minipig plan into action. With Sesi and Hercules following me, I headed out to prepare Butch and Roxi for the short journey ahead. This basically just involved talking to them. In a way, I felt a little guilty about what was about to happen. A pet is for life, as my wife and children reminded me on a regular basis, and yet here I was getting set to see off the two oversized members of our menagerie.

'It's in your best interest as well as ours,' I told them, as they sauntered across to see me. Despite being so big, Butch and Roxi were still sweet-natured creatures. They were horribly trusting too, which just made me feel bad. 'Nice Tom is coming to collect you at any time. It's going to be an adventure, but trust me you'll be fine.'

I said this to assure myself as much as the minipigs. As ever, Sesi watched them with interest. She would miss them, I thought, while Hercules was paying more attention to a rake that was propped against the shed. Somehow, on licking at an icicle that had formed at the base of the handle, he managed to get it stuck to his tongue. In a panic, he tugged back several times before the icicle broke free. I watched him scuttle across the garden, shaking his head frantically until it broke loose.

The dog was an idiot, but a fun one at least.

As I pondered how much longer Hercules would remain in my care, a Land Rover pulled up in the lane. It was towing a stock box. As the vehicle crunched into reverse, the box arrived first in the drive. By the time I had stowed the dogs safely in the house before opening the gate, Tom had already lowered the ramp to the box in readiness for the passengers.

'Have they packed their suitcases?' he asked, as the kids appeared behind me.

May looked a little panicked, until I informed her that he was just joking.

'Roxi won't be needing her bikini,' I told her. 'They both have everything they need.'

When the minipigs arrived, I knew nothing about their upkeep. It proved to be a steep learning curve, with many sacrifices made, but now I considered myself to be an expert. From experience, I knew that bribery was the surest way to encourage a pig to move. With a bucket of chopped apples in one hand, waved under their snouts for a second or so, both Butch and Roxi were happy to follow me from the pigpen, across the garden and into the yard. Lou, May and the little ones stood well out of the way as I led them into the drive, where Tom was waiting to raise the ramp just as soon as they had climbed inside. Butch was a little hesitant, but couldn't resist the lure of an apple segment that I tossed inside the box. Roxi required the contents of the bucket, but she climbed in eventually.

'What about seat belts?' asked May as Tom locked up the ramp.

'I'll drive very slowly,' he assured her, with a wink to me. 'Right, if you'd like to follow me down in your car, we'll get this holiday under way.'

As he had promised, Tom negotiated the hill at about ten miles per hour. I listened out for any sound of upset from the stock box, but heard only the rumble of our engines. At the foot of the lane, I followed Tom through the gate he had opened in advance. I pulled up just inside, and walked across with the kids while Tom manoeuvred his Land Rover so the stock box faced the front of the enclosure. By the time we joined him, he was ready to lower the ramp. I peeked through the slats in the side of the box. Butch and Roxi looked quite calm, if a little baffled.

'This is all going a little too well, don't you think?'

I grinned at Tom, as he prepared to open the ramp.

'Nothing can go wrong,' he said. 'Once they're safe and sound inside the enclosure, we can stop fretting.'

*And start enjoying the rest of our lives*, I thought to myself.

Butch and Roxi took a moment to exit the stock box. First they looked around. Then they locked onto the pear that Tom produced from his pocket and tossed upon the pressed earth.

'Fantastic,' I said, applauding as they trotted into their new home. 'What do you think, kids? How cool is it down here?'

The little ones looked up from their DS's, and then returned to the game, while Lou and May just nodded in approval. For once, nobody had any objections. I noted that my eldest hadn't taken any photographs. Given that Butch and Roxi just looked like normal-sized pigs in their natural environment, I figured their online appeal among the teenage community had probably dwindled quite a bit.

'Shouldn't you call Emma and let her know it's all gone to plan?' Tom closed the gate to the enclosure. 'She'll be worried.'

'She's probably sleeping,' I reasoned, unwilling to admit to him that I wasn't entirely sure my wife was aware that her minipigs were moving.

Having wolfed down the pears, the minipigs turned to investigate their new surroundings. This involved Roxi searching out the feeding trough while Butch headed straight for the straw bed inside the ark.

'Just bring down your feed bin and we're good to go,' said Tom, before crossing to the stock box and closing the ramp once more. 'I'm sure as soon as Butch and Roxi have settled in we won't even know they're here.'

Back home, having deposited the kids, I decided to bring Hercules and Sesi on my return journey to the smallholding.

I figured they could run around the fields while I unloaded the bin, thereby exercising themselves. It was a small act of multitasking that would've made Emma proud.

The bin, however, was a bitch. It was almost full, which left me with no option but to drag it across our garden to the car. This just served to leave behind an ugly furrow in the grass, which was already in a fragile state after so much snow. The chickens peered at the damage, and then at each other in silent disapproval. Still, I told myself, there would be no further minipig-related grief. Butch and Roxi had gone on holiday. Our lives could begin again.

With Sesi in the boot alongside the bin, and Hercules on the passenger seat with his front paws on the dash, we set off down the lane. Along the way, I wondered how best to get the bin in place beside the enclosure with the minimum of damage to the ground. I didn't want to give Tom or his wife any reason to regret their kind invitation to look after our minipigs. At the gate, I decided that once inside I would reverse the car across the smallholding. That way, I only had to slide the bin from the boot and it would be in the right position.

'Stay down,' I instructed Sesi, as I eased the car backwards.

Through the rear window, beyond my dog's pointed ears, I could see Butch and Roxi in their new enclosure. They looked completely at home, I thought to myself. While bumping backwards over the grassland, I noticed how Hercules was taking in the surroundings with great interest. He swapped the dash for the edge of the window, and barked excitedly. As if in response, one of the minipigs squealed dramatically. I glanced from the sausage dog to the rear-view mirror. What I saw led me to jam on the brakes, curse out loud and turn in my seat.

We were no more than twenty metres from the enclosure, which was close enough for a clear view of Roxi scrambling over the wire fence at the back. I watched her considerable backside wriggling for freedom before jumping out of the car. As I did so, Butch issued a cry of what sounded like sheer panic, and followed her over.

'Hold it right there!' I sprinted towards the enclosure, clambering over the gate with a little more grace than Roxi, only to double back on remembering that my mobile phone was in the car.

I don't think Tom expected me to call him so soon after he had left us.

'What's up?' he asked, only to break off so he could yell at his son, Jake, to switch off the angle grinder. 'Everything OK?'

'It's Butch and Roxi,' I said. 'They've escaped.'

'That's impossible. I've kept pigs in there for years.'

Hurriedly, I told him how I had been reversing across the smallholding when the pair took flight.

'They just freaked out. I guess it was the first time they'd actually seen a car.'

'So where are they now?' he asked.

I peered into the woods behind the enclosure.

'Not a clue,' I reported. 'They just bolted.'

'Hold on.' Judging by the muffled conversation I could hear, it sounded like Tom was relaying what had happened to his son. I'm not sure what Jake called me, but it sounded a lot like a clown. 'We'll be there in a couple of minutes,' he said with a sigh.

Unlike me, who just stood around getting cold, Tom used his initiative. As well as bringing his wife and son with him, several neighbours also piled out of his Land Rover.

'A search party,' I said, nodding my approval. 'Good thinking.'

Tom strode across to the fence, scouring the area as if it were a crime scene.

'Frankly, I'm amazed,' he said eventually. 'Butch and Roxi must've been completely terrified to have attempted that kind of jump.'

'I had no idea the car would have that effect on them,' I protested, but nobody was listening.

'So, this is the situation,' said Tom, addressing us all now. 'We have two minipigs on the loose someplace. Butch is black, about eighty pounds and quite cute. Roxi is double the size and twice as ugly.'

'Steady on,' I said, but thought better of pursuing it. Pacing as he put forward a plan, Tom had comfortably taken charge of the situation. His son, Jake, was a close-cropped, former paratrooper who looked like he had done things in combat I could only hope to replicate on the PlayStation. Jake often worked with his father, whose only apparent paternal failing was in not teaching him to smile.

'You know these woods,' said Tom, addressing Jake first. 'See if you can track them. We'll all fan out and meet in the clearing at the top.'

Jake was alone in vaulting the fence. Tom followed him over with a little more care, and then helped everyone else in turn. I was the last to make the climb, having gone back to the car to collect something.

'Hercules can help,' I said, and handed Tom the sausage dog. 'He found our neighbour in the snow the other day.'

Tom looked unconvinced, but took him nonetheless.

'What about Sesi?' he gestured towards the boot of the car. 'Wouldn't she be more useful to us?'

With two minipigs at large I just wanted to start searching.

'Sesi won't track Butch and Roxi,' I explained. 'She'll just hunt down other dogs. It's better we leave her here with the window open. If Butch and Roxi return, she'll soon let us know.'

As I said this, Hercules wriggled around in Tom's arms and licked at the bristles under his chin. It sounded like Velcro parting. Tom put up with it for a couple of seconds before planting the sausage dog on the woodland floor. At this time of year, amid the oak, birch, holly and hornbeam, the ground was covered in leaf mulch and evergreen shrubs. It was also very wet from the thaw. If I'm honest, Hercules didn't look like he was enjoying the feeling under his paws.

'Go on, then!' said Tom, peering down at him. 'Do your thing.'

'Give him a chance,' I said, and scaled the fence myself. I clipped the leash on Hercules, and twitched it tight a couple of times to encourage him into action. Eventually, with no more time to waste, I picked him up and tucked him under my arm. 'OK, let's move.'

Already Tom's wife and neighbours had set off up the slope. The woodland here was several acres wide and divided farmland from the village playing fields. Some way beyond the crest, the trees bordered a road that was long, straight and notorious for speeding traffic. Although our search began in high spirits, I had a nagging feeling that this might not end well. The minipigs were licensed to move down to Tom's smallholding, but had no authority to roam freely without any human supervision. Even if they were still safe, I dreaded to think what damage they might be doing. It was enough for me to keep calling out for them, and encourage everyone else to use their eyes and ears. This extended to Hercules, though he seemed quite content to be carried along. At one point my mobile phone rang. The screen told me it was Emma. I put it straight through to answermachine.

'Everyone stop for a moment,' said Tom, midway towards the crest. He then cupped his hands to his mouth and issued a screech not unlike a bird of prey preparing to strike.

'What are you doing?' his wife asked.

'Asking Jake to report in.' He paused to listen, but heard nothing. 'Must be out of earshot.'

She tutted, sighed, and pulled her phone from the pocket of her coat. Tom looked at me sheepishly, and continued to trudge up the slope. While his other half called their son, I decided to give Hercules a second chance to move under his own steam. I wanted him to prove himself to everyone, just as he had done with me.

'Man up,' I whispered. 'Show him what you can do.'

Fortunately, Tom was focused on listening in to his wife when Hercules dug in his paws and refused to move. By now, I was beginning to regret bringing him with me. I just felt silly with a sausage dog under my arm. More than anything, however, I was deeply worried about Butch and Roxi. Not just for their welfare but what Emma would say if I had to confess to losing them. They had been quite secure at the bottom of our garden. We had moved mountains to make sure they couldn't escape, and now both minipigs had vanished.

In climbing the slope, we had to negotiate several sprawling rabbit warrens. With so much foliage it was hard to spot the entrance holes in the ground. I worried what injuries they could cause to a misplaced trotter. Quite simply, the longer this went on, the gloomier I became about the outcome. I knew my children were safe at home under Lou's care. Sesi would also be quite happy in the boot of the car. Free from the attentions of a sausage dog, she could sleep in peace. It meant I could stay out looking for a long time to come. What was beginning to trouble me was the light. The sun was low from dawn to dusk at this time of year. We only had a couple of hours at most before darkness settled.

'Jake's not having much luck,' Tom's wife reported, on pocketing her phone. A woman who lived for her horses, it was unusual for me to see her moving without the accompanying clip-clop of hooves. I didn't know her very well at all, but as with her neighbours, I was hugely grateful for such help. Not that I felt any less anxious by what she had to add about her son. 'He's gone all the way to the main road at the top. Hopefully, they won't have got that far and he can stop them from wandering into the traffic.'

'There's no guarantee they've travelled in that direction,' said Tom quickly, as if to stop me from fearing the worst. 'They could be anywhere.'

The farmer's fields were bordered on the far side by yet more woodland and rolling hills that stretched for miles. If Butch and Roxi evaded our search, there was a good chance we had lost them forever. I started wondering whether random sightings would earn the village a reputation for being home to two legendary creatures. Bodmin had its fearsome black beast. We would have wild minipigs.

'Let's not give up now,' said Tom, who had just relayed the message to the rest of the search party. 'Jake is an excellent tracker,' he added, with a disparaging glance at the sausage dog I had now slung around my neck for comfort. 'If anyone can find them, my boy is the man.'

A few minutes later, we reached the clearing. Kids came out here to play quite a bit, as was evident in the dens built from fallen branches and the ropes that hung from a couple of branches in the trees. In my mind, I had hoped to find

Butch and Roxi here, as if this was where they would run out of steam. I placed Hercules on the ground, in the vague hope that he might pick up on their scent and lead us to them. I could only think he was feeling a bit self-conscious at being carried so far, because when I moved off once more he did at least walk beside me.

'We should all fan out from here,' Tom suggested. 'If anyone sees anything, just shout.'

'Or call me,' his wife added, and showed them her phone.

I chose to head for the farmer's fields. I felt sick at the thought that I might have to admit to my family that I had lost the minipigs. Once again, I had been trying to do what I believed to be the right thing, and it had all gone wrong. Hercules had at least found his stride now. I barely noticed the leash unspooling as he scampered ahead. Then it reached its full extent, and the tug brought me back to my senses.

'Hercules!' I called out, as the sausage dog stopped and buried his nose into something. 'What have you found?'

As it turned out, much to my disappointment, he had discovered the sight of a woodpigeon ambush. The scattering of feathers had clearly tweaked his senses. Unfortunately, it had nothing to do with our missing minipigs. I figured a fox must've got it, or even a kestrel. I even heard one screeching in the distance as I trudged on towards the fields, only to stop dead in my tracks. For it was a call answered by much excitable shouting, which is when I realised that Jake might just have been behind it.

# 30

# Stubborn, Selfish, Smart

As soon as he saw me, sprinting towards him with Hercules at my side, Tom's son gestured wildly for me to lie low. He was crouched behind the roots of a toppled tree, stripped down to his vest despite the cold weather. Using a series of hand signals he could only have picked up from his time in the Forces, he drew my attention to the creature in the middle distance.

'Roxi!'

I kept my voice to a whisper, but the surge of excitement and relief on seeing one of our minipigs was hard to contain. As his father crept into Jake's view, and communicated with a series of yet more hand gestures, I worried that she was about to find herself the target of a military-style assault. I glanced back at Roxi, and was delighted to see that Butch was close by. He too had buried his snout into what was basically ancient and protected woodland, but I couldn't fret about that now. Having found them, more than a mile from where they were supposed to be, I realised we hadn't given any thought as to how we might get the two runaways back to Tom's enclosure. It wasn't like walking Hercules. I couldn't just clip one onto the retractable leash. Not without it breaking within seconds. A pig had a reputation for being selfish and stubborn for good reason. Right now, with so much foraging potential on offer, I had every reason to believe that Butch and Roxi had no plans to move any time soon.

Jake was still gesturing to his father in a way that made me think he had just radioed out for a drone strike. I decided that Hercules and I should creep up and find out exactly what he had in mind. As soon as I did so, the minipigs picked up on the crackle of twigs under my feet and retreated by several paces. Jake wheeled around, glaring. Then he saw the sausage dog, and appeared to weigh up what this said about me.

'We're going to need a gun,' he said, much to my alarm. Not least because I imagined he probably had one holstered down the back of his pants.

'We can't go shooting minipigs,' I told him, as Tom, his wife and neighbours regrouped behind us. 'It's bad enough they've escaped. How would I explain that to my wife?'

'I meant with a tranquilliser,' said Jake, shaking his head at his father.

'I know a vet who is licensed to do that,' Tom suggested. 'The trouble is, how do you shift a minipig as big as Roxi when she's out for the count? We're better off getting them to move under their own steam.'

Looking around, I realised several other villagers had joined the search party. Above all, they seemed amused by the fix we were in here. Still, I was grateful that they were prepared to lend a hand. I did a quick head count, in fact, only to concede that there were nowhere near enough people to mob-handle two minipigs clear of the woods. Even if we managed to sedate them, they were too hefty to be carried out strapped to a pole by their trotters. It left me thinking we had just one option. Handing the dog leash to Tom's wife, I rose to my feet and climbed over the fallen tree.

'What are you doing?' Jake struggled to keep his voice in

check. He also looked like he was a heartbeat away from pulling out that gun – assuming that he had one.

'Butch and Roxi trust me,' I said. 'They're smart animals. They must know we want to help.'

Reasoning with a minipig wasn't something I'd attempted before. I just didn't see we had any other option. I approached Roxi first. She continued digging, deep into the rich, pungent soil that contained what looked like next year's bluebell bulbs. Still, she was well aware of my presence. She looked wary, which was unusual for such a big, bold creature. I was close enough now to place my hand on her flank. She started immediately, and trotted from my reach. Butch was equally wired. As soon as he saw Roxi move he also shifted position. Only he didn't stop. The end result, after my brief attempt at shepherding, was that I had caused the minipigs to scatter.

'We really should call the vet,' said Jake, and glanced up through the bare branches overhead. 'The light is going.'

Over the course of the next half an hour, every member of the growing search (and now rescue) party tried out their own means of getting the minipigs to move. A couple of people attempted to shove Roxi as if she were some kind of broken-down car, but it didn't get them anywhere. A few others tried coaxing her from the front. One of the younger members of the party, possibly familiar with managing a dog and not a pig, threw a stick for her to retrieve, but nothing would persuade her to move. Tom's wife returned Hercules to me before heading back to the smallholding for a bucket of pig feed, which also failed to tempt my single-minded minipig. I couldn't blame Roxi. Here she was amid acres of mineral rich woodland, untouched by any other pig since medieval times, most probably. Why would she be interested in a bucket of processed cereal feed?

Our other problem concerned the fact that Butch and Roxi had decided to split. It forced our group to divide in two, some five hundred metres from each other. While Roxi resolutely stuck to turfing up woods, Butch took himself into the brambles that bordered the top of the playing fields. There he remained stock-still, as if believing himself to be invisible to everyone around him. I switched my attention from one pig to the other, finally joining Tom as he attempted to tie his leather belt around Roxi's neck.

'Now this is a long shot,' I observed. 'If she runs off with that she's going to look like the victim of some horrible S&M practice.'

'I'm hoping it'll give me something to hold onto,' he said, grunting just like Roxi as he attempted to secure it. 'If you see what I mean.'

With the belt secured, Tom tried to lead her forward. By now, Roxi was clearly getting fed up with being told what to do. She reacted angrily, startling Hercules and squealing as she shook Tom's hand free. Sighing to himself, he released the belt.

'I'm all out of ideas,' he said, and looked at me uncomfortably. 'Apart from the one involving a gun.'

I had no wish to shoot the minipigs, using tranquilliser darts or something altogether more final, if that's what he was suggesting. Without replying, I turned my attention back to Roxi. She stood beside me with her head bowed, honking quietly to herself. She looked tired, which was understandable. I really didn't want to stress her any further. Being shot in the rump probably wasn't going to help in that respect, even if it was just to knock her out.

'Will you give me a moment?' I felt foolish asking this. Like Tom, however, I just had no idea what else to do.

I didn't actually spell out that I planned to talk to her, but clearly he could see this was something I wanted to do on my own.

'I'll be up at the brambles with Butch,' he said. 'Hopefully his powers of invisibility will be starting to fade.'

Given that the runaway beast before us could've crushed him under one trotter, Hercules was remarkably relaxed in such close quarters. I could only think he had spent enough time on the other side of the pigpen fence, peering into Roxi's snout. I crouched before her. Once again, I placed my hand on her back. This time, she didn't move. I was close enough to look into her eyes. Her long gingery lashes made her look half asleep. Despite the energy she had spent in getting here, however, I could tell she was more alert than ever before.

'This is my fault,' I began, speaking low so as not to be overheard. 'But, Roxi, you can't stay here. It's going to get dark soon, and the temperature is dropping. Anything could happen to you. All you have to do is come with us. We'll take care of you, I promise.'

Roxi grunted, though I was well aware she didn't understand a word I had just said. My hope was that she would simply pick up on the tone of my voice. Having been surrounded by a crowd of people trying out different ways to move her, it seemed like a way of giving her some time to think. Up ahead, I realised that Tom's wife was watching us. She still had the feed bucket with her. I looked around at her, and then stood back from the minipig. Taking her cue from me, she shook the bucket. Roxi huffed, dropped her snout to the ground, only to lift her head and advance by several steps. I followed at her side, swapping the sausage dog for a wooden board that one of Tom's neighbours had fetched. In theory, it was possible to use one to steer a pig. Earlier, Tom had showed me how it was done. Not that Roxi had paid any attention. Another shake of the feed bucket prompted her to lumber towards Tom's wife. Quickly, I grabbed a stick and tapped Roxi's behind with it. At the same time, I held the board close to the right hand side of her head. In response, seeing only a dead end on that side, Roxi turned away to the left just a little, towards the brambles where Butch was hiding. From there, working with Tom's wife, and with a trail of cheering villagers behind us, we began to steer the minipig out of the woods.

'Take it easy,' I said, as Roxi picked up the pace and promptly stumbled in a gully. 'Let's make it back in one piece, eh?'

I could see Tom up ahead, watching proceedings. He peeled away as we approached, picked his way into the brambles behind where Butch was hiding, and attempted to shoo him out. I can't say whether he was successful, or if our male minipig just picked up on Roxi's approach. Whatever the case, by the time we reached the edge of the woods Butch was waiting for her.

The playing fields are a popular feature of the village. As well as a football pitch for Sunday League soccer, it also houses the tennis courts and a little wooden clubhouse. You'll always find something going on down there, from kids kicking a ball around to dog-walkers coming and going from the woods. What you wouldn't expect to see, of course, is a ragtag procession of people, enjoying a kind of carnival atmosphere, parading after two pigs.

'I can't believe we've nearly pulled this off,' I called across to Tom, who had also borrowed a board to steer Butch. 'It's as if they realised we're just trying to help.'

'Pigs are smart creatures,' he reminded me. 'Even the pet ones.'

I smiled, tapping Roxi's rump with my stick at the same time. It was frankly weird to be out walking her. Three children on BMX bikes had stopped to watch us pass. Tom waved at them like we did this kind of thing every day. His house backed onto a footpath across from the entrance to the playing field. Our plan was to direct Butch and Roxi through the rear gate. In doing so, we could at least contain them in his garden while he went to collect his Land Rover and stock box from the smallholding. So far, it looked as if everything was going to plan. Every now and then, one of the minipigs would threaten to wander off course, only to come back on track with the help of the board. Still, they learned fast. By the time we crossed the concrete track from playing field to footpath, both Butch and Roxi were moving with the minimum of guidance.

Tom's back garden was much like his smallholding minus any animals. It was a beautifully designed, low-maintenance affair filled with mature plants and ornamental ironware. The moment Butch followed Roxi through the back gate, a heartfelt cheer rose up behind them.

'We did it!' I said, extending handshakes and accepting the odd high-five. 'I can't believe so many people came out to help.'

'I'm sure you'd do the same thing,' said Tom.

'Sure,' I agreed. 'Assuming anyone else had minipigs on the loose.'

Butch and Roxi looked exhausted. With the feed bucket empty, having successfully deployed the pellets as an additional incentive to move, Tom's wife went off to fill it with water.

The drink was gratefully received, not just by the minipigs but also by Hercules. This involved tipping the bucket low enough for him to place his front paws on the edge, but once there he lapped eagerly. It had been a long and testing afternoon for us all, but it wasn't over for everyone. As the party slowly disbanded, Tom and I turned our attention to the wayward pair once more.

'You stay with them,' he suggested. 'I'll go fetch the stock box.'

'Don't be long.' I felt a little nervous being left with Butch and Roxi. Hercules was a far cry from a sheepdog. His herding instinct was non-existent. His only interest, in fact, was in being picked up by me for a cuddle. 'Be quick, in fact.'

As Tom's wife retired to the house, I was left alone with three animals who had each challenged me in different ways. I had never expected to find myself in a position like this, standing in someone else's garden with a sausage dog and livestock that once hung out with us in the living room. As much as I moaned about them, an episode like this made me realise how much I cared about their welfare. I was also concerned about Tom's grass just then, as Roxi appeared to revive sufficiently to realise she had a potential feast on her hands here.

'Can't you just stay out of trouble for a couple of minutes?' I pleaded, as she tested the ground with her snout. From experience, I knew there was no way that I could stop Roxi from undercutting a sizeable strip. Frankly, it was just a question of damage limitation. By the time Tom reversed through the gates of his drive, he found Hercules and me guarding four ragged rolls of turf. Roxi had created quite an impressive crater in the short time he had been away, but I assured him that he wouldn't know the difference once I replaced it all.

'That's good thinking,' he said, looking less than impressed by the minipig's actions. 'And so is this.'

From his coat pocket he produced a handful of pig nuts. Dropping one on the ground was enough to attract Butch and Roxi's attention. This time, it seemed both minipigs knew the drill. It wasn't long before they followed the little trail he made for them, all the way into the stock box. When Tom raised the ramp and bolted it, with both minipigs inside, I just wanted to hug him. What stopped me was my sense of reserve, plus the sausage dog who was back in my arms once more. I took Hercules around to the passenger side, and climbed into the seat with him. Tom joined me on the other side. Closing the door, he sat back and just breathed out for a moment. I did exactly the same thing. It had been a long afternoon. One that looked like it might have a bleak outcome, but which instead was about to see a happy ending.

'Emma must know nothing about this,' I said, when he finally reached for the ignition key. 'It's our secret, right?'

Tom tapped his nose, before shifting the Land Rover into gear.

'It's a *village* secret,' he said. 'If you can trust your friends and neighbours, this never happened.'

Having been in the woods all afternoon, I was cold, hungry, a little shaken up but above all deeply relieved. I was pretty sure that's how Butch and Roxi felt too. As Tom drove towards his smallholding, I figured he would know what measures to take so they didn't stage another getaway attempt.

It was only when he drove past the entrance, following the lane up the hill, that I realised what measures he had in mind. It was nothing to do with electrifying the fence, as I had assumed. This was a more extreme solution, and one that would ensure our minipigs never again escaped the small-holding on Tom's watch. The opportunity was just no longer there, given that Butch and Roxi were about to find themselves where they started – in the back of our garden, a place they call home, and there they remain to this day.

# 31

## Did You Miss Me?

Butch and Roxi had blown it. Faced with the holiday of a lifetime, and the possibility of no return ticket, they had comprehensively rejected Tom's hospitality. Not that he ever extended the invitation again, and I understood his reasons. He reared pigs from scratch, not as pets but for a very different purpose. His livestock were aware of nothing else but the first-class enclosures he provided, unlike our pair, who knew how it felt to once lounge in front of the TV waiting for the lottery results. Now they had discovered that there was yet more fun to be had in the wider world. Ultimately, they still had the potential to break free, run riot in the woods and redesign all the gardens in the village in an unprofessional way. As a worst-case scenario, there was always the chance that Butch and Roxi could break into a house and turf out the occupants.

Lou and May looked a little mystified when the minipigs trotted past the kitchen window once again, heading for the bottom of the garden with me close behind. As for the little ones, I don't think they even noticed that Butch and Roxi had come back. When I finally closed the door on the day, having retrieved the feed bin, Sesi and the car from the smallholding, I found Frank and Honey in the front room, pretty much as I had left them.

'Have you actually switched these off today?' I asked them,

and repeated myself when they failed to turn their eyes from their DS screens. The little ones glanced at one another, then they faced me and shook their heads. I had seen and heard enough. 'Things are going to have to change,' I declared. 'When your mother comes home from hospital, I want you to welcome her back and take good care of her. *Talk* to her. Ask how she's feeling. If there's anything she needs, I shouldn't have to ask you ten times to help out. At least give her the impression that we've been functioning as a normal family. And if you can do that for me,' I said to finish, before extracting both consoles from their hands, 'I'll let you have these back.'

The next morning, as the early birds found their singing voices, I awoke with a start. It wasn't because Butch and Roxi had joined in the dawn chorus with all the grace of two drunks at a church mass. Quite the opposite, in fact. Not a grunt, honk or squeal could be heard from the foot of the garden.

Immediately, I worried that they really had developed a taste for escape. As I hurried to investigate, bringing both dogs with me, I had visions of them on a rampage through the village, forcing people awake to the sound of breaking glass and car alarms. As soon as I reached the garden, however, and saw the snout peeping out of the side of the shed, I slowed to a walk and breathed out in relief. Roxi watched me approach from the floor of their sleeping quarters.

'Morning,' I said, and received a half-hearted honk in reply. 'Everything OK?' It wasn't until I let myself in to feed them that both minipigs stirred. Unlike the usual bundle, it took a good half minute for Roxi and then Butch to exit their quarters. When they did emerge, I realised why they were both so subdued. 'Word of advice,' I said, standing back to watch them moving stiffly into the daylight. 'If you're going to run away again, be sure to do some warm-up exercises first. You two need to take it easier than normal for a while. Let those aching muscles rest.'

I expected them to grunt at me at least. Instead, Hercules made all the noise. I turned to hush him, only to come around full circle when a voice addressed me from over the fence.

'He's only a dog,' said Roddie. 'Barking is in his nature.'

'Should you be on your feet?' I asked my neighbour. 'I wasn't even aware that you were back from hospital.'

'My niece collected me yesterday,' he said. 'Amazing what they can do to patch you back together nowadays.'

I smiled, thinking of Emma. At the same time, I was relieved that Hercules had decided to abandon his guard dog duties in favour of a tennis ball.

'Well, it's good to see you,' I said as peace returned. 'You gave me quite a scare.'

Roddie pressed his lips together and nodded just once. I sensed he had something to say. A moment passed before he offered it.

'I believe I owe you my thanks,' he said quietly. 'I will always be grateful for what you did.'

At the time, I had been so focused on Emma that I hadn't really dwelled on the incident. Hearing him say this, however, caused a catch to form in my throat.

'It wasn't really me,' I said eventually, and gestured at the Dachshund.

'My niece told me the story,' said Roddie, and watched Hercules as he drove the ball around the garden with his snout. 'It seems a sausage dog saved my life.'

\* \* \*

For the rest of that day, both Butch and Roxi lay outside the shed and dozed in the winter sun. They didn't even stir at a cheer that went up inside the house when I called Emma and learned that she was ready to come home. Every now and then, as we set about tidying up, I'd glance out of the window and smile to myself. I really didn't think they'd try to break out from their pigpen. Why would they? Here, in what used to be a nice garden, they had enough space, a shelter cushioned with fresh straw and a personal servant at their beck and call. In short, Butch and Roxi had everything they could possibly want in life.

As I worked with the children in putting the house back together, Hercules did his level best to undo it all again. I couldn't watch him all the time, which meant two sofa cushions and another curtain ended up in shreds. Lou had gone to great lengths to protect Justin from the fate that had befallen his twin sister. Unfortunately, as I found out on breaking up a shouting match in the kitchen, he was accidentally used up in a homecoming cake that May decided to bake for her mother.

'She wasn't to know,' I said in May's defence. 'To be fair, you had stored him in the cupboard.'

'Next to the baking soda,' May added, and looked to the floor. 'I feel bad now.'

I made a face at Lou, silently pleading with her not to let this minor incident turn into a catastrophe that would leave her sister in a stew for weeks on end.

'It's fine,' Lou said after a moment. 'I'll explain what happened to my teacher.'

'You could even bring in some cake,' I suggested. 'It's what Justin would've wanted.'

Emma was ready for me when I arrived to collect her. She was sitting on the edge of the bed with her bag beside her, along with a pair of crutches, and her leg in a bandage. Above all, it was a relief to see her with a little colour in her cheeks.

'Promise me something,' she said, as I kissed her on the forehead and arranged her crutches so she could stand. 'Never, *ever* make me a hot-water bottle again.'

I stood aside as Emma said goodbye to the staff at the burns unit. It was an emotional moment for her, which was understandable given what she'd been through. When the nurse with the pen in her hair gave her a heartfelt squeeze, I kept my head down and purposely avoided her eye. I'd had enough of being branded as the brander. I just wanted things to return to normal.

The kids had asked to stay behind for a good reason. I knew just what we could expect when they opened the front door to us. Even so, the extent of their preparation still came as a surprise.

'I've missed you all so much!' cried Emma, enjoying what was basically a group hug from her children. Balloons filled a hallway that was rich with the smell of freshly baked Justin cake, while a home-made *Welcome Home* banner was strung at an angle from the kitchen door to the staircase. 'And how are the animals?' she asked, looking around now.

Sesi was in the boot room, behind the child gate with Hercules. As he had at last learned not to provoke my Canadian Shepherd by repeatedly jumping at her face, I no longer needed to crate him in my absence. The pair of them had picked up on the activity going on in the hall, because both were barking excitedly.

'Everyone is just fine,' I said. 'Including Butch and Roxi.'

Emma looked at me as if she'd just remembered something.

'I tried to call you about them yesterday,' she said. 'Am I

right in thinking you suggested sending them to Tom's small-holding for a holiday? I swear I heard you talking about it when you visited me the other day.'

I glanced at Lou and May, and found them both awaiting my response.

'I did,' I said, uncomfortably. 'But it was just an idea.'

'A *stupid* idea.' Emma turned to May and Lou, who nodded treacherously. 'Why would I want them anywhere else but here?'

The dogs were still making a big noise from the boot room, which was fortunate as it gave me a chance to move away from the subject of the minipigs.

'Hercules has been pining for you,' I said, largely because I figured it would make her feel good. 'He isn't interested in anyone else.'

'Really?' Emma sounded doubtful, which was no surprise. I just hoped that I was right about the sausage dog. 'I've been worrying that he might've forgotten me,' she added.

'Never!' I tried to sound incredulous, and suggested we head into the kitchen for the sake of the two dogs. 'All that barking is because they want to see *you.*'

I pulled back on the door to find Sesi sitting at the child gate. Hercules had adopted exactly the same position, directly in front of her. Even so, they couldn't have looked more different.

'Awww!' Emma stood before them, leaning on her crutches. 'Remember me?'

I crossed to open the child gate. At once both dogs rushed to greet her, much to my relief. As Hercules, Sesi and the children vied for her attention, I remembered that I had left Emma's bag on the doorstep. When I came back into the kitchen with it, I found everyone facing me. Sesi had taken up position at Emma's side, and was gazing up lovingly. Emma's hand rested on the dog's head, but her attention was locked on Hercules. He was standing at the threshold to the hall, clearly having ventured after me when I left. I looked down at the sausage dog, who wagged his tail in response.

'Fine,' said Emma. 'Maybe I'll just take Sesi to work with me.'

I scowled at Hercules, and stepped around him. He followed me dutifully.

'Don't leave that dog here with me,' I cautioned, and collected the kettle to make us a cup of tea. 'Remember the terms of the deal.'

'But you *adore* him!' said Lou, and faced her mother. 'Dad talks to him when he thinks there's nobody listening. He's even got a special name for him.'

'What?' Without turning off the tap, I glared over my shoulder at my eldest. 'I have not.'

'He so has,' said May, grinning now. 'He doesn't call him Hercules. He calls him Minky . . . Minky *Dinks*.'

'That's a lie!' I protested. 'OK. Not quite a lie, just a private thing we have going.'

'Sometimes,' said May, if only to stir up the little ones' laughter, 'he picks up Hercules for a cuddle and calls him The Minkster.'

'Also Mister Pinkle,' Lou added, clearly relishing this moment. 'In a silly voice.'

Emma listened to all this with rising amusement. I could feel myself practically incinerating with embarrassment, but I was all out of protests for the simple reason that it was true.

'But he answers to it,' I said weakly. 'Don't you, Minky?'

In response, the sausage dog padded towards me. It felt wrong not to pick him up, seeing that's what he expected.

Emma watched me cuddling him, and asserted her grip on the handle of her crutches.

'Whatever you choose to call him,' she said, still smiling as she joined the children in petting Sesi. 'It's good to know that your dog has a loving home.'

# Epilogue

*Health and safety nightmare.*

When I agreed to let Emma bring a sausage dog into our lives, I had no idea of the consequences. Then again, sometimes things pan out in ways you least expect. A case in point occurred the following summer, shortly after Hercules crossed my path on the landing and sent me tumbling down the stairs. As a result of the injury I sustained, I found myself in the seat of a vehicle I never dreamed that I would drive.

\*     \*     \*

'This is ridiculous,' I grumbled, on trundling behind my family in the mobility scooter they had just made me hire. 'I feel like such a tool.'

It didn't help that Hercules was stationed in the front basket. With his forelegs planted on the edge, he was looking around like I'd ordered him there as some kind of lookout. We were on a family day out at a country fair. We'd booked tickets before my fall, which had left me with a broken joint in my big toe. It hadn't sounded like that big a deal when the hospital consultant viewed the X-rays. Nevertheless, he had gone on to explain that as a load-bearing bone, I would be unable to walk for six months without crutches. I'd arrived at the fair on a pair, but shortly after passing through the entrance it was clear that I would be holding everyone back. That's when May had spotted a roped-off area offering scooters for hire. I had dismissed the idea out of hand, of course, which didn't go down well with the man in charge.

'There's no shame!' he had said pointedly at me when Emma checked out the different models.

I had hung back, mortified that my wife was even entertaining the idea of putting me in one for the day.

'I know that,' I agreed, thinking that the inexplicable presence of a sticker for mint-choc-chip ice cream on the back of each chair wouldn't exactly lend itself to the preservation of my dignity. I glanced at the line-up of scooters. Several at the end looked like they might be packing a punch. The sun was beating down and I had started to sweat with the effort of using the crutches. Even so, I declined the offer.

Ten minutes later, as I struggled to keep up with the family, I relented.

'Very well,' I sighed, and waited for them to turn around.

'Just this once, and only because I don't want to stop you from having a good time.'

'At last,' said Emma. 'A sensible decision.'

The man in charge looked totally unsurprised when I returned. In fact, he was very helpful in explaining how to operate the vehicle. Not that it was particularly difficult. You grasped the handles and then turned the dial to go.

'Can I have a fast one?' I asked.

'Oh, no,' he said, a little affronted. 'They're for the war vets.'

I looked to the foot of my crutches, and submitted without argument when he picked out a rickety model that looked like it had last been driven into a ditch.

'Thanks,' I said, on sitting astride my battery-powered charger. 'What kind of horsepower are we talking about here?'

'Not a lot,' he said, and clapped me on the back. 'Giddy up!'

I told myself I'd done the right thing as I hummed along to catch up with Emma and the kids. Unfortunately, that entirely failed to hold my resolve. As soon as I began to weave around people, I realised I was destined to spend my day wishing I'd stayed at home. I had nothing against anyone who used mobility scooters. It's just I'd never imagined myself to be among their number.

It didn't help when Emma planted Hercules in the front basket. He hardly passed muster as an assistance dog. All I could do was focus on the heels of my wife and children and avoid eye contact with anyone else. People chuckled, of course, but that was on account of my four-legged travelling companion. If anything, I gained an insight into how it must feel being Hercules. There I was, low down to the ground, inviting looks of amusement as I trundled along. Every now and then,

Hercules himself would glance back at me, as if to check I hadn't just bailed out.

On several occasions that day, I had to turn the dial beyond the recommended setting just to catch up with my family. At one point, a man with both legs removed at the knees, mirrored glasses and a cigar between his teeth beetled across my path in a machine that outshone my own. To my eye, he was travelling at an irresponsible speed. Nevertheless, I watched him bounce over the grass with envy.

'Have you seen everything yet?' I asked Emma, having finally drawn level with her.

'Everything but the rare breed pigs,' she told me. 'They're up at the top field along with the craft stands. Apparently there's a table selling sausage dog draft excluders!'

I glanced at the children. They all knew what this meant. Having lived with porcine trinkets on every shelf and surface for several years, it was no stretch to imagine what it would look like with the addition of some Dachshund paraphernalia.

'These rare breed pigs,' I said warily. 'They're not for sale or anything, are they?'

Emma grinned before setting off to lead the way. She had recovered remarkably well, much of which I put down to her determination to get on with life just as soon as she returned from hospital. To begin, it had been a daily battle to encourage her to rest. Eventually, along with Lou and May, we had just let her get on with things, and that's how we put the whole episode behind us. What was a crater in the back of her leg had slowly filled out over time. Despite the scar, her spirit was intact. Unlike me, however, her injuries had no effect on her mobility. As we hit the incline that led to the rare breed pigs I even had to ask her to slow down.

'Why didn't you get a zippier model?' she asked, though I chose not to reply.

Instead, as we trundled diagonally up the hill, I stopped moaning about the lack of speed and began to fret instead about my centre of gravity. Even Hercules looked concerned as the scooter leaned heavily to one side.

'She's tipping,' I said with some anxiety. 'I'm sure I can feel her tipping.'

'Nonsense.' Emma turned to assess my claim. Immediately, she looked alarmed. 'OK,' she said, and clamped her hand around my shoulder. 'You're tipping.'

From there, I completed the ascent with my children trailing at a distance behind the scooter, which was understandable, while their mother valiantly propped me up.

'I'm so humiliated,' I muttered over the whine of the engine, and motioned at the sausage dog in the basket. 'For once even Hercules looks like he feels the same way.'

Emma didn't answer for a moment. She was too busy stopping the scooter from flopping sideways and tipping me onto the grass.

'We'll get there,' she assured me, and gestured towards the stock pens through the crowds. 'We always do.'

'We're a team,' I agreed through gritted teeth.

Emma faced me side on.

'We're a good team,' she said pointedly. 'In sickness and in health, remember?'

'For better or worse.'

'To love and to cherish?' she asked, laughing.

'So long as you call a halt to more pets,' I said, only to withdraw the terms when Emma momentarily lifted her hand from the chair of the scooter.

'You can't blame Hercules for everything,' she said, and

leaned across to ruffle his head. 'Without him, we wouldn't be sharing moments like this.'

I glanced up at her. Emma looked back without any hint of irony about what she had just said. I didn't comment. There was no need. Not because she was right. It's just we were within sight of the rare breed pigs and Hercules decided that what I really needed from the seat of a mobility scooter with a choc ice advert on the back was a lot more attention. This he achieved by stretching up on the edge of the basket, squaring his shoulders and barking lustily.

I made no effort to stop him. If people thought that he was my dog then so be it. I was beyond embarrassment. Having spent a long time coming to terms with walking him in public, I now felt no sense of shame. Having said that, I'd undertaken just one change so I felt more comfortable in his company. Hercules no longer sported the hot pink collar. Instead, he wore a manly leather number with a buckle and a circular chrome tag. If ever a dog had been designed with the potential for self-esteem issues, it was a miniature Dachshund, and I had no doubt that he was grateful. I could see it in his eyes, which was frequently seeing that he spent his days with me. Emma was correct when she said that the breed tended to bond with one person. It just so happened that my wife and I were each in the wrong place at a critical time in his development.

We'd been to hell and back with Hercules, but as a family we were closer, stronger and wiser for the experience. As for that bond between man and sausage dog, it was one that had grown to work both ways.

## Sesi
### 2004–2011

Soon after I started writing this book, Sesi began treatment for inflammatory bowel disease. It isn't uncommon in German Shepherds, and largely treatable with medicine for life. Sadly, this didn't prove to be the case for Sesi. Her condition took a turn for the worst towards the end of 2011, which left her in a great deal of pain. Eventually, on the vet's advice, she was put to sleep – but not before enjoying one last walk with her family that none of us will ever forget.

Sesi was an unruly nightmare in many ways, but at heart a dream of a dog. The house has felt very empty without her. All of us, not least Hercules, miss her hugely.

# Acknowledgements

Having spent my career writing thrillers for teenagers, I never thought I'd see my name on a book called *Walking With Sausage Dogs*. However, like its predecessor, *Pig in the Middle*, the whole experience has been hugely enjoyable. So much is down to the fact that everyone on the publishing side has shown such enthusiasm, good-humour and commitment from the start. In particular, I am grateful to Julian Alexander, Philippa Milnes-Smith, Ben, Holly and all at LAW, as well as Rupert Lancaster, Kate Miles and the entire team at Hodder. When I visit my publisher's office and find pictures of Hercules as a puppy on the walls, you know they're rooting for the long dog.

On the home front, I'd like to thank my wife, children, wider family, friends, neighbours and villagers who helped to shape this story. In order to protect identities and privacy, I have changed some details of events, people and places. For the same reason, I have adapted the chronology where necessary and also recreated some dialogue based on memory. One thing I can't forget is the contribution made by the animals featured in this book. Without the challenges so many pets present, the noise, defiance, misbehaviour and mayhem, our lives would be so much easier – but it wouldn't be the same.

# PIG IN THE MIDDLE

## Matt Whyman

'What a fabulous, funny read! I enjoyed every page.' Sophie Kinsella

'Move over Marley, a pair of cute mini-pigs are about to take over the world!' *New York Post*

The hilarious tale of how two minipigs took over one family's life.

Matt Whyman is a writer and house husband. He enjoys the quiet life. His career wife, Emma, prefers the chaos a big brood can bring. On top of four challenging children, one freaked-out feline, a wolf-like dog and a wild bunch of ex-battery chickens, she brings minipigs Butch and Roxi into the fold.

But can the new arrivals really cuddle up on the sofa, or will their growing presence spark a battle of hearts, snouts and minds?

*Also available as an ebook*
www.hodder.co.uk